The Echoes of Fitna

Islamic History and Civilization

STUDIES AND TEXTS

VOLUME 197

The titles published in this series are listed at *brill.com/ihc*

The Echoes of Fitna

Accumulated Meaning and Performative Historiography in the First Muslim Civil War

By

Aaron M. Hagler

BRILL

LEIDEN | BOSTON

Cover illustration: *First volume of a Tarikhnama (Book of history) by Balami (died ca. 992–997)*, dated from the early 14th century. It is in the Freer Gallery of Art and Arthur M. Sackler Gallery at the Smithsonian Institution.

The Library of Congress Cataloging-in-Publication Data is available online at https://catalog.loc.gov
LC record available at https://lccn.loc.gov/2022044561

Typeface for the Latin, Greek, and Cyrillic scripts: "Brill". See and download: brill.com/brill-typeface.

ISSN 0929-2403
ISBN 978-90-04-52423-1 (hardback)
ISBN 978-90-04-52425-5 (e-book)

This book is printed on acid-free paper and produced in a sustainable manner.

This book is dedicated to my Papa Ernie, who taught us all to leave the campsite better than we found it, and who made everything possible

Contents

Acknowledgements XI

Introduction: Making Use of Uncertainty 1
1 The Later Historians: Ibn al-Athīr and Ibn Kathīr 6
2 Their Source 10
3 Establishing the Texts' Relationships 15
4 Methodology: Performative Historiographical Analysis 17
5 Mapping the *Fitna* 22
6 Structure 27

1 **Historical Background of the *Fitna* and Its Histories** 29
1 A Brief History of Islam before Our Extant Sources and the Emergence of Sectarian Rivalry 29
2 The Raw Data: The Sectarian Narratives 32
3 The *Fitna* as Narrative 35
4 Historical Context: Damascus during and after the "Sunnī Revival" 40
5 Conclusion 46

PART 1
The Slaughter at Karbalāʾ

2 **The Karbalāʾ Narrative** 51
1 The Story of Karbalāʾ 51
2 Ibn Kathīr on al-Ḥusayn ibn ʿAlī 53
3 Ibn al-Athīr on Karbalāʾ 59
4 Conclusion 60

3 **The Fight and Its Aftermath** 61
1 The Immediate Preparation 61
2 The Battle 64
3 Conclusion 66

4 **Approaching Karbalāʾ** 68
1 Towards Karbalāʾ 68
2 Umayyad Representatives, Softened and Erased 69

3 Al-Ḥusayn is Detained and Denied Water 75
4 Conclusion 75
5 Next Stop 77

PART 2
The Betrayal at Ṣiffīn

5 **The Ṣiffīn Narrative** 83
1 Sourcing Ṣiffīn 86
2 The Elements of the Story 88
2.1 *The Journey of ʿAlī from Baṣra to Kūfa to Ṣiffīn and Muʿāwiya's Journey to Ṣiffīn* 89
2.2 *The Battle by the Water* 89
2.3 *The Makeup of the Armies and the Early Skirmishes* 89
2.4 *Laylat al-Harīr—the Main Battle* 90
2.5 *Call for Arbitration; Appointment of Arbiters; Withdrawal of the Armies* 90
2.6 *Negotiation, Ruling, and Reneging* 91
3 The Stakes 92

6 **The Battle of Ṣiffīn: Fight and Conclusion** 94
1 Introduction 94
2 A Broken Link to the Prophet: The Battlefield Death of the Elderly ʿAmmār ibn Yāsir 96
3 Arbitration, Negotiation, and a Portentous Stalemate 100

7 **Preparing the Battle** 109
1 Introduction 109
2 The Battle of the Camel 109
3 The Allegiances of ʿAmr ibn al-ʿĀṣ and Abū Mūsā al-Ashʿarī 110
4 The Correspondence between ʿAlī and Muʿāwiya 114
5 The Battle by the Water: Softening Umayyad Villainy at Ṣiffīn 118
6 Conclusion 120

PART 3
The Election of ʿUthmān

8 **The Story of ʿUthmān** 125
1 The *Shūrā* 126
2 Six Good Years, Six Bad Years 127
3 Muʿāwiya on the Minbar 128
4 The Stakes 128
5 Six Good Years and Six Bad Years: The Caliphate of ʿUthmān ibn ʿAffān 131
5.1 *The ʿUthmān Interlude* 131
5.2 *ʿUthmān's Alteration of the Pilgrimage Rites* 133

9 **The *Shūrā* of ʿUthmān** 136
1 Introduction 136
2 Narrating the *Shūrā* 139
3 ʿAbd al-Raḥmān ibn ʿAwf: Cynical or Sincere? 140
4 ʿAlī's Reactions: Playing the Wild Card 143
5 Looking Backward 148

PART 4
Further Ripples

10 **The Stories of Succession** 151
1 Introduction 151
2 The Death of the Prophet and the *Sāqifa* 152
3 The Caliphate of ʿUmar ibn al-Khaṭṭāb 156
4 The Stakes 157

11 **The Prophet Muḥammad and His Role in the Narrative** 158

Conclusion: The Tapestry of History 161
1 Karbalāʾ the Pebble 163

Bibliography 165
Index 172

Acknowledgements

This book, like most academic books, had to be written and rewritten a few times before reaching a publishable state. It began its life as a PhD dissertation under the wise and kind advisership of Professor Paul Cobb at the University of Pennsylvania. Paul was a constant source of support (when it was needed) and direct, helpful criticism (when it was needed). The seeds of this study would not have existed without him.

While I am thanking teachers, I would like to acknowledge a number of instructors past who helped shape me into the scholar I am today. So, with that in mind, I offer my thanks to Beth Montgomery, my 12th-grade AP European History teacher, who gave me a "zero" when I deserved one; Adrianne Krstansky, my undergraduate theatre professor at Brandeis University, who helped me learn how to interpret intention behind words; Reuven Amitai and Moshe Sharon, Islamic history professors at Hebrew University, who opened my eyes to the wonders of this field; and to Roger Allen, Joseph Lowry, Heather Sharkey, Jamal Elias, Jamal Ali, and Emad Rushdie, all of the University of Pennsylvania, who, along with Paul, helped me through graduate school and out the other side. I would be remiss if I did not mention Linda Greene, Peggy Guinan, and Diane Moderski, the combined heart and soul of Penn's NELC department when I was enrolled. I would also like to acknowledge all of the colleagues with whom I have worked at Cornell College and Troy University for offering two marvelously collegial environments in which to produce scholarship. Special thanks to James Lindsay of Colorado State University, who has offered friendship, support, and wonderful conversation ever since I met him. He, and Suleiman Mourad of Smith College, were particularly helpful in the transition of this project from dissertation to monograph.

In the publication process, I am very grateful to the two reviewers, both of whom offered fair and helpful critiques. I did not agree with all of their suggestions, of course, but even the comments with which I disagreed pointed out weaknesses in my presentation. Teddi Dols, my publisher at Brill, has been helpful, communicative, and kind. My very patient copyeditor, Rebekah Zwanzig, has an astounding attention to detail and an eye for errata that rivals that of eagles.

There are others deserving special mention for their assistance and support of both me, and this project, in ways both tangible and intangible. These include Nathaniel Allen, Tam Baig, Scout Blum, Antoine Borrut, Cathy Bronson, Tim Buckner, Hal Fulmer, Allen Jones, Rob Kerr, Rabbi Scott Kramer, Sarah Gibson-Daly, Margaret Gnoinska, Windham Graves, Sarah Graves, Rob Kruckeberg, Joungbin Lim, Phil Lucas, Joe McCall, Martin Olliff, Elisabeth Palmer, Dan Puckett, Luke Ritter, Karen Ross, Kris Sanchack, Steven Taylor, Kathryn Tucker, Jay Valentine, Leslie Warden-Anderson, Kenny Whitlock, Adi Zarchi, and the people of Maverick Night and the Cloverdale Playhouse in Montgomery.

I take great joy in knowing that my grandparents, *zichronam l'vrach*, Ann and Sidney Edelman and Ernest and Norma Hagler, would all be proud of this book. My grandparents-in-law, Haim and Sara Bronshtein, treated me like a son from the moment they realized I was serious about their granddaughter, which is to say, from about two days after meeting me; I have never known anybody, anywhere, with greater determination and dedication to family than they had. My parents, James and Vivien, supported me (and continue to support me) in my various endeavors in life; thanks to them, I have the freedom to take risks and pursue a life that is meaningful to me. My children, Asher and Dina, motivate me to achieve and distract me from achievement in equal measure (I am grateful for both). Last, but not least, I would like to thank my wife, Elana Hagler, for too many things to mention; if I were to start listing the ways I am grateful for her, it might make the binding of this book unwieldy. I have learned much from her, but of all the things I could mention, the most relevant is the first time I saw her work for days on a section of a painting and then, ultimately dissatisfied with the outcome, scrape off her work with a palette knife, sandpaper it down, and start on that section anew, without even a small hesitation. Her example kept me from becoming disheartened when, inevitably, I needed to do the same with a section of text and the delete key.

The standard disclaimer naturally applies. Although I am indebted to the brilliant work of a number of great scholars, none of them bears any responsibility for any possible errors I have made.

INTRODUCTION

Making Use of Uncertainty

In the study of early Islamic history, the problem with the sources is by now a cliché. Most books in this genre place an apology somewhere in the pages numbered with single digits, surveying the contributions of Schacht, Goldziher, Wansbrough, Donner, Cook, Crone, and others—drawing the battle lines, as it were, in the discussion of whether the Islamic sources are to be trusted or not. Obviously, the present study is no exception; we begin with the standard disclaimer. But perhaps we should think more positively about it: the historiographical challenges are, in fact, an opportunity.

It is the problem that has both bedeviled and energized the field. No narratives about the rise of Islam that were written before about the early second/eighth century survived to the present day in their original forms. We have such sources as we have only in the form of later citations, reproductions, references, and (for all we know) fabrications. Those early written sources that do appear are almost certainly incomplete. To take a common, and well-known, example, we know that Abū Mikhnaf (d. 157/774) wrote a lot, and we possess a lot of what he wrote, but as of now we have no way to know what *else* he might have written. The early sources exist only insofar as they serve the interests—pious or impious, public or private, official or otherwise—of later scholars.[1]

Once extant, the emergence and evolution of the sects of Sunnīsm and Shīʿism in Islam colored the memory of all that had come before. It is in this context, after the sectarian conflict had become occasionally violent and always socially and politically salient, that the historians ʿAlī ʿIzz al-Dīn ibn al-Athīr al-Jazarī (d. 630/1233) and ʿImād al-Dīn Ismāʿīl ibn Kathīr (d. 774/1373) wrote their histories. Based largely, if not exclusively, on the earlier history of Abū Jaʿfar Muḥammad ibn Jarīr al-Ṭabarī (d. 310/923), the two texts—Ibn

1 A notable exception is Ibn Aʿtham al-Kūfī's *Kitāb al-Futūḥ*, which Conrad suggests was overlooked due to its reliance on "fanciful material," and its overtly Shīʿī perspective. It was also ahead of its time stylistically, synthesized in a way that may have made it appear less "scholarly" to later historians. See Lawrence I. Conrad, "Ibn Aʿtham and His History," in *Al-Uṣūr al-Wusṭā* 23 (2015), 87–125. Cf. Mónika Schönléber, "Notes on the Textual Tradition of Ibn Aʿtham's *Kitāb al-Futūḥ*," in *Contacts and Interactions: Proceedings of the 27th Congress of the Union Européenne des Arabisants et Islamisants*, Jaako Hämeen-Anttila, Petteri Koskikallio, and Ilkka Lindstedt (eds.) (Leuven: Peeters, 2017), 427–438.

 | DOI:10.1163/9789004524255_002

al-Athīr's *al-Kāmil fī al-taʾrīkh* (the immodestly titled "The perfect work of history," or perhaps less grandly, "The complete history") and Ibn Kathīr's *Kitāb al-Bidāya wa-l-nihāya* (The book of the beginning and the end)—bear a striking, indeed often identical, resemblance to al-Ṭabarī's sweeping chronicle of world and Islamic history written in the second/ninth century, *Taʾrīkh al-rusul wa-l-mulūk* (The history of the prophets and the kings). In their hands, the early narrative of Islam's beginnings became an intellectual battlefield, ripe for the deployment of whatever picture of the past they wished to present. The two later historians have much in common: both were ardent Sunnīs, both saw in the existing historiographical corpus an overtly anti-Umayyad (and thus an anti-Syrian and, while not anti-Sunnī, perhaps to their minds an insufficiently Sunnī) bias, both utilized al-Ṭabarī's work heavily. Indeed, the differences among the three men are often difficult to spot, so alike is their treatment of the period.[2] Nevertheless, Ibn al-Athīr and Ibn Kathīr had profoundly different goals from each other. Ibn al-Athīr's *Kāmil* was a version of the historical narrative that emphasized unity, cooperation, and the fundamental oneness of the *umma*, despite its history of significant, and occasionally violent, sectarian and theological disagreements.[3] Writing at a time when the Crusades were well underway—and, much more troubling for Ibn al-Athīr, at a time when he could only watch with horror, and even abject terror, as the Mongols slowly approached Baghdad, biding their time in Iran before their devastating incursion into the heartlands of *dār al-islām* on behalf of *dār al-ḥarb*—such niggling details seemed trivial. Ibn Kathīr wrote a century later, when the Crusaders were on their way to defeat. The fight was not over, but the outcome was assured. Furthermore, by Ibn Kathīr's time the Mongols had done their devastating worst, but then ultimately, many of their governors and rulers had converted to Islam, a faith and community that survived the onslaught and was thriving again. Writing from the relatively safe harbor of the Sunnī courts of the Mamlūk dynasty, Ibn Kathīr was free to turn the history into a divisive tale of

---

2 Whether the two later works should be said to resemble al-Ṭabarī's opus or—perhaps more accurately—the works of al-Ṭabarī's now-lost sources, such as Abū Mikhnaf, Naṣr ibn Muzāḥim, ʿUmar ibn Saʿd, etc. is ultimately irrelevant to this study. The two men were clearly utilizing al-Ṭabarī's text as their main source, and so, despite the fact that the words Ibn al-Athīr and Ibn Kathīr copied were not originally al-Ṭabarī's, they do represent the product of al-Ṭabarī's editorial thinking. The construction of al-Ṭabarī's chronicle is not the focus; the way his work was utilized by later historians, regardless of how he constructed his work, is. For more on al-Ṭabarī's process of construction, emendation, and compilation, see Boaz Shoshan, *The Poetics of Islamic Historiography: Deconstructing Tabari's History* (Leiden: E.J. Brill, 2004).

3 I explored this question in Aaron Hagler, "Unity through Omission: Literary Strategies of Recension in Ibn al-Aṯīr's al-Kāmil fī l-Taʾrīḫ," in *Arabica* 65 (2018), 285–313.

Shīʿī duplicity, idiocy, and treachery.[4] Ibn Kathīr is careful—as a good Sunnī—to avoid criticizing the polarizing figure of ʿAlī ibn Abī Ṭālib, the fourth Sunnī caliph and first Shīʿī Imam, but takes every opportunity to point out not only that ʿAlī's followers have made too much of him but also that ʿAlī himself would likely be appalled at their overveneration.

The question of ʿAlī's proper role in early Islamic history had already become a key political fault line by the time of al-Ṭabarī, even if the development of that question had not yet coalesced into the full-blown sects of Sunnīsm and Shīʿism by his lifetime; it was a question of life and death for Ibn al-Athīr and Ibn Kathīr.[5] It is certain that the sectarian environment tinted their view of the meaning of events; it probably tinted their view of which early events were important, and which were not. As Haider puts it, "there was no definitive moment when the Muslim community split into two irreconcilable factions; such a perspective was anachronistically posited by later Sunnī and Shīʿī scholars."[6] This is correct; Ibn al-Athīr and Ibn Kathīr were two such scholars, and this book is a study of how their histories both reacted and contributed to that evolving split.

Sectarianism is not the only factor that can account for the differences in presentation in the works of Ibn al-Athīr and Ibn Kathīr, both from each other and from al-Ṭabarī. Geography played an important role as well, particularly

---

4 Aaron Hagler, "Sapping the Narrative: Ibn Kathir's Account of the *Shūrā* of ʿUthman in *Kitab al-Bidaya wa-l-Nihaya*," in *IJMES* 47 (2015), 303–321.

5 Conrad demonstrates that Ibn Aʿtham al-Kūfī's (pre-Ṭabarī) *Kitāb al-Futūḥ* cites Shīʿī Imams as part of the larger *isnad* collection surrounding Karbalāʾ, an event that is the focus of the present study. However, he does so only after listing a set of more standard Sunnī *isnād* chains. To Conrad, this is indicative of Ibn Aʿtham's desire to normalize emerging Shīʿī narrative tropes (as Shīʿī identity was emerging, not fully formed, at the time of his life and work) within a normative Sunnī historiographical milieu. This is one way of making sense of the large collections of *isnād*s that appear, somewhat haphazardly, in Ibn Aʿtham's work, interpolated into the text rather than some sort of systematic attempt to establish the authority or veracity of a given account. The notion that Ibn Aʿtham was name-dropping stock Sunnī *isnād* chains is supported by the fact that Ibn Aʿtham's version of the Karbalāʾ story is utterly dissimilar to the ubiquitous al-Ṭabarī version, and is utilized as a source only by later authors of a decidedly Shīʿī bent, such as the *Maqtal al-Ḥusayn* of al-Khwarizmī (d. 568/1172); had he actually utilized the same accounts as al-Ṭabarī, his narrative would have been more similar to al-Ṭabarī. Regardless, Ibn Aʿtham's self-conscious citation of sources he did not really employ in a serious way, probably for the purpose of signaling a broader acceptance of what later generations would come to assess as overtly Shīʿī perspectives, indicates at least that the historiographical push-and-pull between Sunnī and Shīʿī tropes was well underway by Ibn Aʿtham's time, and had taken much of its concrete shape by al-Ṭabarī's.

6 Najam Haider, "The Myth of the Shīʿī Perspective," in Herbert Berg (ed.), *Routledge Handbook on Early Islam* (New York: Routledge, 2018), 210.

for Ibn Kathīr, whose pro-Syrian sympathies are evident. However, there was significant overlap between Syrian/Sunnī and Iraqi/Shīʿī identities. This overlap is general but important; its largest, most significant, and primary cause was the particulars of the Arab conquest. After the deaths of the Prophet Muḥammad and Abū Bakr, during the reign of ʿUmar ibn al-Khaṭṭāb, the early Muslims emerged from Arabia and conquered Syria (then part of the Byzantine Empire) and Iraq (then part of the Sassanian Persian Empire), the two most proximal territories to Arabia. The names and identities of the conquerors of those two territories are well-attested in a number of Arabic chronicles, including those of al-Ṭabarī, Ibn al-Athīr, and Ibn Kathīr. Syria being the expedition planned by the Prophet before his death, the invasion of that territory represented the more official military action undertaken during ʿUmar's reign. As such, Kennedy points out that the Muslim conquerors of Byzantine Syria tended to represent "large numbers of Qurashīs, volunteers from Yamāma tribes who had been sent up after the end of the *Ridda* in their homeland, and some members of tribes from the northern Ḥijāz who had presumably joined up *en route*. Conspicuous by their absences were the *Anṣār* of Medina and members of the Najdī and eastern Arabian tribes."[7] In other words, the conquerors and settlers of Syria represented the privileged Umayyad and Qurashī (often pre-Islamic) elite, and the men most likely to oppose the rise of a more egalitarian figure like ʿAlī ibn Abī Ṭālib. As such, the initial conquerors of Syria made the land fertile for resistance to Shīʿī ideas when they developed centuries later. By contrast, Iraq was a land largely ignored by the Prophet.[8] Perhaps the agricultural landscape was less appealing to the nomadic Arabic tribesmen than the pasturelands of Syria. Of the army that took Iraq from the Persians, Kennedy writes that "the Quraysh were hardly represented at all whereas there was a considerable number of *anṣār* from Medina and Thaqafīs from Ṭāʾif [...] [in other words] those who were already second-class citizens in the new regime while the élite turned their attention to Syria."[9] The leadership among the conquerors of Iraq, in other words, tended to be from among those who were already less privileged than the leadership among the conquerors of Syria.[10] Such men were more likely than their elite Syrian counterparts to support ʿAlī's claims

7 Hugh Kennedy, *The Prophet and the Age of the Caliphates* (Harlow: Pearson Longman, [2]2004), 61.

8 Conrad points out that Ibn Aʿtham al-Kūfī traces the beginnings of the Islamic conquest of Iraq to a dispute between the Rabīʿa tribe (a northern tribe) and Sasanian officials over grazing rights. See Conrad, "Ibn Aʿtham and His History" 124.

9 Kennedy, *The Prophet and the Age of the Caliphates* 66.

10 This is a vast oversimplification, of course. See Michael G. Morony, *Iraq after the Muslim Conquest* (Princeton: Princeton University Press, 1984).

and those of his descendants, and in that fact we see the seeds of the strength of emerging Shīʿī ideas in Iraq. Whether the rivalry that developed between Iraq and Syria was geographical (Iraqi/Syrian or Meccan/Medinan), political (Umayyad-ʿAbbāsid), *sābiqa*-related (muhājirūn/anṣār), tribal, or sectarian is a tangled question. The first *fitna* itself already possessed many of these divisions as salient factors;[11] by the time of Ibn al-Athīr and Ibn Kathīr, many of them had become intertwined and calcified. Thus, while Ibn al-Athīr and Ibn Kathīr had clearly discernable strategies of compilation and narrative performance to which they were notably loyal (as we will see), their rehabilitative projects were not single-mindedly devoted to one form of rivalry but rather to a tapestry of interrelated rivalries. Ibn Kathīr could, at one and the same time, challenge the negative historical reputation of Syria, the disparaged legacy of the Umayyads, and the glut of Shīʿī narrative tropes in his source material simply by amending his narrative performance of critical moments. Sometimes those rehabilitative priorities are separable and detectible, and sometimes not. This complication should not dissuade us from seeking a greater understanding of historians' strategies of narrative performance.

It should also be acknowledged that sectarianism was not the only complexifying factor in the histories that Ibn al-Athīr and Ibn Kathīr, and al-Ṭabarī before them, consulted and constructed. As Noth has eloquently demonstrated, the "salient themes of the early historical tradition" include not only *fitna* but also *ridda* (apostasy), *futūḥ* (conquests), administration, and genealogy, all while historians made different organizational choices related to chronological and stylistic concerns.[12] However, as time passed, the sectarian question maintained its salience (or perhaps increased in importance), while questions of apostasy, conquest, and genealogy all faded in terms of their relative importance. They did not disappear, but apostasy (as the *ridda* wars came to be remembered) became less of an immediate threat to the increasingly self-assured Islamic commonwealth, and questions of *sābiqa* became increasingly academic as generations passed and the Islamic enterprise grew past its infancy. What makes the sectarian question the primary focus of the present study is its durability in the face of an evolving set of progressive Islamic societies and its utility in providing an explanatory model for understanding the alterations Ibn al-Athīr and Ibn Kathīr make to al-Ṭabarī's narrative.

We will now begin by getting to know Ibn al-Athīr and Ibn Kathīr. Later, we will examine the raw material with which they had to work. The ubiquitous

11 Martin Hinds, "The Murder of the Caliph ʿUthmān," in *IJMES* 3 (1972), 450–469.

12 Albrecht Noth, *The Early Arab Historical Tradition: A Source Critical Study* (Princeton: Darwin Press, 1994), *passim.*, but especially 26–108.

"problem with the sources" means that there was a narrative opportunity in the story of the first century of Islam: since no definitive written sources survived (the fact that they relied so heavily on al-Ṭabarī rather than directly on his sources or other, even earlier, sources is telling), there was a great proliferation of written opinion on the period in the form of different, and occasionally dueling, accounts. However, there was no possibility of any later scholar creating an iron-clad, irrefutable narrative. That uncertainty was useful if one had an axe to grind, and by the time of Ibn al-Athīr and Ibn Kathīr, the axe that needed grinding was primarily a sectarian one.

We begin with the men themselves.

1 The Later Historians: Ibn al-Athīr and Ibn Kathīr

Obviously, the scope of a study such as this one could easily spin out of control with the addition of ever more worthy authors and their histories, and so it is worth discussing not only these two historians but also defending this self-imposed limitation. The Arabic textual tradition is famously complex and interconnected, and attempting to make good sense of the relationship among a large number of sources, while worthwhile, will provide a conclusion that is better described through statistical analysis than through the more human question of authorial intent. A clear portrait of any authorial intent may only be discerned when an appropriate framework is applied. These historians share their generally acknowledged Sunnīsm, the fact of their work in Syria, and their general reliance on al-Ṭabarī, which will be established. This study focuses on two famous historians, the first from the thirteenth century and the second from the fourteenth: Ibn al-Athīr and Ibn Kathīr, respectively. The choice of these men as the focus of this study should not be understood as a rejection of other contemporaneous, and equally worthy, historians. Of the two, Ibn al-Athīr's inclusion here is easier to justify: largely relying on al-Ṭabarī's material for the first three centuries of Islamic history, Ibn al-Athīr's work largely supplanted al-Ṭabarī's from the time of its publication onward. Ibn Kathīr's historical work, too, was widely published. He was chosen for inclusion here because his authorial voice is so strong, and as such he provides a clear counterpoint to Ibn al-Athīr, who mostly (as we will see) omits problematic material rather than altering the words of his major source. But there are other authors whose works could easily and justifiably and profitably be included. Sibṭ ibn al-Jawzī (654/1256) and al-Dhahabī (748/1348), in particular, spring to mind. However, both men had a biographical, rather than a narrative, focus to their works. Even in the case of al-Dhahabī, who did have a narrative section that, like the narratives of Ibn al-Athīr and Ibn Kathīr, relied heavily on the work of al-Ṭabarī, the narrative was considerably truncated. In De Somogyi's words, "In the first three centuries A.H. the records are very short, not detailed, and only give the gist of the matter. They can be styled a concise compendium of the *Ta'rīkh ar-rusul wal-mulūk* of aṭ-Ṭabarī, the general use of which was so common and well known that adh-Dhahabī considered it superfluous to give a detailed narrative of the events in this period."[13] As a biographically focused work, the relevant section of the *Ta'rīkh al-Islām* in al-Dhahabī's narrative is not so much a repetition of al-Ṭabarī's account as a *mukhtaṣar*. The case is even more pronounced in fully biographical works like those of Ibn al-ʿAdīm and Ibn ʿAsākir. Because those works focus on men rather than stories, many of the relevant pieces of the narrative become homeless. Karbalāʾ, for example, may be referenced by name, and the reader will be expected already to know the narrative, which never needs to appear in full detail. Thus, Ibn al-Athīr and Ibn Kathīr are included because they provide a clear example of the phenomenon to be described: the large impact of minor alterations to a fully detailed source text, which is in the same literary style and possessing the same basic structure as that source.

ʿIzz al-Dīn al-Ḥasan ʿAlī ibn Muḥammad ibn ʿAbd al-Karīm ibn al-Athīr (d. 630/1233) was a historian of Kurdish ethnicity born in Cizre, in present day Şirnak province in Turkey, who spent much of his scholarly life studying *ḥadīth*, *fiqh* and *uṣūl al-fiqh* under the shaykhs of Damascus. He spent a great deal of time in Mawṣil as a private scholar, and he also spent some time working in Baghdad. He fought against the Crusaders with Salāḥ al-Dīn, and was personally acquainted with Yāqūt, author of the *Irshād*.[14] Unfortunately, the circumstances of his life are "most imperfectly known as compared to the extent of his fame and influence that were his on account of his works."[15] Ibn al-Athīr was a world historian in the style of al-Masʿūdī and al-Maqdisī and, like them, devoted much of his time to his literary work in the fields of history and biography. However, "being an expert on the important theological discipline of the biographies of the men around Muḥammad and of the religious scholars, he also was a successful lecturer, and he was supported by his ruler."[16] The status of history as a field of study was very important to Ibn al-Athīr, and he defended

---

13 Joseph De Somogyi, "The 'Ta'rikh al-islām' of adh-Dhahabī," in *Journal of the Royal Asiatic Society of Great Britain and Ireland* 4 (1932), 831.

14 Franz Rosenthal, "Ibn al-Athīr," in *EI*² iii, 723.

15 Ibid.

16 Franz Rosenthal, *A History of Islamic Historiography* (Leiden: E.J. Brill, 1952), 55.

it as possessing examples for kings to follow in order to avoid tyranny, and for men to follow in order to achieve a praiseworthy character.[17]

The early part of *al-Kāmil fī al-taʾrīkh*,[18] according to Lewis and Holt the "chief example" of Zangid- and Ayyūbid-era universal histories,[19] is heavily indebted to al-Ṭabarī's *Taʾrīkh al-rusul wa-al-mulūk*[20] and, like the works of other *muʾarrikhī*s, entirely omits the *isnād*s and displays a more fluid narrative style. On this point, Rosenthal states: "His great compilation entitled *al-Kāmil*, an annalistic history from the beginning of the world to the year 628 [1230 CE], represents the high point of Muslim annalistic historiography. [It is] distinguished by the well-balanced selection of its vast material, by its clear presentation, and by the author's occasional flashes of historical insight," although it possesses a "noticeable partiality for the Zangids,"[21] as one might expect. Ibn al-Athīr set out to correct what he perceived to be the inadequacies of prior historical works, stating that "facts were overlaid in many of them through their repetition, ornate style, or through the long chains of *isnād* to be cited: and so many important events had been intentionally passed over or omitted through prejudice."[22] The work is organized chronologically by year. The significance *al-Kāmil fī al-taʾrīkh* is demonstrated by the fact of its ubiquity. As late as the nineteenth century, it was studied in Mecca by those "who wanted to shine in conversation."[23] Significantly, by its obvious dependence on al-Ṭabarī's *Taʾrīkh al-rusul wa-al-mulūk, al-Kāmil fī al-taʾrīkh* is a *muʾarrikhī* work that bridges the pro-Syrian biographical works with the *muʾarrikhī*-style pro-Syrian Ibn Kathīr.

ʿImād al-Dīn Ismāʿīl ibn ʿUmar ibn Kathīr (700–774/1301–1373) was a Syrian historian, traditionist, jurist, and exegete who flourished in Damascus under the Baḥrī Mamlūk dynasty.[24] Born to a family of Sunnī religious scholars who claimed Shīʿī ancestry in the Syrian town of Buṣrā, Ibn Kathīr moved to Dam-

---

17 Lewis, Bernard, and P.M. Holt (eds.), *Historians of the Middle East* (London: Oxford University Press, 1962), 81.

18 The most recent edition of *al-Kāmil fī al-taʾrīkh* was published in Beirut in 1988 by Dār al-Kitāb al-ʿArabī, and edited by Dr. ʿUmar ʿAbd al-Salām Tadmurī.

19 Lewis and Holt (eds.), *Historians of the Middle East* 82.

20 Rosenthal, *A History of Muslim Historiography* 108, and esp. 146–147; Lewis and Holt (eds.), *Historians of the Middle East* 89. For Ibn al-Athīr's relation to al-Ṭabarī, see C. Brockelmann, *Das Verhältnis von Ibn al-Aṯîrs Kâmil fit-taʾrîkh zu Ṭabarîs Aḫbâr er rusul wal mulûk* (PhD Diss.: Strasbourg, 1890). For other eras, Ibn al-Athīr relied upon the works of Ibn al-Jawzī, Ibn Shaddād, Ibn ʿAsākir, al-ʿĀẓimī, and Ibn al-Qalānisī, among others, for times and places where appropriate.

21 Rosenthal, "Ibn al-Athīr," *EI*^{2}.

22 Lewis and Holt (eds.), *Historians of the Middle East* 89.

23 Rosenthal, *A History of Islamic Historiography* 53.

24 Carl Brockelmann, *GALS* Supplementband ii, 48–49.

ascus at a young age with his family. He studied law with the Shāfiʿī Burhān Dīn al-Fazārī, under whose tutelage he produced some sizable commentaries;[25] he also attended lectures of some famous jurists, including the Shāfiʿī scholar Kamāl al-Dīn al-Iṣbahānī (d. 1348) and Shams al-Dīn al-Iṣbahānī (d. 1348). However, despite his early interest in law, it was the Qurʾān, and especially the *ḥadīth*, that captivated Ibn Kathīr. In addition to being a "direct heir to the legacy" of the scholars Jamāl al-Dīn al-Mizzī (d. 1342) and Shams al-Dīn al-Dhahabī (d. 1348),[26] he also studied closely with the Ḥanbalī scholar and jurist Ibn Taymiyya.

Ibn Taymiyya's influence on Ibn Kathīr's thought is clear not only from the latter's *Tafsīr*[27] but also from his historical writing.[28] Under the influence of Ibn Taymiyya, he had developed a sense of deep hostility to non-Sunnī perspectives on law, *ḥadīth*, and history, to the extent that, in composing *al-Bidāya wa-l-nihāya*, Ibn Kathīr stated that he carefully avoided sources like the *Qiṣaṣ al-anbiyāʾ* (stories of the prophets) and the *Isrāʾīliyyāt* (extra-biblical prophetic legends) when they were not corroborated by the Qurʾān or the *ḥadīth*, particularly if potential sources were deemed to be the result of *taḥrīf* (deliberate Jewish and Christian corruption of their respective scriptures) or posed theological challenges to his perception of Qurʾānic doctrine.[29]

Given his background, one would expect harsh views of Shīʿism; that, and his life in Damascus, probably accounts for some of the sympathy he shows Muʿāwiya's camp in the narrative of the first *fitna*. Most relevantly, "despite his commitment to the thought of [Ibn Taymiyya] on many levels, Ibn Kathīr approached politics with a certain measure of caution, displaying an attitude which privileged conciliation and compromise along lines typical of the *jamāʿī-sunnī* ideal that a bad ruler was better than anarchy and that as long as the ruling powers made effort to ensure the continued rule of *Sharīʿah* they were due loyalty and respect."[30] This ideal would play a critical role in shaping his presentation of the denouement of the Ṣiffīn story.

His great history, *al-Bidāya wa-l-nihāya fī al-taʾrīkh*, was one of the principle works of history composed during the Mamlūk period. It is similar to the biographical dictionaries of Ibn ʿAsākir and Ibn al-ʿAdīm in terms of its pro-Sunnī

25 Erik S. Ohlander, "Ibn Kathīr," in Joseph E. Lowry and Devin J. Stewart (eds.), *Essays in Arabic Literary Biography* (Wiesbaden: Harrassowitz Verlag, 2009), 150.

26 Ibid. 149.

27 Ibid. 149.

28 See Aaron Hagler, "Sunnifying ʿAlī: Historiography and Notions of Rebellion in Ibn Kathīr's *Kitāb al-Bidāya wa-l-Nihāya*," in *Der Islam* 97 (2020), 203–232.

29 Ohlander, "Ibn Kathīr" 154.

30 Ibid. 156.

tone, although naturally different in structure and reliant, much like Ibn al-Athīr, on al-Ṭabarī's work. By Ibn Kathīr's time, he probably utilized Ibn al-Athīr for his perspective on the historical course of events that occurred after al-Ṭabarī's death. As the title suggests, *al-Bidāya wa-l-nihāya*[31] covers the story of the creation of the world, a Prophetic biography based upon both the *sīra* and *ḥadīth*, the Umayyads, the ʿAbbāsids, and up through his time, and then even speculates about the future, up to the Day of Judgment. The coverage of Islamic history from the time of Muḥammad's death onward tends be very heavily focused upon the territory of Syria.

2 Their Source

Muḥammad ibn Jarīr al-Ṭabarī (d. 310/923), one of the giants of Arabic historiography, was born in Āmul, Ṭabaristān during the reign of the Caliph al-Muʿtaṣim.[32] Before considering his biography, it is worth noting that the real challenge that comes from working with al-Ṭabarī is just how little we actually know about him. Unlike many other Muslim annalists, al-Ṭabarī included no autobiographical details in any of his works, and most of what is known about both his life and his lost works comes from later biographers.[33] This is true of his general philosophy of history writing as well: almost none of his material constitutes his original words but rather takes the exclusive form of authority citation. Trying to pin down his perspective on this or that historical event is complicated by the fact that his cited authorities frequently disagree with each other, in particular on the events discussed in this study: Abū Mikhnaf, Madāʾinī, and al-Wāqidī had pro-ʿAlīd perspectives that would have been rejected by Ṣayf ibn ʿUmar, who was pro-ʿUthmānī, and al-Ṭabarī used all of them with no compunction. Al-Ṭabarī as compiler rather than al-Ṭabarī as author, the standard view of the field before El-Hibri[34] and Shoshan,[35] holds true for matters in his works of history until about the time of the ʿAbbāsids (and, as Shoshan points out, al-Ṭabarī does construct, in his own words or at least

31 The second edition of *al-Bidāyā wa-al-nihāya* (used here) was published in Beirut by Dār al-Kutub al-ʿIlmiyya in 2005, and edited by Dr. Aḥmad Abū Mākim, Dr. ʿAlī Najīb ʿAṭawī, Professor Fuʾād al-Sayyid, Professor Mahrī Nāṣir al-Dīn, and Professor ʿAlī ʿAbr al-Sāʾir.

32 See Fuat Sezgin, *GAS* i, 323–328; Brockelmann, *GALS* i, 148–149.

33 Chase Robinson, "Al-Tabari," in Michael Cooperson and Shawkat M. Toorawa (eds.), *Arabic Literary Culture, 500–925* (Detroit: Thompson Gale, 2005), 334.

34 Tayeb El-Hibri, *Reinterpreting Islamic Historiography: Hārūn al-Rashīd and the Narrative of the ʿAbbāsid Caliphate* (Cambridge: Cambridge University Press, 2009).

35 Shoshan, *Poetics* xxxi–xxxii.

without attribution, his own history of the period of the 30 years or so prior to the opus's completion). This dark spot when it comes to al-Ṭabarī's personal historical opinions on the early Islamic narratives stands in stark contrast to his legal thoughts; we have no trouble, in his juristic works, determining his opinions of the four major *madhhab*s.

Al-Ṭabarī's silence regarding his opinions of historical matters is a great lacuna in our knowledge of him. Fortunately, for the purposes of this study, his personal perspective hardly matters. The mere existence of his historical work as a bottleneck of the (now-lost) authorities he cites, and the unavoidability of this work as a key, nay, *the* key, reference for later historians like Ibn al-Athīr and Ibn Kathīr, means that we do not have to concern ourselves with questions of what al-Ṭabarī really thought (although, occasionally, it is reasonable to make educated guesses). Although it may be unsatisfying, we will therefore treat al-Ṭabarī as a text that was considered authoritative for centuries and comprised of the cited works of earlier informants, rather than concern ourselves with the unknowable man himself, whenever possible. We may content ourselves with the likelihood that al-Ṭabarī would have accepted being equated with the work itself; as Khalidi points out, "al-Ṭabarī would probably have insisted that he *was* his scholarship, that his words are all there is."[36]

He was educated in Rayy (present-day Tehran) before moving to Baghdad at the age of sixteen. He moved there with the apparent intention of studying with Aḥmad ibn Ḥanbal,[37] but the latter died shortly before al-Ṭabarī arrived. He continued his education in Baṣra and Kūfa, and then in Palestine and Egypt. His educational goal seemed to be to collect as many famous teachers as possible; his teachers tended to be authorities whom he cited to establish authenticity in his work.[38] He returned to Baghdad when his education was complete.

In Baghdad, al-Ṭabarī did not accept a position with the government or the judiciary, as might be expected for a man of his skill and stature, but rather chose to devote himself entirely to his intellectual pursuits,[39] and he seems to have enjoyed a private income from his estate in Ṭabaristan. The primary focus

36 Tarif Khalidi, "Al-Ṭabarī: An Introduction," in *Al-Ṭabarī: A Medieval Muslim Historian and His Work*, Hugh Kennedy (ed.) (Princeton: Darwin Press, 2008), 1.

37 Franz Rosenthal, "The Life and Works of al-Ṭabarī," in *The History of al-Ṭabarī*, i (Albany: SUNY Press, 1989), 19. Rosenthal points out that this story may have been invented to defuse later Ḥanbalī animosity towards al-Ṭabarī.

38 Ibid. 18–31.

39 Ibid. 36. See D. Sourdel, "Ibn Khāḳān," in *EI*², iii, 824, s. v. Ibn Khāḳān (3), for a story in which al-Ṭabarī angrily rebukes his friends and students for encouraging him to accept a position with the *maẓālim* court, a body that dealt with cases outside the competence of the *qāḍī*s of the *sharīʿa* jurisdiction.

of his output was jurisprudence, although, like many of his teachers, contemporaries, and students, he was an expert in a wide range of topics, including *ḥadīth*, *tafsīr*, medicine, poetry, and, naturally, history. As a citizen of Baghdad during an era of securely centralized ʿAbbāsid rule, he lived and wrote in a time and place where Shīʿism was seen as a potential subversive threat, and was himself accused of Shīʿism by Ḥanbalī opponents. Despite his obvious admiration for the character of ʿAlī—an admiration that was shared by many Sunnīs, both before him and after him[40]—his perspective was not really a proto-Shīʿī one, notwithstanding claims to the contrary by his Ḥanbalī opponents, "who were to stir up the Baghdād mob against al-Ṭabarī on more than one occasion."[41] Indeed, the sects as such did not yet exist in anything but a chrysalis form when al-Ṭabarī was alive; the internal political divides that al-Ṭabarī emphasized in his narrative of the *fitna* were the political and tribal factions that dominated the Umayyad period and the ethnic and military feuding that featured prominently into his own era. On the contrary, al-Ṭabarī probably held mainstream beliefs[42] and wrote with an avowed Shāfiʿism in the early part of his career before his independent views caused him and his students be referred to as a separate *madhhab*, the "Jarīrī" *madhhab*. In fact, despite how posterity recalls him, al-Ṭabarī almost certainly considered himself a *ḥadīth* scholar and a jurist before a historian or an exegete. He is remembered by Ibn al-Nadīm as a jurist[43] and by al-Masʿūdī as the author of the *Taʾrīkh*, though he identifies al-Ṭabarī expressly as "the jurist of his day, the ascetic of his age, where the sciences of the world's jurists and Hadith scholars were mastered."[44] Al-Ṭabarī was remembered this way until the twelfth and thirteenth centuries, by which time his reputation as a historian overshadowed his reputation as a jurist. This is in no small part due to the regrettable fact that his juridical work survives only in part, while his historical and exegetical work survives in full.

Ḥanbalī hostility towards al-Ṭabarī was based largely on the publication of his book *Ikhtilāf ʿulamāʾ al-amṣār fī aḥkām sharāʾiʿ al-Islām* (The disagreements of the scholars in the major garrison towns with respect to the laws of the

40 Robinson, "Al-Tabari" 335.

41 E.L. Petersen, *ʿAlī and Muʿāwiya in Early Arabic Tradition* (Copenhagen: Munksgard, 1964), 148.

42 Yāqūt al-Rūmī, *Irshād al-arīb ilā maʿrifat al-adīb (muʿjam al-udabāʾ)* (W. Gibb Memorial Series 6), ed. D.S. Margoliouth (Leiden and London: E.J. Brill, 1907–1927) 453 f.

43 Ibn al-Nadīm, *The Fihrist*, trans. Bayard Dodge (New York: Columbia University Press, 1970), 563–565.

44 Robinson, "Al-Tabari" 337.

Muslim religion), which disregarded Ibn Ḥanbal; the only reference to him is an indirect one.[45] Al-Ṭabarī seems to have considered Ibn Ḥanbal a *ḥadīth* scholar rather than a jurist and also claimed that he had not seen anyone transmitting any of Ibn Ḥanbal's legal opinions authoritatively, a clear slight against contemporary Ḥanbalīs.[46] Al-Ṭabarī and his followers had other disagreements with the Ḥanbalīs, including the proper understanding of certain Qurʾānic passages, as well as deep disagreements about the "relative merits of rationalism and Hadith-based learning."[47] This eventually led to an incident where Ḥanbalīs stoned al-Ṭabarī's residence and had to be removed by force. Again, it should be noted that al-Ṭabarī's writings show a man far more concerned with legal and jurisprudential conflict than with any emerging conflicting identities that pitted proto-Sunnīs against pro-ʿAlīds.

To say that al-Ṭabarī was prolific would be a great understatement.[48] Besides his history, his most famous work was *Jāmiʿ al-bayān ʿan taʾwīl āy al-Qurʾān*, his famous *tafsīr*, or Qurʾānic commentary. Interestingly, he also composed a work called *Tabṣīr ulī al-nuhā wa-maʿālim al-hudā*, apparently a treatise addressed to his hometown, warning them against the erroneous doctrines of the Muʿtazilīs and Khawārij.[49]

Al-Ṭabarī's great history, *Taʾrīkh al-rusul wa-al-mulūk*,[50] is a historical account that quickly grew to enjoy "an almost canonical validity"[51] and, in time, became "the first port of call for virtually all Muslim annalists of the classical period."[52] It is among the most extensive and detailed works of Islamic history ever composed, preserving many citations from sources that would otherwise be lost. Al-Ṭabarī relied on a wide spectrum of written sources that were available to him, likely including the works of his contemporaries, al-Dīnawarī's *al-Akhbār al-ṭiwāl* and al-Yaʿqūbī's *Taʾrīkh*. He expressed his own views "prin-

45 See Joseph Schacht, "Introduction," in Joseph Schacht (ed.), *Ikhtilāf ʿulamāʾ al-amṣār fī aḥkām sharāʾiʿ al-Islām* (Leiden: E.J. Brill, 1933), xv.

46 Rosenthal, "Life and Works" 70. See Yāqūt al-Rūmī, *Irshād* vi, 436, ll. 5f.

47 Robinson, "Al-Tabari" 338.

48 For an alphabetized list and discussion of al-Ṭabarī's known and suspected works, see Ibid. 80–134.

49 Ibid. 335.

50 The field is indebted Ehsan Yarshater, who was the general editor, and the team of translators who edited the 40 volume English translation of *Taʾrīkh al-rusul wa-al-mulūk*, based upon the collated text that was the fruit of the efforts spearheaded by M.J. de Goeje and his colleagues, printed by E.J. Brill in Leiden. The Arabic version of the text used here is al-Ṭabarī, *Taʾrīkh al-rusul wa-al-mulūk* (Beirut: Dār al-Kutub al-ʿIlmiyya, 2012).

51 Petersen, *ʿAlī and Muʿāwiya* 148.

52 Robinson, "Al-Tabari" 341.

cipally through selecting, redacting, and arranging reports," as opposed to his methodology in his legal, theological, and exegetical work, where he frequently states his positions outright, clearly, and explicitly.[53] He was not as fastidious about *isnāds* in *Taʾrīkh al-rusul wa-al-mulūk* as he was in his other works and satisfied himself with incomplete *isnāds*, relying (in the sections relevant to this study) upon eighth- and ninth-century transmitters, such as Abū Mikhnaf, Sayf ibn ʿUmar, and al-Madāʾinī.[54]

Like the other historians examined in this book, al-Ṭabarī organized his historical opus annalistically. Petersen writes: "Year by year and event by event he builds up his exposition by means of—often several—parallel or co-ordinate traditions, normally supplemented with comments of his own; he lays down categorically how each event is to be placed and interpreted. This is one reason why Ṭabarī gives his reader, immediately and overwhelmingly, the impression of final authority."[55] Unlike the other men examined in this study, al-Ṭabarī does regularly include *isnāds* in his retelling. Regarding his use of the tradents, Petersen explains:

> Ṭabarī follows the conservative traditional technique, and he does it fairly loyally; even his occasional tendentious abridgements will hardly reveal any actual falsification. The difficulties do not appear until we are to explain his peculiar choice of sources, and especially why he in long passages prefers a corrupt source like Sayf b. ʿUmar to the pure ones, Abū Mikhnaf, ʿAwāna and others, which he knows and frequently employs. It applies generally that Ṭabarī's depiction of the revolution against ʿUthmān and of the first year of ʿAlī's caliphate follows Sayf, and that his discussion on the preparations for the showdown between the Caliph and Muʿāwiya entirely follows Abū Mikhnaf, merely now and then interrupted by other sources.[56]

Without endorsing Petersen's description of Sayf ibn ʿUmar as "corrupt,"[57] it remains true that al-Ṭabarī is the most important source for medieval Arab scholarship on the entirety of early Islamic history. He also wrote from a pious and scholarly vantage point, a perspective that employs later ideas to "seek to

53 Ibid. 338.
54 Ibid. 341.
55 Petersen, *ʿAlī and Muʿāwiya* 150.
56 Ibid. 150. See also Shoshan, *Poetics, passim*.
57 For a rehabilitation of the reliability of Sayf ibn ʿUmar, see Ella Landau-Tasseron, "Sayf ibn ʿUmar in Medieval and Modern Scholarship," in *Arabica* 67 (1990), 1–26.

extract tidy legal theories from messy past *Realpolitik*,"[58] with an apparent larger goal, Robinson argues, of "serving an emerging orthodoxy" that did not exist in al-Ṭabarī's time.[59]

3 Establishing the Texts' Relationships

For many of the Arabic historians of the Islamic past, the process of composing a work was less akin to writing and more akin to compiling narrative reports, while rejecting other such reports, and stitching the selected text together into a considered order. The percentage of authors' texts that represent their own composed language is therefore clearly smaller than one might expect from historians occupying a similar scholarly niche in other traditions. Presumably, each author selected those earlier accounts he thought "best," although whether that meant most trustworthy, most eloquent, most pious, most entertaining, or some combination thereof is beyond our ability to discern confidently (although we can hypothesize). Then, he put them in what he deemed the proper order, copied those parts he wished to, removed or amended other parts, and interjected his own thoughts (if at all) irregularly, though not necessarily infrequently. This process might have happened in a couple of ways: the author could have determined to use specific sources at the beginning of his process, copied them, and then added his interjections later; or, alternatively, he could have written a section at a time, combining the actions of compiling and composing into a single creative endeavor. The order of his creative process hardly matters of course. Our interest lies in the changes themselves, since those are the natural expressions of ultimate authorial approval or disapproval of earlier sources. If nothing was wrong with an earlier version, no new version would be required. Nothing would need to change; indeed, most things did not change.

What this means is that the way to establish the exact relationship between a text and its sources is to compare each text of interest with every prior text in the historiographical corpus. A map of each text's sources, created by comparing earlier texts, still presents a set of methodological difficulties. For example, there will be no shortage of selections from, say, Ibn al-Athīr that are identical to corresponding sections from al-Ṭabarī, but without further information there will be no way to ascertain whether Ibn al-Athīr was consulting a copy of *Taʾrīkh al-rusul wa-l-mulūk* itself or whether he was looking at the now-lost work of

58 Andrew Marsham, *Rituals of Islamic Monarchy* (Edinburgh: Edinburgh University Press, 2009), 15.

59 Robinson, "Al-Tabari" 342.

ʿUmar ibn Saʿd or Ṣayf ibn ʿUmar or a more specialized earlier work, like Naṣr ibn Muzāḥim's *Waqaʿat Ṣiffīn*.[60] The relative indistinguishability of sources in terms of text alone is one of the key linguistic and stylistic factors that allows for a study such as this; however, if our goal is to discover which specific sources later historians consulted, the digital approach made possible by databases like kitab-project (an eminently useful and quite exciting application) leads to compelling big-data conclusions that nonetheless fall somewhere short of definitive when seeking to answer questions about individual texts.

Sourcing specific textual passages is not our goal, but merely a useful tool. The important distinction for our purposes is not one between al-Ṭabarī and Ṣayf ibn ʿUmar but rather between sections of text that are traceable and those that are not. A traceable textual selection gives us insight into a later author's intentions. Reused text may be understood as having been considered unproblematic (if there is no change) or (if there is a change, and depending on the nature and scope of the change) a guide to the author's thought process in terms of his compilation and recension. A section of text with small omissions may have been altered for brevity; on the other hand, if (as we will see in the case of Ibn al-Athīr) there is a discernible pattern to the omissions, they may offer a valuable glimpse into literary-narrative strategy, communal sympathy, and overall perception of the historical narrative itself. Changes in the narrative relating to the attribution of quotations or ideas, larger omissions (say, of entire episodes), addenda, and other emendations offer further insights when compared to the textual baseline provided by the source text. By contrast, untraceable text fragments—though admittedly few in number—are invaluable to this study because they are the most likely to present us with not only the original words of the authors but also with a marker noting a place where the authors felt it sufficiently necessary to buck the standard conventions and offer words or interpretations of their own.

The relationship of our two later historians to al-Ṭabarī is evident and widely acknowledged. This does not mean, however, that modern historians have dealt with these sources in the same way. Just as (as we will see) Ibn al-Athīr and Ibn Kathīr shaped the sources they employed to create a narrative that suited their purposes, modern historians have seen in the early Islamic narrative an opportunity to append any desired meaning to their sources. Accounts range from the

---

60 The relationship between Ibn al-Athīr's text and that of al-Ṭabarī has been long noted, including in Carl Brockelmann's PhD diss., *Das Verhältnis von Ibn-el-Aṯīrs Kāmil fit-taʾrīḫ zu Ṭabarīs Aḫbār errusul wal mulūk*. Cited in R. Stephen Humphreys, *Islamic History: A Framework for Inquiry* (Princeton: Princeton University Press, 1991), 130.

nakedly polemical[61] to the theologically patronizing,[62] from the deeply experimental[63] to the straightforward translation.[64] Obviously, there is no single correct way to engage in historiographical scholarship; while some, like the works of Muir and Andrae, tell us more about the scholars themselves than the period they treat, very little of the scholarship is entirely without value. The standard cautious approach always applies: seekers of knowledge must bear in mind the biases of the authors, the biases of the sources, and the intellectual and social milieus in which each wrote. In our case, those milieus will be discussed in the next chapter.

4 Methodology: Performative Historiographical Analysis

At its heart, the history writing in which Ibn al-Athīr and Ibn Kathīr engaged was less an act of storytelling and more an act of successive editorial decisions strung together.[65] In this case, we will focus on Ibn al-Athīr's[66] *al-Kāmil fī al-taʾrikh* and Ibn Kathīr's[67] *Kitāb al-Bidāya wa-l-nihāya*—both histories rely heavily on al-Ṭabarī's *Taʾrīkh al-rusul wa-al-mulūk*. In fact, their texts are often indistinguishable from that of al-Ṭabarī, and thus often from each other. At first glance, this is a daunting obstacle. Since Ibn al-Athīr tended only to omit mater-

61 William Muir, *The Life of Mohammed* (London: Smith, Elder, and Co., 1851).

62 Tor Andrae, *Mohammed: The Man and His Faith*, trans. Theophil Menzel (New York: Books for Libraries Press, 1971).

63 Michael Cook and Patricia Crone, *Hagarism: The Making of the Islamic World* (New York: Columbia University Press, 1977).

64 For example, Sean W. Anthony (ed. and trans.), *Maʿmar ibn Rāshid: The Expeditions, an Early Biography of Muḥammad* (New York: New York University Press, 2014).

65 I originally discussed this notion in Aaron Hagler, "The Shapers of Memory: The Theatrics of Islamic Historiography," *Journal of Islamic and Middle Eastern Multidisciplinary Studies* 5 (2018), 1–28. Much of this section reflects the research and conclusions that were published in that article. The treatment of the texts as literary creations has a long provenance; most influential is the approach of Tayeb El-Hibri, *Parable and Politics in Early Islamic History: The Rashidun Caliphs* (New York: Columbia University Press, 2010). See also Aziz Al-Azmeh, *The Times of History: Universal Topics in Islamic Historiography* (Budapest: Central European University Press, 2007).

66 For a more detailed biography of Ibn al-Athīr than the one provided here, see D.S. Richards, "Ibn al-Athīr and the Later Parts of the *Kāmil*: A Study in Aims and Methods," in D.O. Morgan (ed.), *Medieval Historical Writing in the Christian and Islamic Worlds* (London: SOAS, 1982), 76–108.

67 For a more detailed biography of Ibn Kathīr than the one provided here, see Henri Laoust, "Ibn Kaṯir Historien," in *Arabica* 2 (1955), 42–88.

ial from al-Ṭabarī, and only rarely added words of his own,[68] examining his choice of primary sources reveals much more about al-Ṭabarī than it does about Ibn al-Athīr (and, taken further, because al-Ṭabarī was such a loyal recounter of his sources, it tells us even more about them). We are thus left somewhat in the dark about Ibn al-Athīr; although he is a later figure, Ibn al-Athīr himself remains veiled behind the words of al-Ṭabarī. In turn, al-Ṭabarī is himself obscured by the limited sources *he* chose to use, and by his unwavering fidelity to their texts.[69]

The similarity of these texts, however, is not an impenetrable veil blurring the differences between them into undifferentiable literary mud. Rather, the fact that they are so similar, but not identical, means that when either of the later writers departs from al-Ṭabarī's text, it is a signpost for us that the narrative moment in question represented, for the author, one of those authorial or editorial decisions. The discrepancies themselves are the keys to understanding the authors' aims, motives, and literary-narrative strategies.

At its core, therefore, the methodology for approaching these texts is relatively straightforward. The task before us is to seek out the discrepancies (and determine if Ibn Kathīr and Ibn al-Athīr were relying on any other sources besides al-Ṭabarī), explore what impact the change has on the wider narrative, and hypothesize (bearing in mind the specific situation in which each man was writing, and the *oeuvre* of each) about the motive or motives behind the change. Elsewhere, I have called this approach "theatrical," noting the similarities between the creative process of an actor in possession of a script and our authors in possession of a source.[70] So as to maintain the integrity of the model without getting bogged down in the unfamiliar terminology of the craft of the actor, here we will use the term "performative," in view of the fact that the recycling of al-Ṭabarī's material was more than the mere revision of a text. Ibn al-Athīr and Ibn Kathīr consciously and purposefully brought the presentation of the past into alignment with the exigencies of their political, legal, and theological predilections,[71] and they did so with the intent of communicating those predilections to an audience through the medium of their texts.

This "performative" approach treats later texts as "performances" of earlier ones. The term performance might imply "orality" to some. It should therefore be made clear going forward that when the term is used here, no orality

68 Hagler, "Unity through Omission," *passim.*

69 Hagler, "The Shapers of Memory" 3–4.

70 Ibid., *passim.*

71 Ibid. 24.

is implied. On the contrary, the act of copying and then altering the source text of al-Ṭabarī was done in a manner that was clearly considered in solitude and then written; never was it actively performed for an audience (to the best of our knowledge). In this case, "performance" refers to the fact that both men saw, in al-Ṭabarī's text, enough that it was worth (to use the modern movie-industry term) *rebooting*. These *reboots* constitute a new performance of a well-known text.

Because the narratives would certainly have been familiar to at least the majority of readers of the later texts, and even the earlier texts, such as that of Abū Mikhnaf, might have been familiar as well, the changes that the later authors make mark, for us, moments of performative disagreement: they wanted their discrepancies noticed by the educated, and the "incorrect" views presented in earlier sources kept hidden from the historical neophytes. Ibn al-Athīr and Ibn Kathīr, when they make changes to their source material, may or may not be attempting to signal to their readership/audience that they have found some element of their source wrong; that would no doubt depend on each individual reader's familiarity with the material in question. However, they certainly made the decision, within their own mind, that a moment within their source was insufficient, erroneous, or otherwise undesirable for the picture of the past they wished to communicate. When a decision has clearly been made, we may—like an audience viewing a play—search behind the words for the motive. Unlike actors, though, these authors are in control of the performance of the entire story; thus, to determine what the motive for the decision to change a moment was, we must examine the changed moments and their impact upon the entirety of the narrative. Even small changes to the narrative have echoes and ripples that extend in both directions of the narrative. Such changes were certainly purposeful.[72]

The temptation in a study like this one is to proceed through the narrative chronologically, marking the differences in the narratives and discussing them as we go. Once we have defined (with apologies to Ibn Kathīr) the begin-

72 On the terminology of authors as actors, cf. Konrad Hirschler, *Medieval Arabic Historiography: Authors as Actors* (London: Routledge, 2006); and Konrad Hirschler, "Studying Mamluk Historiography: From Source-Criticism to the Cultural Turn," in Stephan Conermann (ed.), *Ubi sumus? Quo vademus? Mamluk Studies-State of the Art* (Bonn: Bonn University Press, 2013), 159–186. Hirschler does not mean to imply any theatricality to the focuses of his study, Abū Shāma (d. 665/1268) and Ibn Wāsil (d. 697/1298). Hirschler wishes to assert (correctly) that authors possessed individual agency within their societies and were thus "actors" within it. Obviously, the term is used here in a different sense. See Hagler, "The Shapers of Memory" 4ff.

ning and end of the narrative to be examined, in a chronological approach, it would make sense to proceed from the beginning (the election of ʿUthmān) to the end (Karbalāʾ) in order, examining the changes that occur when the earlier source text is adapted and recycled by a later author. To proceed in this manner, while it would emphasize the linearity of the narrative, would leave our analysis improperly centered on the chronology of the events described, which has little bearing on the meaning of each site of memory.

The starting point for an analysis that is centered on the authors' intentions should proceed from the authors' own conceptual starting points. Since the creation of any author's version of the narrative proceeded conceptually from the most important event outward (to events both antecedent and subsequent to it within the narrative), and not the chronologically earliest event, that must be our order as well. Authors may have written their texts in chronological order; or they may have written them out of order and then compiled them into an appropriately chronological presentation later in the process. They certainly did not *think* of their narratives chronologically, though; as the example of the Wahb ibn Munabbih papyrus shows, and as Keshk's framework[73] demonstrates, earlier events in the narrative were deployed and shaped to give the "proper" meaning to later events from a very early date. This analytical model will demonstrate that the *fitna* is the most important episode in the early Islamic narrative and that concerns that we call "sectarian" were of primary importance to Ibn al-Athīr and Ibn Kathīr. Their narratives swirl around such questions, and the events that treat such questions, like matter drawn into a vacuum.

There are some events even within the narrative, such as the Battle of Ṣiffīn, that are more important than others, such as the Battle of the Camel, in that the former's course ultimately played a decisive role in the formation and emergence of "sectarian" communities while the latter did not. The Battle of the Camel, to put it another way, could easily be excised from the narrative, and while we would lose the conclusions to the stories of Ṭalḥā and al-Zubayr, the emergence of sectarian identity would still make complete sense to subsequent generations.

Not so the Battle of Ṣiffīn, or Karbalāʾ, or the *shūrā* of ʿUthmān. To approach the stories in such an "event-centered" manner places us in the position of needing to determine which episode each author thought was the most important element of the narrative. This difficulty is compounded by the fact the historians in question may not have agreed on the matter; one may find the

73 Khaled Keshk, "How to Frame History," in *Arabica* 56 (2009), 381–399.

murder of ʿUthmān to be of primary importance, while another sees that assassination as nothing but a step on the road to ʿAlī's loss of the arbitration at the Ṣiffīn. A third might see Ṣiffīn as nothing but a prologue to ʿAlī's assassination, while a fourth finds the appalling slaughter at Karbalāʾ the event with the greatest impact. And, of course, each of these discrete episodes have elemental sub-episodes or "sub-narratives" within them. The Ṣiffīn story, for example, has six such elements. Keshk may call such elements "set-up stories."[74] There are two shortcomings to Keshk's incisive approach. The first is that he assumes that such "framing" must precede "momentous events" in Islamic history,[75] when in fact the framing elements may be found immediately preceding, or they may appear far in advance, or even following such events. The second is less a shortcoming than a missed opportunity; what Keshk sees as "momentous events," like the Battle of Ṣiffīn, may have an alternative function as "set-up stories" in and of themselves.

Although imperfect, the approach of this study will be to focus on events. There are some key events that make the *fitna* narrative the *sine quibus non* of the story: without these events, it is not the *fitna* story. These events are the dramatic climaxes, the local maxima of the linear narrative. These events—the murder of ʿUthmān, the Battle of Ṣiffīn, and the death of al-Ḥusayn at Karbalāʾ—are (somewhat counterintuitively) presented strikingly consistently from al-Ṭabarī's account to the later accounts written by Ibn al-Athīr and Ibn Kathīr. Nonetheless, the impact of these events on the characters is what drives the narrative forward, and so the meaning behind them (discernible in their context and their impact) is what reveals the authors' agendas. Therefore, this book is organized into sections, one each for each of these events. Rather than proceeding in chronological order, however, the analysis will begin at the end—the Karbalāʾ narrative—and then work progressively backward, highlighting how each site's narrative contributes to what comes after it chronologically, which will have already been discussed in prior chapters. The ostensibly less-important sections of the event narratives—the moments that give these sites their meaning relative to the larger narrative of early Islam—will be compared. The differences in the accounts of the more minor, lower-stakes moments give the consistent accounts of those climaxes different contexts and different effects—and thus different meanings. In each narrative the altered meanings of those smaller moments cumulatively change the meaning of the entire early Islamic narrative itself. Less important events, such as the Battle

74 Keshk, "How to Frame History," *passim*.
75 Ibid. 383.

of the Camel, will be treated superficially; like the limitation of the analysis of Ibn al-Athīr and Ibn Kathīr, the limitation of sites to be discussed will hopefully serve to clarify the argument.

There is, admittedly, a large amount of circularity to this approach. At the outset, the reader is being asked to take on faith that Karbalā' trumps all other moments as the authors' conceptual starting point and to proceed through the narrative in reverse order based upon that assumption. Please consider this a request to (momentarily) suspend disbelief for the sake of argument, even though this is not the first study to claim such a central narrative position for Karbalā' by any means.[76] The point of the study is not to prove Karbalā''s importance, either in general or to Ibn al-Athīr and Ibn Kathīr specifically, but rather to demonstrate the process by which these authors shaped their narratives around conceptually important moments. Indeed, Ibn al-Athīr and Ibn Kathīr both put their pins in Karbalā', so to speak, but they did so for different reasons and utilizing different literary-narrative strategies. Not all historians, even of their era, would choose Karbalā', although most would likely choose something—not all polemics were against Shīʿa or the general disunity of the *umma* after the Shīʿī emergence after all, and not all historical works had polemical elements to them.

5 Mapping the *Fitna*

Once the methodology is established, we may proceed to the task: assigning the *fitna* its external meaning within the broadly conceived narrative of Islamic history, and determining which aspects or episodes of the *fitna* story are instrumental to determining the narrative's internal meaning. The first trap one must avoid falling into is the temptation to view the *fitna* as a linear story, with the linearity functioning as the operative font of narrative meaning. It would be an error to assert that two events are of equal importance just because they both appear as necessary parts of the narrative. It would be equally erroneous to say that earlier events eclipse later events in importance, even if the later events are falling dominos caused by the earlier events. Linearity is not the key element.

Because the *fitna* is a narrative sequence that has profound consequences for the rest of "Islamic history," the events that inform upon the most important themes of the story turn out to be the highest stakes moments for our authors.

76 Most recently, see Antoine Borrut, "Remembering Karbalā': The Construction of an Early Islamic Site of Memory," in *Jerusalem Studies in Arabic and Islam* 42 (2015), 249–282.

A performative, event-centered approach will naturally emphasize the high-stakes moments and demonstrate how both preceding and subsequent events are captured by the gravity of those higher-stakes moments.

Trying to pin down the critical elements of the narrative depends upon one's opinion of what is thematically important. In the *fitna* narratives, two themes easily emerge as the most important: the question of political legitimacy following the death of the Prophet Muḥammad, and the trope of the betrayal of ʿAlī and his descendants. For our purposes, it is best to start with something basic, and perhaps obvious: the related questions of succession and legitimacy. That such issues play a critical, if not a decisive, role in Islamic history is practically a truism. We enter the narrative, in other words, mindfully focused upon the same problem that caused the sectarian divide in the first place: the Prophet Muḥammad, when he died, seems not to have had a unanimously accepted successor. The crisis moments within the early Islamic story as it is recorded all center around transitions from one leader of the *umma* to his successor. While there was grumbling about the elections of Abū Bakr and ʿUmar, it was really ʿUthmān whose (perhaps dubious) election shaped the debate surrounding political legitimacy.

The identity of the Prophet's successor is a central question, but it is not the only question. While the nature of caliphal authority was not a source of disagreement—there was communal division over ʿUthmān's effectiveness and legitimacy, but not much recorded over the nature and scope of his office—the process by which the next leader should be chosen was not standardized, either in the Qurʾān or in the Prophetic *ḥadīth* (although, of course, later dynasties had their own rules). In addition to the political uncertainty that was consequently endemic to each succession episode within the narrative in question, the accession of a ruler became a stand-in for his legitimacy. It is not surprising, then, that the *shūrā* of ʿUthmān was a target of each author's editorial performance of the narrative. By establishing legitimacy, not only of rulers and pretenders but also of the political theory that necessarily accompanied their accession, moments of succession and attempted succession provide a key battleground for the meaning of the entire *fitna* narrative.

The other key theme, namely the repeated betrayal (as the Shīʿa see it) of ʿAlī and his descendants, requires less elucidation. In this study, the focus will be on the denouement of the episode at Ṣiffīn, although others, including the *shūrā*, could easily stand in.

With these criteria, the key moments, what Nora calls "sites of memory," are easily discernable. They do not all take place within the internal confines of the *fitna*, but because of the *fitna*'s external influence on the wider narrative of Islamic history, those that come either before or after are included because they provide the *fitna* with its context and demonstrate its impact. These key moments are: 1) the *shūrā* of ʿUthmān, which sets the dynamics for the debate surrounding political legitimacy; 2) the Battle of Ṣiffīn, which exemplifies the trope of the betrayal of ʿAlī (and his family), and also provides important narrative context for very important subsequent events; and 3) the Battle of Karbalāʾ, which serves as a climax for both of those thematic threads.

A critic would undoubtedly (correctly) point out that there are moments of absolutely critical importance absent from this list, including any mention of the second caliph, ʿUmar ibn al-Khaṭṭāb, or the seizure of power by Muʿāwiya and his subsequent appointment of his son Yazīd, which violated previous norms of succession, or even the assassination of ʿAlī. Even critical moments within the *fitna*, such as the Battle of the Camel, do not make this list. This list of key moments, however, is not meant to linearly survey the entire early Islamic narrative and ensure equal treatment to all indispensable moments. This list is meant to single out those moments whose narrative prerequisites are the foundation of the *fitna* narrative's meaning.

In this case, it is the chronologically last of these events, the Battle of Karbalāʾ and the martyrdom of al-Ḥusayn ibn ʿAlī, that becomes the focal point of the entire narrative for Ibn al-Athīr and Ibn Kathīr. This event would not have been their focal point of choice if it were not for the ultimate division of Islam into the sectarian communities of Sunnīsm and Shīʿism. Karbalāʾ became important because the Shīʿa argued vociferously for its importance; to ardent Sunnīs like Ibn al-Athīr and Ibn Kathīr, it was not a narrative battlefield of their choosing, laden as it was with ready-made Shīʿī narrative tropes, like the martyrdom of ʿAlī's family and the villainous character of ʿAlī's family's opponents. That Ibn Kathīr and Ibn al-Athīr spent, as this book argues, much of their narrative effort seeking to contextualize and repurpose the Karbalāʾ narrative is testament to the successful proliferation of Shīʿī grievances in the written historical tradition that preceded them.

The selection of an event, in this case Karbalāʾ, rather than a conceptual or spiritual division, as the central focus of the Sunnī-Shīʿī divide is problematic. After all, many if not most self-identified Sunnīs and Shīʿa, throughout history and today, would describe the differences between them in conceptual rather than historical terms. Dakake points to the critical concept of *walāya*, which to Shīʿa came to mean "an all-encompassing bond of spiritual loyalty that describes, simultaneously, a Shiʿite believer's allegiance to God, the Prophet, the Imām and the community of Shiʿite believers, collectively."[77] A dispute

77 Maria Massi Dakake, *The Charismatic Community: Shiʿite Identiy in Early Islam* (Albany: SUNY Press, 2007), 7.

over the proper meaning of the term in the Qurʾānic context is actually be a key element of the Ṣiffīn narrative, as we will see. From a practical standpoint, Dakake is correct, and her work on the development of Shīʿī identity is excellent. Her forefronting of spiritual, theological, and conceptual divergences between the evolving Sunnī and Shīʿī communities downplays the historiography at Karbalāʾ. To Dakake, Karbalāʾ is an episode where, even in the narratives of pro-ʿAlīd or downright Shīʿī historians,[78] the critical concept of *walāya* has temporarily lost its importance, having been largely replaced with the concept of *nuṣra*, a term less pregnant with theological meaning (although it would make a return later in the narrative). As such, she reasons, Karbalāʾ is a less important site of memory than, for example, the movement of the Penitents, the *tawwabūn*, whose narrative of suicidal rebellion for the cause of the already-deceased al-Ḥusayn was rife with the critical sectarian language of *walāya* and *ʿadāwa*[79] ("enmity" to the enemies of ʿAlī), and thus was far more important to the development of sectarian identity than Karbalāʾ. The present study, by contrast, is less concerned with the actual development of sects in Islam than it is with later understanding of the relative importance of events. Al-Ḥusayn was no more a Shīʿī than Jesus was a Christian; the development of both Shīʿism and Christianity was accomplished by their post-death followers. It was explicitly Karbalāʾ that motivated the *tawwabūn* and the later ʿAlīd or pro-ʿAlīd rebellions. So while the *historical* Karbalāʾ was not, as Dakake infers from the Shīʿī presentation of it, necessarily a sectarian event in and of itself, the *historiographical* Karbalāʾ—as the narrative motive for the *tawwabūn* for al-Mukhtār, and for Zayd ibn ʿAlī and Muḥammad al-Nafs al-Zākiyya for the sectarian violence and the emergence of the Fāṭimids—became the moment that these particular Sunnī historians were most concerned with "landing."[80] The centrality of the Karbalāʾ narrative, and its unparalleled importance within the

78 Dakake draws most heavily from al-Ṭabarī, al-Masʿūdī, Ibn Aʿtham al-Kūfī, al-Balādhūrī, and especially the cited words of Abū Mikhnaf, a group that ranges from sympathetic to the pro-ʿAlīd cause to self-identified Shīʿī. It is no surprise that the ardently Sunnī historians Ibn al-Athīr and Ibn Kathīr see matters differently.

79 See Dakake, *Charismatic Community* 63–64.

80 Abbas Barzegar, "'Adhering to the Community' (Luzūm al-Jamāʿā): Continuities between late Umayyad Political Discourse and 'Proto-Sunni' Identity," in *Review of Middle East Studies* 49 (2015), 140–158. Barzegar convincingly shows that one of the most important concepts that shaped emerging Sunnī identity was the norm of *luzūm al-jamāʿā*, which emerged not under the ʿAbbāsids but under the later Umayyads, particularly the Marwanids. The concept is supported by a great number of *mutāwatir aḥādīth* and places the emergence of Sunnī identity under the Syria-based Umayyads.

wider early Islamic narrative, is not an assumption of this study; it is a focus and, eventually, a conclusion.

Working backward from that point in the story, the importance of the other events, Ṣiffīn and the *shūrā* in particular, will become clear. Karbalāʾ may well be the "point of no return," from which those who later came to consider themselves Sunnīs and those who later came to consider themselves Shīʿa could no longer be reconciled, so its narrative importance to subsequent events (as just discussed) is self-explanatory. The standard narratives generally present Karbalāʾ, at its most basic, functional narrative level, as an attempt by al-Ḥusayn to revolt against the iniquitous Umayyad usurpers and overthrow them. For this uprising to make any kind of narrative sense, the iniquity of the Umayyads and their usurpation from ʿAlī's family must be established. This trope is visible in the Ṣiffīn narrative; Muʿāwiya managed to politically outmaneuver ʿAlī at Ṣiffīn (a battle Muʿāwiya had been losing, if the standard is success of arms). This provides the spark for a sequence of events that led to the emergence of the Khawārij and the resultant assassination of ʿAlī. The assassination created a leadership vacuum, the narrative tells us, that only Muʿāwiya was in a position fill (thus setting the stage, eventually, for Karbalāʾ). Tracing the roots of Ṣiffīn backward, the meaning of the battle changes depending on one's opinion of ʿAlī's complicity or noncomplicity in the murder of his predecessor, ʿUthmān. It had been, of course, Muʿāwiya's demand for justice on the heads of ʿUthmān's killers, and ʿAlī's reticence to turn over his supporters, that provide the battle with its catalytic context. The question of whether killing ʿUthmān may have been lawful, although almost all agree that it was not, raises the question of ʿUthmān's legitimacy in the first place, which is far more contentious. This question, in turn, is tied to ʿUthmān's own election. Each narrative moment is designed to "set up" the proper meaning for events after it. The focal point of all of these historiographical endeavors is Karbalāʾ.

One consequence of choosing those narrative moments as the organizational principles of the study is that we are left comparing discrete episodes that do not vary greatly from version to version. These extremely important moments function like signposts: markers of progress along the way from the beginning of the story to the end. As we will see, the routes taken by the authors to get from one to the other *do* vary, sometimes greatly, oftentimes quite subtly, but always with an impact on the internal meaning of the story (and thus, its external function within the wider narrative).

Another consequence of proceeding in this manner, with Karbalāʾ acting in the central dramatic role of the early Islamic narrative, is that it makes the most sense to begin with Karbalāʾ and then proceed backward from there (in reverse chronological order). This is why the first section is on Karbalāʾ, the second on Ṣiffīn, and the third on the *shūrā*. One could easily proceed chronologically forward from Karbalāʾ, as well, through the (mis)treatment of the ʿAlīd Imams and their betrayals by the ʿAbbāsids; but once Karbalāʾ's narrative is concluded, tracing its impact requires a much more perfunctory and straightforward approach.

Looking at the story in reverse order requires some discussion, as it is admittedly unorthodox in a book discussing a historical narrative. The goal of this approach is to highlight the authors' narrative priorities (specifically, presenting a narrative whose meaning conforms to their preexisting intellectual preferences) and to demonstrate how earlier sections of the narrative set up the Karbalāʾ narrative to have the intended narrative impact. By beginning with Karbalāʾ, the reader can bear in mind the narratives' intended conclusion, even as we explore the set-up stories that are presented earlier in the narrative (such as Ṣiffīn and the *shūrā*). This is easier, in my opinion, than reading the narratives in chronological order, bearing in mind all the foreshadowing, and recalling it when we arrive at Karbalāʾ. It is easier and better to start with the conclusions in mind and then see, at various points in the narrative, how they impacted the presentation of earlier events.

6 Structure

The first chapter will discuss the historical background of the *fitna*, placing it in both its historical and historiographical context. It will establish the role sectarianism played in the narratives of the *fitna*, in particular the narratives found in *al-Kāmil fī al-taʾrīkh* of Ibn al-Athīr and *Kitāb al-Bidāya wa-l-nihāya* of Ibn Kathīr. It will also discuss the milieu in which Ibn al-Athīr and Ibn Kathīr were writing: Damascus during and after the "Sunnī Revival."

The next three chapters will discuss Karbalāʾ itself. Chapter 2 will discuss the Karbalāʾ narrative in a general sense, focusing on the goals of each author in presenting the story the way they do. Chapter 3 will discuss the fight and its immediate aftermath, and Chapter 4 will discuss the approach of the armies to Karbalāʾ in the battle's narrative run-up. This reverse chronological approach allows us to see the "pay-off" moments that are foreshadowed earlier in the text; this way, when we see the foreshadowing, it will be easy to know its intent.

The next section, on Ṣiffīn, will follow the same structure, with Chapters 5, 6, and 7, respectively, covering the general intent in the Ṣiffīn narrative, the battle of Ṣiffīn, and the run-up to the battle (including the Battle of the Camel). The third section, on the election of ʿUthmān, will follow suit, with Chapter 8 on the story of ʿUthmān overall and Chapter 9 covering the specific incident of the *shūrā*.

The fourth section will look at "further ripples" of the narrative enterprise, touching upon the stories of succession to the Prophet, briefly surveying (in Chapter 10) to what extent the pull of the Karbalāʾ is still active at the times of the death of the Prophet, the Saqīfa event, and the Caliphate of ʿUmar ibn al-Khaṭṭāb. Chapter 11 will look at the impact on the narrative of the Prophet Muḥammad himself.

CHAPTER 1

Historical Background of the *Fitna* and Its Histories

1 A Brief History of Islam before Our Extant Sources and the Emergence of Sectarian Rivalry

If the problem with the sources is a cliché, then so, too, is the fact that between the time of the life and mission of the Prophet Muḥammad and the appearance of surviving sources, a lot happened in (and to) Islam. There was, so the "ecumenical" version of the narrative tells us, a heroic campaign of proselytizing and warfare by the Prophet and his Companions, a series of assassination-instigated succession struggles (those struggles focusing primarily on the Prophet's cousin and son-in-law, ʿAlī ibn Abī Ṭālib) that pitted those Companions against each other multiple times, the expansion of the local monotheistic religion of Islam into a regional, and then a world, empire, a civil war known as the first *fitna*, the accession of a dynasty made up of the Prophet's original enemies, the Umayyads, and the murder of the Prophet's grandson, al-Ḥusayn. Following that, the Umayyad dynasty was overthrown by the ʿAbbāsids, close (but perhaps not the closest) relatives of the Prophet—an echo of the original succession struggle. Only after all this turmoil does a light trickle of sources, demonstrably from the era represented, begin to reach us in the present.[1] The expert on Islamic history may choose to skip this section, as it will already be known to them.

It would be wrong to say that the succession struggle, and the nature and person of the Prophet's rightful successor, was the initial divide that bedeviled the new faith. The initial partisan divide within Islam was between the *muhājirūn*—the Meccan followers of the Prophet—and the *anṣār*—the Medinese converts who welcomed the Prophet, already established as such, to rule over the new community of believers, the *umma*. After that, a series of other issues came to afflict the politics of what came to be known as *dār al-islām*, "the abode of Islam," referring to those lands ruled by Muslim rulers in accordance with Islamic law (in contrast to *dār al-ḥarb*, "the abode of war," or everywhere else). Without getting into the weeds too much, the Umayyad state was troubled by a dispute between large, ancient tribal confederations

1 The Qurʾān is almost certainly a product of its time; however, it is not a history book, and as a sacred text, its use carries with it a host of methodological challenges to a secular historian that can, in the case of the present study, be mercifully omitted.

 | DOI:10.1163/9789004524255_003

known as Qays and Yamānī; additionally, descendants of ʿAlī or their supporters vied for political leadership in a series of doomed rebellions against the Umayyads, starting with al-Ḥusayn but also including the rebellions of al-Mukhtār (d. 65/685),[2] Zayd ibn ʿAlī (d. 76/695), and Muḥammad al-Nafs al-Zākiyya (d. 145/762). Immediately after the ʿAbbāsid overthrow of the Umayyads, the most divisive political issue was essentially a taxation dispute between descendants of the Khurāsānīs for whom the ʿAbbāsid caliph al-Manṣur (136–158/754–775) had built the city of Baghdad, known as *Abnāʾ al-Dawla*, and the Khurāsāniyya still in Khurāsān. This was the dispute that ultimately led to the civil war between the two brothers, al-Amīn (d. 198/813) and al-Maʾmūn (218/833), sons of Hārūn al-Rashīd (d. 193/809), that caused the first collapse of central ʿAbbāsid authority. Even if ʿAbbāsid power was restored by their younger brother, Caliph al-Muʿtaṣim (d. 227/842), he was forced to rely on outside military force—specifically his mercenary-slave army of Turkish cavalry archers—to do so. The Turks were a double-edged sword for the ʿAbbāsids; they were the premier military units of their day, but it only took them about a generation to achieve a dominant position in ʿAbbāsid politics. It was probably more out of fear of losing their position than an expression of their own strength that they assassinated al-Muʿtaṣim's son, Caliph al-Mutawakkil, in Sāmarrāʾ in 246/861. The Anarchy at Sāmarrāʾ (246–256/861–870), as the following period is known, is marked by the fighting, within the temporary capital, of specific Turkish factions and the rapid turnover of the ʿAbbāsid caliph.[3] Three of four caliphs were assassinated in a nine-year period. The result of this anarchy was not a civil war in the rest of the ʿAbbāsid polity. However, the collapse of ʿAbbāsid power in and around Sāmarrāʾ did mean that, increasingly, outlying regions were forced to fend for themselves, and locally powerful notables stepped in to fill the role that the chaos in the capital had forced the ʿAbbāsids to abdicate. Iraq fell under the sway of the Daylāmī Persian Būyid dynasty; most of Syria came to be ruled by a network of the extended Hamdānid family. Egypt, having been dominated by ʿAbbāsid-allied potentates such as the Ṭulūnids and the Ikhshidids, soon fell to the Fāṭimids. What these new groups all had in common was that they were Shīʿī: they believed that ʿAlī had been the rightful successor to Muḥammad, and ʿAlī was succeeded in legitimacy by a line of divinely inspired Imams (although they sometimes disagreed on the nature and identity of those Imams). They were not, of course, descendants of ʿAlī themselves.

---

2 Mukhtār's rebellion was not an ʿAlīd one but an ʿAlīd-sympathizing one.

3 Matthew Gordon, *The Breaking of a Thousand Swords: A History of the Turkish Military of Samarra* (A.H. 200–275/815–889 C.E.), (Albany: SUNY Press, 2001).

Even so, violence in the early Islamic period before the fourth/tenth century generally did not pit Sunnīs, as they came to be known, against Shīʿa. The other political divisions, already mentioned, were far more likely to cause inter-Muslim violence. Even violent events of massive sectarian importance were certainly, at the time, perceived as political rather than theological disputes. This includes the Battle of Ṣiffīn (36/656)—both the Sunnīs and Shīʿa would come to see their ancestors on the same side of the fight against Muʿāwiya—and the martyrdom of al-Ḥusayn at Karbalāʾ (61/680), which, at the time, was the brutal suppression of a straightforward political rebellion, rather than an attempt to defeat and discredit a sectarian theological rival. The sects that came to see such moments as watershed events did not yet exist at the time they occurred. For the most part, from their earliest attestations until the fourth/tenth century, Sunnīs and Shīʿa more often than not lived together in an environment of peaceful, if begrudging, mutual tolerance, a *modus vivendi* likened by Cobb to a cold war (at worst).[4] There was the occasional outbreak of sectarian violence, such as the Baghdad crisis of 361–364/972–975, wherein Sunnī sectarian sentiment was stoked by the Turkish leader Sabuktakīn against his rival, the Shīʿī Būyid prince Bakhtiyār and his supporters. The result was armed fighting and the permanent division of Baghdad into sectarian quarters. Even so,

> representatives of both sects rarely clashed in open combat, but [...] rivalries were fought in the open through learned polemic and public spectacles [...] and covertly through the use of clandestine agents and missionaries. All this while Sunnis and Shiʿis continued to trade, work, and live with one another. However, this Sunni-Shiʿi cold war did not, and perhaps could not, last. It became white hot toward the middle of the eleventh century, long after Shiʿism found not just a dynasty, but also [the Fāṭimid] empire.[5]

It was in this milieu, after the Pandora's box of sectarian violence had been opened, that all three of the histories examined in this book were written.

The conflation of *fitna* and sectarian conflict is more tenable in the contexts of Ibn al-Athīr's and Ibn Kathīr's writings; by their time, the Sunnī and Shīʿa were certainly distinct communities of religious ideas and practice, and occasionally violently opposed to each other. Those categories were not nearly

4 Paul M. Cobb, *The Race for Paradise: An Islamic History of the Crusades* (Oxford: Oxford University Press, 2014), 41–49.

5 Ibid. 44.

so well-developed during al-Ṭabarī's career, even if the disputes that ultimately coalesced into dueling sectarian identities were already extant. The real crisis for al-Ṭabarī was likely *fitna* itself. Correcting what they considered to be erroneous sectarian ideas that had emerged since al-Ṭabarī, and neutralizing or accounting for the disunity they engendered, were (as we will see) a primary motive of both Ibn al-Athīr and Ibn Kathīr for making the changes that they did.

2 The Raw Data: The Sectarian Narratives

The first *fitna*, or Muslim civil war, had its seeds in the question of succession to the Prophet Muḥammad, who died without communal unanimity on the nature and person of his successor.[6] As the "Seal of the Prophets," God's last warning before the age of prophecy ended forever, Muḥammad had provided the incipient Islamic polity with a truly inimitable pattern of executive leadership: God Himself had provided much of the legislation for the state, largely in the form of the Medinan *surāt*, but now the hotline to the Almighty was forever disconnected. Interestingly, the question of the nature of authority after the Prophet seems not to have engendered a great deal of immediate discord (that would come later). The early office of the caliph, or "successor," reflected a community needing both political and religious leadership—not a pope to legislate the divine will infallibly but a political leader and spiritual guide who would steer his community on the right path.[7] The disagreement, rather, lay in the identity of the Prophet's successor.

The chronology of the first four caliphs, whom Sunnīs call *rāshidūn*, or "rightly guided," is amply attested in any number of easily accessible and well-researched modern works of scholarship,[8] and therefore need not detain us long. If the seeds to the first *fitna*—the first Muslim civil war—were sewn

---

6 For an in-depth discussion of the historiographical concerns that emerged following the Prophet's death, and their impact on the development of Islamic sectarianism, see Wilferd Madelung, *The Succession to Muḥammad: A Study of the Early Caliphate* (Cambridge: Cambridge University Press, 1997), with particular focus on 1–27.

7 Chase F. Robinson, "The Rise of Islam, 600–705," in Chase F. Robinson (ed.), *The New Cambridge History of Islam*, i (Cambridge: Cambridge University Press, 2010), 203. See also Patricia Crone, *Medieval Islamic Political Thought* (Edinburgh: Edinburgh University Press, 2004), 22; Patricia Crone and Martin Hinds, *God's Caliph: Religious Authority in the First Centuries of Islam* (Cambridge: Cambridge University Press, 1986).

8 One such "Islamic history" narrative is that of Kennedy, *Prophet*. The chronology of the *rāshidūn* can be found on pp. 50–81.

when Muḥammad died, it took root when ʿAlī ibn Abī Ṭālib (d. 40/661), the Prophet's cousin and son-in-law, was repeatedly rejected as caliph by powerful forces within the community (if not the majority of the community). There was a faction of early Muslims who preferred ʿAlī to any of the other Companions of the Prophet. The reasons for the support ʿAlī enjoyed are diverse: he was a great warrior; he was known as a very pious (perhaps the most pious) of all of Muḥammad's Companions; he was the Prophet's closest living relative at the time of the Prophet's death, as his first cousin and, since his marriage to the Prophet's daughter Fāṭima, son-in-law. Despite his stellar reputation, however, there was another contingent of early Muslims who were eager to keep authority vested in the same men, or at least the same families, who had held it before the conversion of the Meccan notables to Islam. ʿAlī, for all his piety, was from the same less-favored (but, thanks to the advent of Islam, up-jumped) branch of the Quraysh tribe as the Prophet, the Banū Hāshim. Thus, when ʿAlī was thrice passed over by the power brokers from the Meccan aristocracy it was not without a significant amount of grumbling from his supporters that the newly selected caliphs assumed their role, and ʿAlī was forced to bide his time as loyal opposition.

The first *fitna* began in earnest, not during the reigns of the first two caliphs (successors to the Prophet) Abū Bakr (11–13/632–634) and ʿUmar ibn al-Khaṭṭāb (13–23/634–644), but rather with the assassination of the third caliph of the *rāshidūn*, ʿUthmān ibn ʿAffān (23–36/644–656). Most of the early sources tell us the ʿUthmān was disliked by large segments of the *umma*.[9] Reputedly lazy, nepotistic, gluttonous, and greedy, especially by the second half of his 12 years in office, ʿUthmān was ultimately assassinated at the hands of a Medinan conspiracy in favor of, but not necessarily actively supported by, ʿAlī. However, unlike his predecessor ʿUmar, who had been assassinated by a Persian slave with what appears to be a misplaced personal grievance, ʿUthmān was felled by fellow members of the Arab-Muslim elite. He was succeeded by ʿAlī, but by that time ʿAlī was in late middle age, and the shockwaves from the calamity of the Companions of the Prophet fighting each other was already straining the community's seams. ʿAlī never succeeded in solidifying his power, as he faced opposition first from the Companions Ṭalḥa ibn ʿUbayd Allāh (d. 36/656) and al-Zubayr ibn al-ʿAwwām (d. 36/656), who were joined by the Prophet's widow (and ʿAlī's lifelong rival) ʿĀʾisha bint Abī Bakr (d. 58/678) at the Battle of the Camel (36/656), and then from Muʿāwiya ibn Abī Sufyān (d. 60/680), the

9 Heather Keaney, *Medieval Islamic Historiography: Remembering Rebellion* (New York: Routledge, 2013).

powerful Umayyad governor of Syria and future founder of the Umayyad dynasty, at the Battle of Ṣiffīn (36/656). The first *fitna* finally concluded with the assassination of ʿAlī in 40/661 as a direct result of the course of the Battle of Ṣiffīn, about five years prior. At that point, Muʿāwiya assumed political leadership of the Islamic polity (in fact, he had no rivals), thus ending the *rāshidūn* period and paving the way for the 89-year dynasty of the Umayyads, who had been the powerful Meccan branch of the Quraysh who had most ardently resisted the Prophet's call before converting under the Prophet's benign duress after the first Muslims took Mecca.

It was the assassination of ʿAlī, and then the martyrdom of his son al-Ḥusayn ibn ʿAlī at the Battle of Karbalāʾ (61/680) that turned those initial disagreements over the proper identity of Muḥammad's successor into a schism between what would come to be described as different sects of Islam, known today as Sunnī (i.e., *ahl al-sunna wa-l-jamaʿa*, "those who follow the sunna of the Prophet and the consensus of the community") and Shīʿī (from *Shīʿat ʿAlī*, meaning "partisan of ʿAlī"). Obviously, the division into sects was not immediate but rather the was the end result of a series of confrontations, some physical but mostly intellectual, between those who supported ʿAlī's early right, and after his death the rights of his descendants (the Imams), to leadership on the one hand and those who thought that the *rāshidūn* were legally and properly empowered in accordance with God's divine plan on the other.[10] The first *fitna*, naturally, became an important venue, if not the most important venue, for the expression of each sect's understanding of its beginnings.

That said, it is not as simple as saying that later Shīʿa supported ʿAlī in the set of battles and strife that make up the *fitna* while the later Sunnīs supported his opponents. Both sides would lay claim to ʿAlī as one of their own: to the Shīʿa, ʿAlī was the rightful Imam, or leader of the community, while to Sunnīs, he was the fourth of the *rāshidūn*. Neither branch of Islam ever denied his legitimacy (though they naturally disagreed on when his rightful reign properly began). Nor do we see, anywhere in the surviving early Islamic historiographical tradition, anything beyond lukewarm support of the Umayyads and a grudging acknowledgment of their worldly skills of statecraft. Positive depictions certainly existed. After all, if the Umayyad rulers did not patronize obsequious works of art and scholarship, that would make them unique among ruling dynasties. But the ʿAbbāsid takeover in 133/750, and the probable purge of abruptly disfavored scholarship, left us only the scattered and fragmentary echoes, in

10 Marshall Hodgson, "How did the Early Shiʿa become Sectarian?," in *JAOS* 75 (1955), 1–13. Hodgson described the Sunnī-Shīʿī divide as one in which a piety-minded community diverged over differences with respect to ʿAbbāsid political and religious legitimacy.

later sources, of pro-Umayyad writings.[11] The fact that nobody takes the "anti" position on ʿAlī does not mean that there is not a great deal of historiographical disagreement on the nature and meaning of the first *fitna*, and that disagreement can essentially be expressed by answering the question of just how wicked ʿAlī's opponents really were. Shīʿī scholars call them rebels and perhaps even apostates; Sunnī scholars deny that they were anything of the kind. Many of them, after all, were themselves Companions of the Prophet.

With this dispute at the center of both Sunnī and Shīʿī understandings of their own early narratives, the fact that Sunnīs and Shīʿa tell the story of the first *fitna* differently is no surprise.

3 The *Fitna* as Narrative

If the physical confrontation among Muslims with differing political opinions began in earnest with the assassination of ʿUthmān ibn ʿAffān in Medina in 36/656, at first glance that seems like it should be the point of narrative divergence between Shīʿī accounts and Sunnī ones. In fact, the *fitna*'s gravitational pull on the narrative is significantly stronger than that. In order to address ʿUthmān's assassination and its meaning properly, scholars were required to present the reign of ʿUthmān himself, in its entirety, with a constant eye on the narrative consequences of their presentation of him. Shīʿī historians were eager to highlight his shortcomings, while Sunnī historians often took steps to rectify the unfavorable presentation that was nearly ubiquitous in their pro-ʿAlīd sources.[12]

The need to characterize ʿUthmān's reign, in one form or another, means that it therefore became necessary to discuss the matter of his election. When ʿUmar ibn al-Khaṭṭāb, ʿUthmān's immediate predecessor, was mortally stabbed,[13] ʿUmar had enough time before he succumbed to his wounds to plan for the succession, but he did not do so by unilaterally appointing a specific chosen successor. Instead, he appointed a council, or *shūrā*, of six men—ʿAlī ibn Abī Ṭālib, Ṭalḥa ibn ʿUbayd Allāh, al-Zubayr ibn al-ʿAwwām, Saʿd ibn Abī Waqqāṣ (d. 54/674), ʿAbd al-Raḥmān ibn ʿAwf (d. 34/654), and of course ʿUthmān, the

11 Aram Shahin, "In Defense of Muʿawiya ibn Abi Sufyan: Treatises and Monographs on Muʿwiya from the Eighth to the Nineteenth Centuries," in Paul Cobb (ed.), *The Lineaments of Islam: Studies in Honor of Fred Donner* (Leiden: Brill, 2012), 177–208.

12 Keaney, *Medieval Islamic Historiography* 1–20.

13 History records that the killing of ʿUmar was not a political act but rather the act of a Persian slave with a misplaced personal grievance.

eventual caliph-elect, to choose from among their number the next leader of the Islamic enterprise. The course of the *shūrā* was lightly debated by historians, but the essential facts (as always) were not in dispute, even if their meaning was: ʿAlī and ʿUthmān emerge from the group of six as the two finalists, and through some bald-faced politicking, ʿAbd al-Raḥmān ibn ʿAwf positions himself as the kingmaker, holding in his proverbial back pocket the deciding vote. Through a narrative sequence that includes implied favoritism, impiety, back-room deals, and deceit, ʿAbd al-Raḥmān selects ʿUthmān, bitterly disappointing ʿAlī and his followers for a third time.

But was the *shūrā* process corrupted by all the politicking, or was it a legitimate election of a caliph? Here the histories differ, and it is not difficult to understand why they do.[14] The exemplary life of ʿAlī becomes something less than ideal if his bitterness over his *legitimately elected* predecessor ʿUthmān helped spawn the rebellion that led to ʿUthmān's illicit murder. On the other hand, if the *shūrā* was contaminated by the iniquitous scheming that was to become a recurring motif in Shīʿī presentations of the life experiences of ʿAlī ibn Abī Ṭālib and his descendants, then perhaps the uprising against, and even the assassination of, the usurper ʿUthmān could be presented as perfectly justified. ʿAlī would therefore be excused from culpability for the death of a prominent early Muslim and Companion of the Prophet: if the election was corrupted, ʿAlī's indignation transforms into something righteous. For post-sectarian historians like Ibn al-Athīr and Ibn Kathīr, the presentation of ʿUthmān, and the meaning of his time in power, necessarily draws the narrative of his election into the sectarian framework, despite the fact that the election occurred long before the divisions among the Arab-Muslim elite turned violent.

This phenomenon that sees the sectarian divide enter the early Islamic narrative is by no means confined to the story of the *shūrā* of ʿUthmān. On the contrary, every aspect of the early narrative in the works of Ibn al-Athīr and Ibn Kathīr, from the *Sīra* of the Prophet Muḥammad[15] through the conclusion of the second *fitna* that came with the brutal death of al-Ḥusayn ibn ʿAlī at Karbalāʾ was inevitably colored with the sectarian tint, written, as it was, in a sectarian world. Even for al-Ṭabarī, who wrote at a time when the sectarian divisions were less calcified, the strains and stresses on the community that would ultimately express themselves as sectarian identity were of concern. It would therefore be reasonable to delineate the relevant portion of the narrative of the *fitna* to encompass the election, reign, and assassination of ʿUthmān, the

14 Hagler, "Sapping the Narrative," *passim*.

15 Moshe Sharon, "The Development of the Debate Around the Legitimacy of Authority in Early Islam," in *JSAI* 5 (1984), 121–141.

reign and assassination of ʿAlī, and the reigns of the Umayyads Muʿāwiya ibn Abī Sufyān and Yazīd ibn Muʿāwiya, when the *fitna* itself technically only lasted for a few short years.

Seeing the *fitna* as embedded within the entirety of the early Islamic narrative is justified by the nature of the memory of the *fitna*. The *ex post facto* meaning of a war has little to do with the course of that war. What comes before it, usually presented as the "cause," and what came after it, usually discussed in terms of "impact" or "effects," has far more narrative potency than a play-by-play of troop movements, maneuvers, and skirmishes. At its core, the *fitna* was a dispute over the proper identity of the rightful leader of the post-Prophet Islamic polity, and over the nature of that leader's office. While those disputes neither began nor concluded with the *fitna*, the *fitna was* the section of the narrative where the subsequent split between Sunnīs and Shīʿa became inevitable—or, at least, so the later histories remember it for us. While the notion that the Sunnī-Shīʿī schism was unavoidable, perhaps from the end of the Battle of Ṣiffīn onward, may or may not be true, the fact that our later authors *believed* it to be true is what makes this section of the narrative particularly central to understanding their underlying sectarian message.

The second reason to delineate our narrative focus here has more to do with what we are choosing to exclude than what we are choosing to include. While there were certainly sectarian-based differences in the presentations of earlier figures, like the Prophet, Abū Bakr, and ʿUmar, and later figures, like the Umayyads after Yazīd, this study quickly becomes unwieldy if the line is not drawn somewhere. Students and researchers will have no difficulty applying this study's performative methodology of textual comparison to both earlier and later episodes, should they find it profitable to do so. However, this study will necessarily focus on two eras: twelfth–fourteenth century al-Shām (roughly "Syria," most especially focused on Damascus itself) and the Jazīra, and the narratives of the *fitna*, among the most turbulent episodes of the early Islamic narrative. To add in the narrative of an admittedly relevant figure like the Prophet would open a Pandora's box of other issues that would detract from the intelligibility of the conclusions and complicate them unnecessarily.

Speaking more broadly, in its entirety the early Islamic narrative functions as a literary reflection of a whole host of the author's theological, philosophical, and legal opinions. Much of the intellectual output in the Islamic world derives from one's understanding of the early period. Works of *tafsīr* (exegesis) are obviously tied to one's understanding of the Qurʾān; works on proper behavior are dictated by one's understanding of *ḥadīth*; works of *uṣūl al-fiqh* likewise draws their primary arguments from the Qurʾān and the *ḥadīth*; and works of *fiqh* look to the early *umma*'s example for their most compelling precedents.

The early Islamic narrative functions as *the* source for all other schools of the Islamic sciences. Although never achieving the stature of other fields of *adab* (belles lettres), history, understood to include both chronicles and *ḥadīth* as narrative sources of past events, provided the background, context, and often justification for those other fields. Later thinkers advanced their views on religious practice, sect, jurisprudence, and hermeneutics based on their understanding of this narrative's course (and historians, as we will see, put forward versions of the historical narrative that accorded with their own views of religious practice, sect, jurisprudence, and hermeneutics).

There is naturally some impulse to assume that the narrative the authors are presenting is consistent with their individual estimation of what actually happened, or that their account has not been influenced by preconceptions about sect, *madhhab*, or any other concerns outside of the realm of "pure" history. This is certainly the model with which the authors would prefer that we approach their texts. However, the fact that the narrative changes from author to author, and so frequently reflects a recension totally or partially sterilized of what the author would consider to be problematic source material means that it is more appropriate to approach the narrative in the reverse conceptual order. That is to say, it makes more sense to view later iterations of the early Islamic narrative in general, and the *fitna* narratives in particular, as the products of fully developed *a priori* legal, sectarian, and scholarly opinions, rather than as the *a posteriori* foundation of those opinions. As early as the early first/middle of the eighth century, the sectarian battle had insinuated itself into the act of telling history; for example, the papyrus of Wahb ibn Munabbih, one of the earliest surviving attestations of the *Sīra* of the Prophet, reflects the "sophisticated product of the Shīʿī efforts to establish the exclusive rights of ʿAlī" to the leadership of the *umma*.[16] If the Wahb ibn Munabbih papyrus, which certainly dates from no later than 119/737 (and was therefore almost certainly composed within a century after the Prophet's death), could already be a theater of the sectarian confrontation between Sunnīs and Shīʿa (or at least pro-ʿAlīds, given its very early date), how much more are the histories composed in the twelfth, thirteenth, and fourteenth centuries a product of what Wansbrough terms "the sectarian milieu?"[17]

In fact, later versions of the narrative, always presenting their material with a tone of authority and certainty, tend to contain more detail, not less; they also tend to contain fewer versions of certain key events, rather than more.

16 Ibid. 140. For further discussion, see M.J. Kister, "On the Papyrus of Wahb ibn Munabbih," in *BSOAS* 38 (1974), 545–571.

17 John Wansbrough, *The Sectarian Milieu* (New York: Prometheus Books, 2006).

Both of these facts are contrary to what we would expect to see if the narrative presented were the result of pure, careful scholarly investigation. The addition of details, for example, without the benefit of any new sources the authors care to reveal, "suggests concerns other than historicity."[18]

At the same time, conventions in history writing, and the move towards catering the presentation of the narrative to a broader reading public, evolved to essentially eliminate the *khabar* and the *isnād* as the primary vehicles of information delivery and substantiation. The *khabar* (pl. *akhbār*), which literally means "report," was a discrete, fully self-contained description of an incident, verified by an *isnād* (pl. *asānīd*), or chain of transmittance, which functioned as a kind of genealogy-cum-citation for the report. Usually in the ninth and tenth centuries, *akhbār* would be presented not as part of a linear narrative but alongside other *akhbār* that related other versions of the incident in question. These neighboring *akhbār* could be distinct from the original *khabar* in terms of content, a different *isnād*, or both. The historians who compiled these histories, including al-Ṭabarī, are sometimes called *akhbārī*s for their use of the literary unit. However, the shift towards a more linear narrative, which occurred in the later tenth century, meant that the historians of later ages, sometimes called *mu'arrikhī*s,[19] or "chroniclers," were compelled to pick what they considered to be the single "best" version of events and refrained from including multiple versions. Naturally, if they relied exclusively on the *akhbār* they consulted, the act of selecting one above all the others to which they had access would reflect the historians' best guess at what actually happened. However, the fact that they added information and detail, and sometimes played fast and loose with significant elements of the narrative (such as the order of events), means that the act of composing a narrative of the early Islamic epic necessarily reflected the "Islamic science" biases accumulated from their teachers and societies. In particular, the *fitna* narrative, because it is so central to both Sunnī and Shīʿī sectarian identity, reflects the sectarian biases of the historians.

From as little as 100 years after the death of the Prophet Muḥammad, the sacred history of early Islam did not determine one's opinion on *uṣūl al-fiqh*, *fiqh*, and theology. Rather, a given historian's preconceived notions of proper juris-

---

18 Michael Cook, *Muhammad* (Oxford: Oxford University Press, 1996), 63–64.

19 My use of these terms derives from Chase F. Robinson, *Islamic Historiography* (Cambridge: Cambridge University Press, 2003), esp. 18–54; for a discussion of the development of historiographical writing styles through Arab/Islamic history, see Noth, *Early Arabic Historical Tradition*; Fred M. Donner, *Narratives of Islamic Origins* (Princeton: Darwin Press, 1998); Franz Rosenthal, *History of Muslim Historiography*; and A.A. Dūrī, *The Rise of Historical Writing Among the Arabs* (Princeton: Princeton University Press, 1993).

prudential procedures, legal rulings, and theology, gleaned from one's teachers and society, strongly influenced his narrative choices. In this way, successive presentations of the *fitna* narrative provide insight into the sectarian climates at the time of their composition. The evolution of the narrative reflects the evolution of the sectarian contest.

4 Historical Context: Damascus during and after the "Sunnī Revival"

Since successive versions of the early Islamic narrative reflect the sectarian climate of the time they were composed, it stands to reason that we can employ the early Islamic narrative, and the *fitna* narrative in particular, to gain insight into any time and place where retelling that narrative was considered important. There are compelling reasons to focus on Damascus during the Sunnī Revival era, but first and foremost is the fact that Damascus experienced a turbulent couple of centuries, of the kind that often bears intellectual fruit. For the succession of Sunnī dynasties who ruled *bilād al-Shām* after the era of the Hamdānids—first the Saljūqs, then the Ayyūbids, then the Mamlūks after the Mongol interregnum—Syrian politics were unstable, perceiving (usually correctly) threats from the west, the east, and within. The Crusades were well underway by the time the Sunnī Revival began; in fact, they were already waning, although their influence remained. The cataclysmic invasion of the Mongols, reaching its peak with the destruction of Baghdad and the ʿAbbāsid Caliphate in 1258, and the subsequent rule of the Ilkhāns of Persia further unsettled the country. And in the midst of all of these invasions, sectarian threats from both a Shīʿī polity in the form of the Fāṭimid caliphs of Cairo and a Shīʿī insurrection in the form of the Ismāʿīlī *hashāshīn*, or "assassins," produced for Sunnī Syrians the specter of a world hostile to their political and religious existence. Already tied together by historical chance, the beleaguered Sunnī and Syrian identities of the inhabitants of Damascus found strength in each other. Politically, there was a simple (which is not to say easy) answer to the invaders: they would have to be defeated militarily. The Ayyūbids, most famous among them Ṣalāḥ al-Dīn, ultimately smashed the potential of the Crusaders, while the task of stemming the Mongol flood fell to the Egyptian Mamlūks at ʿAyn Jālūt in 1260 (the Mamlūks thereafter swept aside the weakened remnants of the Ayyūbid dynasty and ruled Syria themselves for roughly three centuries). However, the perceived threat to Sunnī religious identity was not so straightforwardly answered, since ideas, philosophies, and theologies are much more resistant to the potential accomplishments of military force than are invading armies, however formidable.

Syria in general, and Damascus in particular, had been a very energetic venue for the development of Islamic identity since the earliest days of Muslim rule. As Khalek puts it:

> If the religion of the early Muslims had been born in Arabia, its adolescence was Syrian. Like so many adolescences, some aspects of it were formative while others were outgrown and left by the wayside as the faith and culture matured and developed again, beyond Syria and beyond the Umayyad century […]. The core beliefs of the religion, only a few of which went totally uncontested in the first decades AH, certainly did have their origins in the Ḥijāz, in the career of Muḥammad and under the (already divided and divisive) political and spiritual auspices of the first four *Rāshidūn*/"Rightly Guided" caliphs. Yet when the community of nascent Muslims arrived in Syria it was a place that was full of people whose continued presence and surviving communities exerted on one another the kind of bi-directional pressure and influence all heterogeneous environments exhibit […]. The need to draw lines defining the Muslim community eventually arose […] out of competition [and] also out of a type of cultural aging […]. The emerging Islamic society in Syria was a product of its Christian and Byzantine environment in a fundamental sense, not simply because Muslims were borrowing ideas or blindly grafting onto their own old Arabian practices what other people were doing, but because they were cultural producers in a world with which they were, and were becoming increasingly, familiar.[20]

In other words, Damascus and al-Shām had played a decisive role in the evolution of Islam from an Arabian monotheistic faith, by Arabs and for Arabs, to the more cosmopolitan, multiethnic, and universal system of belief and culture it relatively quickly became. The central stature of Syria as the Prophet's last stated foreign policy goal, and the fact that the conquering army happened to be comprised of the pre-Islamic Meccan Umayyad elite of the Quraysh,[21] meant that Syria would begin its Islamic existence as a hub of intellectual activity, and eventually of a specifically Sunnī intellectual culture. The existence of competing monotheistic faiths within Syria, especially the contentious brands

---

20 Nancy Khalek, *Damascus after the Muslim Conquest: Text and Image in Early Islam* (New York: Oxford University Press, 2011), 7–8.

21 Kennedy, *Prophet* 61.

of Byzantine Christianity, meant that the energy exerted to define the Islamic faith, both on its own terms and in relation or opposition to those Christianities, was utmost. It should be remembered that when it came to penning treatises whose purpose was to delineate proper belief and practice, the Byzantine Christians of Syria were not exactly novices.[22]

For all the political and intellectual importance that Umayyad Damascus enjoyed, the winds of political change fated the city to a four-century standing that was something inferior to the metropolis of the Islamic world it had once been, even if it remained something superior to a backwater. The ʿAbbāsid "Revolution" of 133/750, which overthrew the Umayyads after a successful propaganda campaign that employed vague references to the rightful leader as *riḍā min Āl Muḥammad* (a chosen one from the family of Muḥammad), was the knell that sounded the beginning of Damascus's slide into a city of only moderate intellectual importance. The ʿAbbāsid rebellion was couched in Shīʿī terminology, and the reference to *riḍā min Āl Muḥammad* was intended to invoke, by unspoken implication, the descendants of ʿAlī, but in actuality the covert leaders of the rebellion meant themselves: descendants of the Prophet's uncle al-ʿAbbās (hence: ʿAbbāsid).[23] It was, as a result, a rebellion popularly misunderstood even by many of its supporters at the time as a pro-ʿAlīd or Shīʿī rebellion that overthrew the Umayyads, and which weakened the standing of Damascus itself in 133/750. The rebellion ended up being remembered as a Sunnī-on-Sunnī conflict (with the Umayyad branch of the Quraysh being overthrown by a non-ʿAlīd twig of the Hāshimī branch of the Quraysh).

In any event, Baghdad replaced Damascus as Islam's metropolis quickly after it was founded in 762 under the auspices of the second ʿAbbāsid caliph, al-Manṣūr. While the ʿAlīds (and their supporters) were bitterly disillusioned by the perceived betrayal of their cousins, the ʿAbbāsids, it was still the Umayyads and the Syrians who became established as the primary villains of the early Islamic narrative when composed by pro-ʿAlīd authors. These authors became the dominant surviving historiographical voice recounting the early Islamic narrative. After all, the Umayyads had politicked against ʿAlī; Muʿāwiya, their dynasty's founder, had fought against ʿAlī; and, while they were not directly responsible for the death of ʿAlī himself, it was Muʿāwiya's son Yazīd who bore

22 Andrew S. Jacobs, "Adversus Iudaeos," in Roger S. Bagnall, Kai Brodersen, Craig B. Champion, Andrew Erskine, and Sabine R. Huebner (eds.), *The Encyclopedia of Ancient History* (Oxford: Blackwell Publishing Ltd., 2013), 111–113.

23 Moshe Sharon, *Black Banners from the East: The Establishment of the ʿAbbāsid State* (Jerusalem: Magnes Press, 1983).

primary responsibility for the communal catastrophe of Karbalāʾ, and the martyrdom of al-Ḥusayn. Their opposition to ʿAlī's family made them natural foils, or perhaps even villains, to pro-ʿAlīd authors. The ʿAbbāsids would not enter the narrative until later.

Four centuries after the ʿAbbāsid takeover, in 1154, Nūr al-Dīn Zangī entered Damascus and established it as an imperial capital for the first time since the fall of the Umayyads. The intervening pair of ʿAbbāsid centuries (the dates are generally given as 133–325/750–936) came to be remembered as a golden age for Islam. This designation was certainly inaccurate, but understandable, given the politically complex and disunited centuries that followed.[24] The decline of the central ʿAbbāsid government was a phenomenon with complex causes, but it was largely tied to outsourcing the military to the hands of Khurāsānī and then Turkish soldiers.[25] The collapse of the ʿAbbāsid political superstructure triggered extensive social and political changes (and was in turn caused by some of those changes),[26] most relevantly the obliteration of even the pretense of a single Islamic polity in favor of what has come to be known as the Islamic Commonwealth. The ʿAbbāsid caliphs retained *de jure* authority over all of *dār al-islām*, and there was nothing resembling borders between one region of the Islamic world and another, but *de facto* power fell into the hands of sultans, princes, commanders—some Persian, some Armenian, some Berber, and some Turkish, as different (and often rival) ethnic groups from the fringes of *dār al-islām* parlayed their military strength into political influence or authority. Powerful families like the Būyids and Ḥamdānids seized control of regional territories and exercised political authority with the blessing of the caliphs, sending to Baghdad a pittance of a tax collection and dutifully remembering to mention the caliph during Friday prayers in exchange for the religious legitimacy only the caliph could confer.

After about a century of local power magnates ruling over the territory that had once been actively ruled by the ʿAbbāsids (but which now paid them in tax crumbs and lip service), the non-African provinces were reunited to some

24 For a full accounting of the ʿAbbāsid period, see Hugh Kennedy, *When Baghdad Ruled the Muslim World: The Rise and Fall of Islam's Greatest Dynasty* (Cambridge, MA: Da Capo Press, 2004).

25 Hugh Kennedy, *The Armies of the Caliphs: Military and Society in the Early Islamic State* (London: Routledge, 2001), 118–167.

26 Ira M. Lapidus, *A History of Islamic Societies* (Cambridge: Cambridge University Press, [2]2002), 106–111.

extent by the Oghuz Turks under the leadership of Tughril Beg and the Saljūq family. The expansion of Turkish rule was not like the Islamic conquests, which reshaped life in the Fertile Crescent, or the ʿAbbāsid coup, which established important religious norms, or the original influx of Turks, which fundamentally altered the political-ethnic power dynamics of the region. The Saljūq conquest was mostly important, in the grand scheme of things, in that it reestablished Sunnīsm as the politically empowered elite sect after the Būyids and Ḥamdānids had ruled as Shīʿa (though they did not, interestingly, enforce Shīʿī rule—after all, like the Iranian government of today, they were not themselves ʿAlīds, and thus lacked Shīʿī legitimacy. They were happy to settle for a Sunnī brand of legitimacy). Of course, the Shīʿī "threat" to Syrians Sunnīs was by no means gone; mirroring the Sunnī Saljūq takeover in the east, in the west, North Africa had seen the rise of the Fāṭimid dynasty, who followed the Ismāʿīlī ("Sevener") branch of Shīʿism. The Fāṭimids controlled Damascus from 978 to 1076, when the Saljūqs took it from them, a few decades before the First Crusade caused Saljūq authority to splinter.

The Crusades—a series of interregional wars caused by a combination of the Latin-Orthodox rivalry, European concerns about access to Jerusalem, certainly after, but perhaps even before, the Saljūq invasion, and a rising passion for pilgrimage among eleventh-century Christians—did not provoke a rapid response from the Muslims but seems to have been met with a collective shrug of apathy. This was true even in Syria, which would have been (and eventually became) the natural base for resistance to the Frankish interlopers. As Lapidus puts it: "Syria was so fragmented as to preclude any unified opposition to the intruders; several additional small states among many did not much disturb existing interests. The fact that these new states were Christian was not exceptional—the Byzantines had also ruled northern Syria, and there was a substantial, if not a majority, local Christian population."[27] When a Muslim response did develop, it was not motivated by anti-Christian sentiment (or, at least, not immediately), but rather by the governor of Mosul, the Atabeg Zangī (c. 521–541/1127–1146), who seized control of Aleppo and Edessa and seems to have wished to carve out his own empire at the expense of neighboring Muslim and Christian states alike. When he died, his son, Nūr al-Dīn Zangī (c. 541–570/1146–1174) inherited his father's holdings; when a 1154 rebellion ousted the Saljūqid governor of Damascus, the population apparently turned the city over to Nūr al-Dīn. He immediately relocated his imperial capital to the city. Adopting the model that worked in the eastern provinces, the state began patronizing

27 Ibid. 289.

legal scholarship in Damascus. This patronage extended beyond legal scholarship, and Damascus (again) became the primary educational center of the Islamic world.[28]

Under Nūr al-Dīn's successors, especially Ṣalāḥ al-Dīn (Saladin), Damascus's importance as a center of learning and culture increased. Saladin's ultimate defeat of the Frankish Crusaders and the Shīʿī Fāṭimids of Egypt eliminated both Jerusalem and Cairo as potential rivals to Damascus for learning and scholarship. Baghdad, for now, remained—the Mongol sack of the city was still just under a century away—but Damascus, as the forward operating base for the counter-Crusade and the new center of legal scholarship, quickly surpassed its counterpart in Iraq, which had originally been built to replace it.

The period associated with the rise of Sunnī-affiliated scholarship in Damascus following the restoration of its capital status is generally called the "Sunnī Revival," although Bulliet, and Berkey after him, correctly assert that "Sunnī Recentering" is a more accurate, though certainly less evocative, designation.[29] Whatever name we choose to call it (in the present study, we will stick with the conventional "Sunnī Revival"), the goal was the elucidation of Sunnī religious, ritual, theological, and historical norms in response the Shīʿī "challenge" of the prior century.[30] Although the initial aim of most of the scholars who came to work in Damascus (and Aleppo) was to achieve a kind of jurisprudential consensus, the intellectual energy generated by Ayyūbid patronage spilled over into other fields, including literature and history. The fact that it was centered in Damascus meant that the Sunnī Revival carried with it a rehabilitation of Syria's maligned historical role in the narrative that depicts the origins and initial spread of Islam, which is one focus of this work.[31]

It should be remembered that universal chronicles of the type composed by Ibn al-Athīr, as well as, for example, Sibṭ ibn al-Jawzī, were not the only form of historical work. The most popular format was the local history, which could be chronological (such as *Dhayl taʾrīkh Dimashq* by Ibn al-Qalānisī and *al-Rawḍatayn* by Abū Shāma), biographical (such as *Taʾrīkh madīnat Dimashq* of Ibn ʿAsākir and *Bughyat al-Ṭabab fī taʾrīkh Ḥalab* by Ibn al-ʿAdīm), or general works on specialized topics, like Yāqūt's *Irshād* or Ibn al-Athīr's *Usd al-ghāba*.

28 Ibid. 291.

29 Richard Bulliet, *Islam: The View from the Edge* (New York: Cambridge University Press, 1994), *passim*; and Jonathan P. Berkey, *The Formation of Islam: Religion and Society in the Near East, 600–1800* (New York: Cambridge University Press, 2005), 189.

30 Berkey, *Formation of Islam* 190.

31 See Michael Chamberlain, *Knowledge and Social Practice in Medieval Damascus, 1190–1350* (Cambridge: Cambridge University Press, 1994).

In addition, there were monographs on any number of subjects, autobiographies, such as that of ʿUsāma ibn Munqidh, and administrative works.[32] Of course, not all of these works treated the early period (the early Islamic narrative has no real home in the *Irshād*, for example). The fact remains that we have no shortage of options for engaging with the historiographical tradition of the Ayyūbid and Mamlūk periods; the choice to focus on the synthetic histories of Ibn al-Athīr and, later, Ibn Kathīr is a function of the specific questions we are seeking to disentangle. Can the quantitatively minor adaptations made by later synthetic historians to an earlier synthetic historian's account offer significant insight into their milieus? More specifically, can such alterations give us a picture of the later historians' priorities and thought processes?

5 Conclusion

In the two centuries following the Crusades, Damascus was an intermittent imperial capital and constant center of legal scholarship, with the intellectual confrontation between and among Sunnī and Shīʿī scholars taking center stage. The narrative that depicts the origins of Islam became an important theater of that multivalent conflict, as it contained within it all the most important precedents and justifications for proper behavior on all levels, from the highest political authority to the relationships between husbands and wives: the Prophet, his successors, and his Companions provided exemplars of upright moral behavior and precedents for proper personal and political practice.

The historiographical process by which the narrative came to the era under discussion allowed scholars to shape it to fit their preexisting worldview. In other words, the historians presented here studied law and jurisprudence, literature, theology, and history—and only then, as receptacles of doctrines that had evolved as the result of a centuries-long intellectual process of assertion, criticism, refinement, synthesis, and censorship, composed carefully crafted narratives that reflected their understanding of the states of those arts and sciences. The evolution of the narrative was emphatically not the result of what we would today consider to be careful historiographical scholarship. On the contrary, the evolution of the narrative reflects a conscious decision on the part of the compilers and historians to bolster the historical basis of those legal and theological doctrines and political theories they *knew* to be right.

32 M. Holmy M. Ahmad, "Some Notes on Arabic Historiography During the Zengid and Ayyubid Periods (521/1127–648/1250)," in Bernard Lewis and P.M. Holt (eds.), *Historians of the Middle East* (London: Oxford University Press, 1962), 82–83.

Each version of the narrative—Ibn al-Athīr's *al-Kāmil fī al-taʾrīkh* and Ibn Kathīr's *Kitāb al-Bidāya wa-l-nihāya*—reflects the education of each man, and thus, through a careful reading and comparison of each, we can discern the important political, theological, and legal issues of their eras.

One final note must be made before proceeding to the specific case studies. The conclusions drawn in this work are about Ibn al-Athīr, Ibn Kathīr, and their time and place, but a broader set of conclusions would require a different kind of study. Performative historiographical analysis offers a very zoomed-in view on the specific authors studied, and what is true for seventh/thirteenth-century Syria and Egypt may not be true for other times and places, so it is important to note that no universality is implied by the conclusions. For example, tribal divisions were much more important during the Umayyad period than were questions of "sectarianism" (especially given that the Shīʿa were not even a fully defined theological sect before the middle of the eighth century, at the very earliest, and neither were Sunnīs). Hodgson clarifies that there were in fact a large number of "piety-minded" groups under the Marwanids, of which the Shīʿa were one, and so perspectives on what was (then) the more recent past were undoubtedly far more diverse than survived until the times of Ibn al-Athīr and Ibn Kathīr.[33] Dakake's perspective on the historiography of Shīʿism has already been discussed. This project offers a glimpse into the milieus of these two men and, to some extent, their authorial personas. It does not claim any universal truth about the role of sectarianism in an Islamic historiographical context. This is not a bad thing, since any such comprehensive conclusion, based, as it would be, on the limited case studies of two men, would undoubtedly be ill-founded, and would almost certainly be wrong.

33 Marshall Hodgson, *The Venture of Islam: Conscience and History in a World Civilization*, i (Chicago: University of Chicago Press, 1974), 241–279.

PART 1

The Slaughter at Karbalāʾ

CHAPTER 2

The Karbalāʾ Narrative

1 The Story of Karbalāʾ

On the tenth of Muḥarram 61/680, the Battle of Karbalāʾ, the most important event in Islamic history, occurred. This opinion, especially stated so matter-of-factly, is certain to engender dispute and criticism. Indeed, as Borrut points out in his 2015 article on Karbalāʾ, the battle is "frequently regarded by modern specialists as a relatively 'minor' episode [...] [but is in fact] a central event in early Islam."[1] Borrut describes how the memory of Karbalāʾ remains "a bone of contention" between different Islamic communities.[2] It is, in fact, much more than this. As asserted in the introduction, Karbalāʾ is the narrative point of no return that, as remembered, rendered Sunnī-Shīʿī reconciliation impossible.

The basics of the story are well-known. Faced with rebellion from Mecca, led by ʿAbd Allāh ibn al-Zubayr, the Umayyad ruler Yazīd ibn Muʿāwiya (the grandson of Abū Sufyān, the Prophet Muḥammad's chief Meccan enemy before the conversion of that city to Islam) also faced a challenge in the form of al-Ḥusayn ibn ʿAlī (the grandson of the Prophet). Al-Ḥusayn and a small force were intercepted by an Umayyad army while en route to Kūfa from Medina. Al-Ḥusayn and the majority of his force were slaughtered in the ensuing fight, and sources vary, but some kind of mutilation of al-Ḥusayn's body is reported to have occurred. Borrut divides the Karbalāʾ narrative into four subsections: "the problematic succession," in which Muʿāwiya appoints Yazīd; "the Kūfan call," in which some Kūfans write to al-Ḥusayn, inviting him to lead them; "the battle," in which the fighting occurs; and "Commemorations," in which the *tawwabūn* (penitents who failed to come to al-Ḥusayn's aid) are massacred at ʿAyn al-Warda.[3] Al-Ṭabarī's account of these events is not the only one, but his is "arguably the most comprehensive."[4]

However, it is not so much the comprehensiveness of al-Ṭabarī's account that is of interest to us, but rather it is the fact that Ibn Kathīr and Ibn al-Athīr relied so exclusively upon al-Ṭabarī. Al-Ṭabarī's comprehensiveness is part of what

1 Borrut, "Remembering Karbalāʾ" 249.
2 Ibid. 250.
3 Ibid. 255.
4 Ibid. 255. Borrut points out that al-Balādhurī (d. 279/892) and al-Dīnawarī (d. in late third/ninth–tenth c.) "also offer a fairly detailed account."

 | DOI:10.1163/9789004524255_004

interested *them*. After all, especially if Ibn Kathīr and Ibn al-Athīr were searching for a flexible source, al-Ṭabarī's depth and breadth offered the most latitude for interpretation, even if they did not always take advantage of that narrative elasticity. What narrative material, after all, could Ibn al-Athīr or Ibn Kathīr find in al-Dīnawarī's *al-Akhbār al-ṭiwāl* that they could not find in *Ta'rikh al-rusul wa-l-mulūk*, given that the same tradent sources were used in each (ʿUmar ibn Saʿd and Abū Mikhnaf in particular)? As we will see below, Ibn Kathīr especially already found these sources too Shīʿī sympathizing to allow them to pass without comment. This immediately eliminates as a potential source a historian like al-Yaʿqūbī (d. 292/905), who was often considered Shīʿī, but who may not have been one.[5] In any event, al-Yaʿqūbī offered only scant treatment of the episode.[6] Furthermore, to rely on al-Dīnawarī (more noted for his mathematical and scientific work than he is for his histories) or al-Balādhurī (whose *Ansāb al-Ashrāf* was more concerned with preserving the genealogies of the notables, as the title explicitly suggests) over al-Ṭabarī for narrative content would have been out of step with al-Ṭabarī's reputation.

The Karbalā' story was only thinly attested in the earliest preserved narratives, such as the *Ta'rīkh* of Khalīfa ibn Khayyāṭ (d. 240/854),[7] al-Yaʿqūbī, and the Shīʿī al-Masʿūdī (345/956), and "virtually absent from non-Muslim sources" that nonetheless recorded both Yazīd's accession and the revolt of al-Mukhtār.[8] The leanness of the pre-Ṭabarī Karbalā' narrative is perplexing given its impact (Borrut attributes it to a combination of the event being at once too insignificant for its importance to register, and too painful to recount in detail close to the event).[9] However, the paucity of early information is only significant to

5 See Elton L. Daniel, "Al-Yaʿqūbī and Shiʿism Reconsidered," in James E. Montgomery (ed.), *Occasional Papers of the School of ʿAbbasid Studies* (Peeters Publishers: Leuven, Belgium, 2002), 209–232; and Rosenthal, *History of Muslim Historiography* (Leiden: E.J. Brill, 1968), 221–223. Crone puts it most pithily: "Yaʿqūbī gives us nothing like the Shīʿite experience of Islamic history, merely the same body of tradition as the Sunni Ṭabarī with curses in appropriate places." See Patricia Crone, *Slaves on Horseback* (Cambridge: Cambridge University Press, 1980), 11. More recently, Cf. Sean W. Anthony, "Was Ibn Wāḍiḥ al-Yaʿqūbī a Shīʿite Historian? The State of the Question," in *al-Uṣūr al-Wuṣṭā* 24 (2016), 15–41, who argues convincingly that while al-Yaʿqūbī's personal sectarian perspectives are, and are likely to remain, unknowable, the one-sided, invective-filled account of the events in question demands that Shīʿī concerns be borne in mind when assessing the work.

6 I.K.A. Howard, "Ḥusayn the Martyr: A Commentary on the Accounts of the Martyrdom in Arabic Sources," in *Al-Serāt* (*Papers from the Imam Ḥusayn Conference in London, July 1984*) 12 (1986), 124–142.

7 Borrut, "Remembering Karbalā'" 256.

8 Ibid. 258.

9 Ibid. 259.

anyone seeking to discover the truth of the historical event. Ibn al-Athīr and Ibn Kathīr, we will see, were at ease with utilizing al-Ṭabarī's narrative, regardless of how or whether it may have been augmented, as their main source of information.

Divining al-Ṭabarī's sources for the battle is another matter altogether. We have access to the greater part of his source material only insofar as he recorded it for us; whatever ʿUmar ibn Saʿd, Abū Mikhnaf, Naṣr ibn Muzāḥim, and their like might have written that did not get included in the works of second/ninth-century figures, among whom al-Ṭabarī was foremost, is likely forever lost. The sources al-Ṭabarī used for his text can only be reconstructed through a careful process of *isnād* tracing and comparison with surviving accounts in other works (such as ʿAbd al-Salām Muḥammad Hārūn's 1962 reconstruction of Naṣr ibn Muzāḥim al-Minqarī's *Waqʿat Ṣiffīn*[10]). Such efforts are useful acts of compilation, but as attempts to reconstruct earlier sources they are circular, and cannot reasonably claim to have reconstructed such works in their entirety. No such circular intellectual calisthenics are necessary for determining Ibn al-Athīr's and Ibn Kathīr's source. Al-Ṭabarī's text was their history, and the thinness of earlier attestations of Karbalāʾ was of no concern. They were not, after all, intent on disproving the story or calling into question those basic elements of its narrative structure. They wanted to change Karbalāʾ's meaning.

2 Ibn Kathīr on al-Ḥusayn ibn ʿAlī

What sets Ibn Kathīr's account apart from that of al-Ṭabarī and Ibn al-Athīr is a significant section of text written in his own voice. This is a method he returns to, but only at moments of genuine significance; at moments of lesser stake during this period, Ibn Kathīr is generally content to copy or paraphrase al-Ṭabarī. Not so when it comes to Karbalāʾ, and more specifically when it comes to the overveneration of al-Ḥusayn practiced by the Shīʿa ("Rāfiḍīs" in Ibn Kathīr's parlance, or "rejectionists"). Like Keshk's "set-up stories," Ibn Kathīr's long diatribe about the overveneration of al-Ḥusayn has as its main objective the casting of doubt and even scorn upon the historical narrative of Karbalāʾ as asserted by Shīʿī historians. While it is not a perfect "set-up," as Keshk would describe it (since it follows, rather than precedes, the narrative, nor is it a narrative itself), the rant serves the same purpose: to contextualize a critical piece of the narrative and to qualify its meaning.

10 Naṣr ibn Muzāḥim al-Minqarī, *Kitāb Waqʿat Ṣiffīn*, ed. ʿAbd al-Salām M. Hārūn (Cairo: Al-Muʾassassa al-ʿArabiyya al-Ḥadītha, 1962).

He begins disputatiously, but perhaps innocuously enough relative to what follows, by pointing out that there exists a dispute over both the date of Karbalāʾ and the age of al-Ḥusayn at the time:

> The death of al-Ḥusayn (may God be pleased with him) was on Friday, the tenth day (ʿĀshūrāʾ) of Muḥarram in the year 61. Hishām ibn al-Kalbī said it was in the year 62, as did ʿAlī ibn al-Madīnī. Ibn Lahīʿa says it was in 62 or 63, and others say it was in 66, but the first date (61) is correct. It was at an insignificant little spot called Karbalāʾ, in Iraq, that he died at the age of 58 years or so. Abū Nuʿaym erred when he said that he was killed at the age of 65 or 66.[11]

This is a brief, but nonetheless pointed, slap at both the Shīʿī or pro-ʿAlīd historians[12] he names, and at the Karbalāʾ story itself, the locale of which he dismisses as "an insignificant little spot" (*makān min al-ṭaff yuqāl lahu Karbalāʾ*). He follows this with a series of maudlin narratives, his tone mocking, related to the Prophet Muḥammad hearing a prophecy about his grandson al-Ḥusayn's death at Karbalāʾ (the news delivered while the Prophet was bouncing the young boy on his knee). After this, he presents a narrative of Ibn ʿAsākir's in which a delegation to Byzantium finds an inscription critical of the killers of al-Ḥusayn in a Byzantine church, reputed, in a scene that recalls the last day of the Babylonian Emperor Belshazzar in the Book of Daniel, to have been written on the wall by the vision of an iron pen. A variety of stories treating the moment when the news reached, among others, Umm Salāma follow, all of which he frequently characterizes with an *Allāhu aʿlam*: "God knows best," which is tempting to read as dismissive, given his obvious opinion of these stories.

It is when he begins describing the "extreme" Shīʿī rituals that Ibn Kathīr truly seeks to undermine the veracity of Shīʿī accounts of Karbalāʾ. He asserts that the Shīʿa engage in

> some very strange rituals, and that the Shīʿa go to extremes on the day of ʿĀshūrāʾ. They have found many false and marginal *ḥadīths* [relating to

11 ʿImād al-Dīn Ismāʿīl Ibn Kathīr, *Kitāb al-Bidāya wa-l-nihāya* viii (Beirut: Dār al-Kutūb al-ʿIlmiyya, 2009), 206.

12 Hishām ibn Muḥammad al-Kalbī (120–204/737–809) was a Kūfan genealogist and historian whose reliance on pro-ʿAlīd oral sources did not endear him to later Sunnī historians. ʿAbd Allāh ibn Lahīʿa ibn ʿUqba (96–174/688–790) was an ʿAbbāsid-era Egyptian judge and is remembered as pro-Shīʿī.

> the day of ʿĀshūrāʾ], like that the sun was eclipsed that day to the point that the stars were dissipated, and that one could not lift a rock on that day without finding blood beneath it. They say that the skies turned red, and that the sun shone brightly as if its rays were blood, and the skies became stuck that way. They also say that the stars struck each other, and that the skies rained blood and that the red color had never appeared in the sky before that day, and other stories like these. Ibn Lahīʿa narrated, on the authority of Abī Qabīl al-Muʿāfarī, that the sun was eclipsed that day until noon, and that when they brought the head of al-Ḥusayn to the prince's castle, they placed it atop the walls, leaking blood. They say that the earth went dark for three days, and that all the saffron and *wars* (a Yemenite dye-yielding plant) burned up that day. They say that the gates of Jerusalem were closed due to all the as-yet uncongealed blood, and that the camels of al-Ḥusayn that were taken as plunder and cooked yielded bitter meat. There are other lies like this, *ḥadīths* that are to be found that do not have an ounce of truth to them.[13]

Ibn Kathīr, by strangling with his scorn the eschatological and supernatural tone of the pro-Shīʿī accounts of, among others, Ibn Lahīʿa, essentially calls into question the entire veracity of those accounts. He is also setting the table for himself, a few paragraphs later, to mock the Shīʿa who believe this: "None of [the Shīʿa who overvenerate al-Ḥusayn] mention that it should have been obvious that it going to be the date of [the] deaths [of al-Ḥusayn and his compatriots], and that the death of al-Ḥusayn was announced from those matters we discussed before, like the eclipse of the sun or the sky turning red and other things like that."[14] The implication of this is that even if the supernatural weather remembered by the Shīʿa as having occurred on the tenth of Muḥarram that year occurred, then al-Ḥusayn and his compatriots ought to have taken it as a warning and avoided battle.

All of this is not to say that Ibn Kathīr disparages al-Ḥusayn himself. On the contrary, he claims to be grieved by the iniquitous death of the Prophet's grandson, too. Ibn Kathīr reserves his criticism for the Shīʿa and their excesses in weeping for al-Ḥusayn, pointing out that not only are the Shīʿa too enthralled to the al-Ḥusayn narrative, but also that they give his death in particular unwarranted special attention:

---

13 Ibn Kathīr, *Bidāya* viii, 209.

14 Ibid. viii, 210.

> Every Muslim must feel grief at his death, may God be pleased with him. He is one of the great Muslims, one of the wisest of the companions, and the son of [Fāṭima] the most excellent of the daughter of the Messenger of God (may God's prayers and peace be upon him). [Al-Ḥusayn] was pious, valiant, and moving. But it is still unseemly with the Shīʿa have done with him in terms of their demonstration of grief and sadness. It may be that most of it is a sham and hypocrisy. After all, his father [ʿAlī] was more excellent than he, and he was killed, but they do not put on the same kind of annual funerary display for him that they do for the killing of al-Ḥusayn. His father was killed on a Friday as he went out for morning prayers on the seventeenth of Ramaḍān in the year 40 AH. In a similar vein, ʿUthmān was more excellent [*afḍal*] than ʿAlī, according to the people of the Sunna and the consensus [*ijmāʿ*], and he was killed while besieged in his home in the twenties of the month of Dhū al-Ḥijja in the year 36 AH. He was sliced from ear to ear, and nobody makes a ceremony out of his death. Furthermore, ʿUmar ibn al-Khaṭṭāb, who was more excellent than ʿUthmān and ʿAlī both, was killed while he was praying the morning prayers in a prayer niche and reading from the Qurʾān, and the people do not make a ceremony of his murder. Similarly, al-Ṣiddīq [Abū Bakr] was more excellent than [ʿUmar], and the people do not make the day of his death a ceremony. Like this, the Messenger of God, may God's prayers and peace be upon him, who was the greatest of men in the world and the hereafter, was taken by God, just as all the Prophets before him had died, and nobody celebrates their deaths the way these ignorant Rāfiḍīs do on the day of al-Ḥusayn's slaughter.[15]

His assertion that each dead caliph was "more excellent" than his predecessor is an assertion of the Sunnī notion that the "most excellent" living person [*afḍal*] should serve as caliph.[16] Ibn Kathīr also takes a moment to describe some of the history of the ʿĀshūrāʾ commemorations:

15 Ibid. viii, 210.

16 Asma Afsaruddin, *Excellence and Precedence: Medieval Islamic Discourse on Legitimate Leadership* (Leiden: Brill, 2002). Afsaruddin would disagree with the notion that Karbalāʾ was the defining moment of the Sunnī/Shīʿī divergence. She quite clearly places the pivotal moment earlier, at the election of Abū Bakr; however, she would no doubt agree that both moments are rife with sectarian import and narrative potential. *Excellence and Precedence* also seeks—with open eyes to the difficulty of the task—to approach a reconstruction of the earliest debate of Islam, as it actually happened, which is beyond the scope of this book. Whether Afsaruddin is correct or not in her estimation that family ties as a

> In the Būyid lands, in the 400s and thereabouts, the Rāfiḍīs really overdid it, and in Baghdad and places like it in that country, they beat drums on the day of ʿĀshūrāʾ, scattering ashes and straw in the alleys and the markets, and hanging sackcloth on the stores. The people were driven to grief and weeping, and many of them did not drink water that night in solidarity with al-Ḥusayn, who died thirsty. Then the women went out unveiled, wailing, striking their own faces and bosoms, going barefoot in the markets and other things because of their horrid false doctrine, abominable opinions, and their invented divisiveness. In fact, they want by this and similar things to defile the good name of the Umayyads, because he (al-Ḥusayn) was killed by their dynasty.
>
> The Rāfidīs and the Shīʿa were harassed on the day of ʿĀshūrāʾ by the notables of al-Shām. On the day of ʿĀshūrā, they cooked grains, performed ritual ablutions, perfumed themselves, and wore the *thawāb* for the morning prayer. They also undertook that day to arrange a type of meal, demonstrating joy and mirth, wanting by this to harass and oppose the Rāfiḍīs.[17]

Interspersed with his critique of what he considers to be overwrought Shīʿī commemorations of al-Ḥusayn's death, Ibn Kathīr is kind enough to include a rare discussion of his sources:

> As for the *ḥadīths* and the stories of the *fitna* that have been told about his death, many of them are true [...]. The Shīʿa and the Rāfiḍīs, in describing the violent death of al-Ḥusayn, lied with the use of fallacious *akhbār*, some of which we have mentioned. Some of these we have presented but not considered. If [a report] is not [found] in [the work of] Ibn Jarīr [al-Ṭabarī] and other scholars and Imams whom we have mentioned, I have omitted it. Most of these [included reports] are [originally] from the narrative of Abū Mikhnaf Lūṭ ibn Yaḥyā, who was a Shīʿī. His *ḥadīths* are weak among the Imams, but his *akhbār* are considered trustworthy. Anyway, there are not really other sources for these events other than him, and that is why most of the compilers rely on him for these matters. God knows best.[18]

---

means for selection was a later addition to the debate (she presents very compelling evidence that it was), there is no doubt that their entrance into the discourse predated the histories of Ibn al-Athīr and Ibn Kathīr.

17 Ibid. 209–210.

18 Ibid. 209.

This is representative of Ibn Kathīr's general strategy covering the *fitna*. Perhaps as frustrated as the rest of us with the dearth of sources covering the period, he is forced to rely on the accounts of Abū Mikhnaf as reported in al-Ṭabarī. Ibn Kathīr is not as slavish a follower of al-Ṭabarī's narrative as is Ibn al-Athīr, but his respect for al-Ṭabarī's narrative, and, as a corollary, his grudging need to rely on Abū Mikhnaf's record, is quite evident.

The section concludes with a discussion of the fate of al-Ḥusayn's head, reported by the Shīʿī sources he wishes to attack as having been severed and displayed (although there is disagreement over where it was displayed and for how long). To Ibn Kathīr, the entire Karbalāʾ narrative, as reported in the sources, *including* al-Ṭabarī, on whom he relies for most of his information, is designed to libel the Umayyads. In this section, Ibn Kathīr turns the intent of the story upside down. Rather than a narrative that demonstrates the immorality of the Umayyads, it demonstrates the perfidy of the Shīʿa (he reserves special condemnation for the Fāṭimids) and the extent to which these "extremists" are willing to fabricate nonsense in order to give Karbalāʾ its "proper" meaning.

> As for the head of al-Ḥusayn, may God be pleased with him, the common knowledge of men of history and Prophetic biography is that it was brought by Ibn Ziyād to Yazīd ibn Muʿāwiya, but some people dispute this. For my part, I think it is correct, and God knows best. They disagreed, afterwards, about the place where the head was displayed, and Muḥammad ibn Saʿd narrated that Yazīd brought the head of al-Ḥusayn to ʿAmr ibn Saʿīd, the representative over Medina, and that he displayed it to his people.
>
> Ibn Abī al-Dunyā mentioned, by way of ʿUthmān ibn ʿAbd al-Raḥmān, on the authority of Muḥammad ibn ʿUmar ibn Ṣāliḥ—both of those last two are weak links—that the head remained in Yazīd ibn Muʿāwiya's closet until his death. At that point, it was taken out, sanitized, and displayed inside the Farādīs Gate of the city of Damascus. It is said that this place is known as "the Mosque of the Head," today just inside the second Farādīs Gate. Ibn ʿAsākir, in his history, when discussing Yazīd ibn Muʿāwiya, said that when the head of al-Ḥusayn was in his hands, Yazīd imitated the [Jāhilī] poet Ibn al-Zubʿarī, saying:
>
> *Let my ancestors bear witness by the full moon, the Khazraj fear the impact of the family.*
>
> [Ibn ʿAsākir] said that he then placed it in Damascus for three days, then he took a stockpile of weapons, and after a while Sulaymān ibn ʿAbd al-Malik came with them. The greater part of the head was white, and he covered it with a sheet and sanitized it. He prayed over it, and took it to the

> Muslim cemetery. When the ʿAbbāsids came, they exhumed it and took it with them. Ibn ʿAsākir mentions that these women remained after the Umayyad regime, and passed one hundred years, but God knows best. A group who call themselves the Fāṭimids,[19] who ruled over the Egyptian lands from before the year 400 until after the year 560, asserted that the head of al-Ḥusayn was taken to Egypt and buried there, and that they built a famous shrine to it in Egypt called "the crown of Ḥusayn," after the year 500. But others from the learned class assert that it is not to be found there, but rather that they wanted to sell the vain idea of what they were preaching about their noble lineage. In this, they were treacherous liars. The judge al-Bāqilānī, and other members of the learned class, have determined that this is what happened in their regime around the year 400, and we will explain this if we are able to set down an account of them, if God most high wills it. I say that most of the people were duped to believe things like this, but what really happened is that they came with some random head and placed it in the location of this Mosque I already mentioned, and then they said, "This is the head of al-Ḥusayn." They spread this story, and the people believed them, as God knows best.

In this section Ibn Kathīr lets us know, in no uncertain terms, how we should treat the Karbalāʾ narrative he is about to present. He has set up the story with an essay describing what he feels is at stake, what elements of the story he wishes to challenge, and his motives for doing so. He even gives a glimpse into his learning.

The aim of Ibn Kathīr's Karbalāʾ story is to attack the veracity of Shīʿī accounts of history, the honesty and/or the historiographical skill and talent of Shīʿī historians, and legitimacy of Shīʿī polities, like the Fāṭimid regime. As the rest of this study will demonstrate, his charge is not a surprise: he has spent much of the rest of his work building up to it.

3 Ibn al-Athīr on Karbalāʾ

Ibn al-Athīr begins his discussion of the Karbalāʾ story at what is perhaps the most obvious place: the invitation of al-Ḥusayn to come to Kūfa made by men, many of whom would shortly abandon him, repent of their inaction,

19 For an overview of the Fāṭimid period, see Farhad Daftary, *The Ismāʿīlīs: Their History and Doctrines* (Cambridge: Cambridge University Press, 2007), 137–300.

and become the *tawwabūn*. Unlike Ibn Kathīr, there is no departure from the narrative to decry Shīʿī excesses in terms of their veneration for and expressions of anguish over the death of al-Ḥusayn. He does, however, refer to the parties in the story, specifically the party of al-Ḥusayn on its way from Mecca to Kūfa as well as the soon-to-be Penitents, as "Shīʿa,"[20] even though it is clearly too early in the narrative to speak of any such thing, indicating that he is already thinking ahead to the future narrative. Calling the men taking part in the formative events of Shīʿism "Shīʿa" is akin to calling Jesus a Christian: they are obviously critical to the emergence of Shīʿism, but Shīʿism as it came to be practiced required these very specific events to occur and to be properly understood. This mischaracterization aside (al-Ṭabarī obviously does not use the word to describe al-Ḥusayn and his men), Ibn al-Athīr generally sticks close to his source. Diatribes are not his style; a much more conservative historian in terms of his approach, and more genial in tone than Ibn Kathīr, he does not depart from al-Ṭabarī's narrative but rarely, and even then it is usually in the form of omissions, rather than additions, to the text.

4 Conclusion

In discussing the meaning of the battle, Ibn Kathīr provides us with some low-hanging fruit; it is not difficult to ascertain, based on his own words, that he finds in Karbalāʾ a critically important narrative juncture, and one which the Shīʿa have misunderstood and mischaracterized due to their overzealous veneration and grief. Fortunately, the tone implies, Ibn Kathīr will set the record straight. His confidence is striking, given how close to the vest Ibn al-Athīr plays his cards; the earlier man was much more carefully political with his narrative, which, at least on the surface, sticks to what he wants the reader to consider to be the facts. It is only when compared with the work of their source, al-Ṭabarī, that the nature of Ibn al-Athīr's historiographical venture becomes apparent.

20 ʿIzz al-Dīn Abū al-Ḥasan ibn al-Athīr al-Jazrī, *al-Kāmil fī al-taʾrīkh*, eds. ʿAbdullah al-Qāḍī and Muḥammad al-Daqqāq, iii (Beirut: Dar Al-Kotob al-Ilmiyah, ^{5}2010), 385ff.

CHAPTER 3

The Fight and Its Aftermath

1 The Immediate Preparation

If the "Battle of Karbalāʾ" refers to the entirety of the event, including the approach to the battle, which will be discussed in Chapter 4, then the fight refers to the actual military engagement itself. The narrative of the battle itself begins with the morning prayer, which all three historians report was led by ʿUmar ibn Saʿd.[1] All the historians leave in the question about the day of the week; obviously, it was the day of ʿĀshūrāʾ, the tenth of Muḥarram, but al-Ṭabarī records that it happened on a Saturday, although some report that it was a Friday (in actuality, that date was a Wednesday). Similarly, all three historians leave the details of the battle essentially identical, beginning with the detail that after ʿUmar ibn Saʿd led the people in the morning prayer, the military organization began: Zuhayr ibn al-Qayn was placed in charge of the right wing, with Ḥabīb ibn Muẓāhir[2] on the left; al-ʿAbbās ibn ʿAlī, al-Ḥusayn's brother, was given the standard. All then go on to describe the same fight: the tents set up behind the small army, a ditch filled with burning wood created a wall of flame to protect their rear. While the arraying of forces is presented in briefer form in both Ibn al-Athīr's and Ibn Kathīr's texts—nobody, for example, turns to a companion the way somebody does in al-Ṭabarī's text to deliver the helpful expository statement, "When they march against us to fight us, we will have set fire to the ditch, and so we will not be attacked from behind; we can fight those people on only one front!"[3]—the sequence of events and the key players are essentially the same in all three versions.

Al-Ṭabarī spends the most time on the battle itself; the others seem eager to get past the fighting into the aftermath. Al-Ṭabarī includes an exchange between al-Ḥusayn and the enemy soldier Shamir ibn Dhī al-Jawshān—omitted in Ibn Kathīr's text and only alluded to in Ibn al-Athīr's—in which the

1 Al-Ṭabarī, *Taʾrīkh* iii, 316; Ibn al-Athīr, *Kāmil* iii, 417; Ibn Kathīr, *Bidāya*, v. 8, 175.

2 Ibn al-Athīr records his name as Ibn Muṭahhir or Ibn Muṭahhar; obviously, the difference between "Muẓāhir" and "Muṭahhir" is the absence of a diacritical dot over the ṭāʾ and a long alīf, so this change is most likely due to a simple transcription error, be it on the part of Ibn al-Athīr himself or on the part of the scribe who physically wrote Ibn al-Athīr's copy of al-Ṭabarī's text. Ibn Kathīr and al-Ṭabarī agree on the commander's name as Ibn Muẓāhir. See Idem.

3 Al-Ṭabarī, *Taʾrīkh* iii, 316.

 | DOI:10.1163/9789004524255_005

former taunts al-Ḥusayn, prompting one of al-Ḥusayn's soldiers to offer to shoot the "great sinner and one of the great tyrants"[4] for him. Al-Ḥusayn refuses, unwilling to order the commencement of violence. Ibn al Athīr includes the story but omits the dialogue, which includes some colorful insults in al-Ṭabarī's version (such as *Ibn rāʿiyat al-miʿzā*, "son of a goat herdess"). Ibn Kathīr, by leaving out any mention of this spat, leaves open the possibility that al-Ḥusayn's men shot first, explicitly denied in the other two historians.

Al-Ḥusayn then gives a speech, while his sisters—back in the tents—weep and shriek, prompting al-Ḥusayn to send his brother al-ʿAbbās and his son ʿAlī back to the camp to quiet them. The speech essentially seeks to remind those present, both his supporters and his enemies, of who he is: the son of the Prophet's daughter, the son of ʿAlī, the nephew of Ḥamza ibn ʿAbd al-Muṭṭalib and Jaʿfar ibn Abī Ṭālib, all of whom occupy a revered place in the pantheon of martyrs and potentates of the prior few generations. Another key statement that Ibn Kathīr leaves out, which appears in al-Ṭabarī's and Ibn al-Athīr's versions, occurs in this section. Al-Ṭabarī and Ibn al-Athīr record a section of al-Ḥusayn's speech as follows:

> Consider who I am. Then, look at yourselves and repent. Think about whether it is righteous for you to kill me and violate my blessedness. Am I not the son of the daughter of your Prophet, the son of his legatee (*ibn waṣīhi*) and his cousin?[5]

Ibn Kathīr's analogous section of text reads as follows:

> Then [al-Ḥusayn] commenced with reminding the people of his excellence, his honorable lineage, his abilities, and his honor, and said "Look at yourselves and repent. Is it righteous for you to fight me, the son of the daughter of your Prophet? Is there another son of the daughter of the son of the Prophet on the face of the earth? ʿAlī is my father, and Jaʿfar and Ḥamza are my uncles."[6]

Ibn Kathīr's significantly changes *ibn waṣīhi*—the son of (the Prophet's) legatee, or appointed executor of his will—to simply "ʿAlī." It is not al-Ḥusayn's parentage that is in question but rather ʿAlī's status as the Prophet's *waṣī*, a term that has a particular Shīʿī meaning that confers upon ʿAlī the legitimacy

4 Ibid. iii, 318.
5 Al-Ṭabarī, *Taʾrīkh* iii, 318; Ibn al-Athīr, *Kāmil* iii, 419.
6 Ibn Kathīr, *Bidāya* viii, 186.

of specific appointment by the Prophet. The term had already been applied by his supporters to ʿAlī specifically during episodes where his legitimacy was in question, such as the battle of Ṣiffīn.[7]

Indeed, all of Ibn Kathīr's changes to the narrative support his wider anti-Shīʿī mission: he leaves out the assertion that al-Ḥusayn refused to fire the first shot and also replaces the language that asserts ʿAlī's legitimacy, specifically the word *waṣī*. The first change undercuts al-Ḥusayn's innocence in the bloodshed (a key Shīʿī trope) and the second eliminates a specific type of claim of legitimacy, replacing it with ʿAlī's name instead. Ibn Kathīr has a trollish sense of humor—replacing a "rightful title" with just a personal name is a scene the reader has seen before, first with the Prophet Muḥammad accepting the elision of *rasūl Allāh* at Ḥudaybiyya, and then with ʿAlī allowing himself to be named rather than titled *amīr al-muʾminīn* at Ṣiffīn during the arbitration. Ibn Kathīr's Shīʿī readers—assuming they had not already closed his book in disgust—could hardly object to something the Prophet Muḥammad and ʿAlī (to them, his *waṣīh*, after all) had themselves already accepted.

These small but important changes aside, the moments before the Battle of Karbalāʾ are striking for their similarity in all three versions under discussion. Given that the event is the most important site of memory in the early Islamic narrative, one might expect it to diverge significantly. The fact that it really does not do so teaches us two important lessons, which we must apply to the study going forward. First, it is likely that famous events are too famous for significant and noticeable alteration. They may be shortened, or mistakes of transmission may be made, as Ibn al-Athīr's performance of al-Ṭabarī's text summarized the verbal sparring between ʿAlī and Shamir. They may be lightly altered, with the intent of rebranding a character or attacking an abstract idea, as Ibn Kathīr's performance removed the term *waṣīh*. However, the sequence of events at such critical moments must remain relatively consistent, lest they become unrecognizable. The second lesson is that such moments may offer less opportunity for changing the meaning of the narrative than other, ostensibly less important, moments, which provide the context for the famous sites of memory. Those "secondary" moments are both less famous—and thus more mutable—and more impactful, as they offer greater opportunity to delve into the interactions of individual characters. We have already seen one in Ibn Kathīr's rant about Shīʿī unreliability, discussed in the previous chapter.

---

7 See also S.H.M. Jafri, *The Origins and Development of Shīʿī Islam* (Oxford: Oxford University Press, 2000), 101–102.

2 The Battle

Al-Ṭabarī reports that just before the fighting broke out, Zuhayr ibn al-Qayn, a companion of al-Ḥusayn, came out to the enemy delegation, warning them that "we are still brothers in one religion and one sect as long as our swords do not strike [...] [but] when the sword strikes the protection will be completely cut. We will be one community, and you will be another community."[8] All three performances of Zuhayr's warning include an expression of the evil that ʿUbayd Allāh ibn Ziyād and Yazīd ibn Muʿāwiya would commit, including mentioning by name a couple of the *Qurrāʾ* (Ḥujr ibn ʿAdī, who had led, and been executed for, a Kūfa-based rebellion against Muʿāwiya in 51/671, was one of them) as examples of the wicked fate meted out to Umayyad enemies.

The battle begins. The authors go into more or less detail, but the overall impressions of the accounts, again, are the same. Al-Ṭabarī dwells more on the individual experiences of various men at the battle, which include a great number of insults hurled at al-Ḥusayn, which karmically found their way to boomerang back onto their originators. Al-Ḥusayn's supporter Burayr ibn Salīma is challenged to a battle of curses by the Umayyad solder Yazīd ibn Maʿqil; the battle ends with Burayr driving his sword through Yazīd's helmet and so deeply into his brain that Burayr is unable to free his sword before he is speared in the back by Kaʿb ibn Jābir. ʿAbd Allāh ibn Ḥawza yelled to al-Ḥusayn that al-Ḥusayn was destined for hellfire, only to have his horse rear, unsaddling him but for his left foot, which caught in the stirrup; as his spooked horse raced away from al-Ḥusayn, "his head struck every stone and tree trunk until he died."[9] Seeing this was enough for one witness, Abū Mikhnaf informs al-Ṭabarī and posterity, to remove himself from the fighting: "I have seen enough of that family of the Prophet (*ahl hādha l-bayt*) to know never to fight them, ever."[10] But such details are not included in the accounts of Ibn al-Athīr or Ibn Kathīr. They pick up al-Ṭabarī's narrative shortly after al-Ṭabarī lets the reader know: "Then the battle intensified" (*wa-nashaba l-qitāl*).[11]

The first loose end for Ibn al-Athīr and Ibn Kathīr to tie up is the fate of al-Ḥurr ibn Yazīd (no relation to Yazīd ibn Muʿāwiya), whose piece of the narrative will be discussed in the next chapter. Al-Ḥurr had been an envoy sent by the governor of Kūfa, ʿUbayd Allāh ibn Ziyād, to arrest al-Ḥusayn. This Umayyad envoy, despite his allegiances, was presented as reticent to perform his com-

8 Al-Ṭabarī, *Taʾrīkh* iii, 319; Ibn al-Athīr, *Kāmil* iii, 421; Ibn Kathīr, *Bidāya* viii, 187.
9 Al-Ṭabarī, *Taʾrīkh* iii, 322.
10 Ibid. iii, 322.
11 Ibid. iii, 322.

manded duty; he clearly found being in an adversarial position to the grandson of the Prophet distasteful, and had winkingly suggested to al-Ḥusayn a course of action that might prevent battle. Once the battle flared up, however, a neutral course was no longer open to al-Ḥurr; he would have to choose sides. Ultimately, he chooses to abandon his earthly masters and fight for his eternal soul (so al-Ṭabarī tells us) and joins al-Ḥusayn's army. He is killed for his trouble: his horse is shot with an arrow, and he is set upon after he leapt from the dying horse with his sword. The heroic al-Ḥurr takes many of his former comrades, still fighting in the Umayyad army, with him to the grave. This is the payoff of the entire interaction that al-Ḥurr has with al-Ḥusayn.

The fighting subsides for the midday prayer, which al-Ḥusayn leads; then the fight resumes. Al-Ṭabarī gives space to many of al-Ḥusayn's companions, expounding on the specific circumstances of their deaths, noting both their heroism and their killers for posterity. When al-Ḥusayn is finally killed, al-Ṭabarī relates a number of stories about the group of men who killed him, and their relatively immediate fate. Al-Ṭabarī tells of the Kindī man who brought al-Ḥusayn's silk cloak to his wife as plunder and tried to wash the blood from it; she is horrified and makes him take it away. He also records that the man is poor when he dies. According to al-Ṭabarī, he died gruesomely at the hands of followers of al-Mukhtār.[12] He also relates what is by now a trope: al-Ḥusayn dies while trying to reach the Euphrates to get a drink of water (a moment that echoes prior moments, both at Ṣiffīn, which will be discussed in the next section, and at Ḥudaybiyya). Al-Ṭabarī reports that he is shot with an arrow, perhaps in the throat, and with his dying breath curses his killers with a plea to God that they be ever afflicted by unquenchable thirst. Indeed, al-Ṭabarī reports, one man from the Banū Abān ibn Dārim literally drinks himself to the point of his stomach bursting in an attempt to slake his thirst.[13] He goes on for pages, cataloging their names, their wickedness, and their unhappy fates.

The death scene of al-Ḥusayn is significantly shorter in both Ibn al-Athīr's and Ibn Kathīr's accounts than in al-Ṭabarī's. Ibn al-Athīr emphasizes al-Ḥusayn's extreme thirst just before his death and some of the curses he cries as he is dying.[14] It is one of the few times that Ibn al-Athīr goes to the effort to report the cursing of anyone; the killers of al-Ḥusayn were to be remembered as particularly perfidious. The emphasis on the individuals, of course, essentially eliminates the communal guilt at the death of al-Ḥusayn, much as had been done, in some of the accounts, with the killing of the Companion of the Prophet

12 Ibid. iii, 332.
13 Ibid. iii, 333.
14 Ibn al-Athīr, *Kāmil* iii, 432.

ʿAmmār ibn Yāsir at Ṣiffīn. Ibn Kathīr summarizes the whole death scene in a couple of paragraphs. He was clearly following al-Ṭabarī's text, as he lays out the same stories in the same order, but he does so only in the narrative staccato of a list of events.[15]

Once al-Ḥusayn is dead, his head is detached from his body and sent to ʿUbayd Allāh ibn Ziyād. Al-Ṭabarī reports that Zaynab bint Fāṭima, the sister of al-Ḥusayn, disguised herself in dirty clothes and entered the hall where al-Ḥusayn's head was being abused, and when identified by ʿUbayd Allāh, she decrees that she and her family will be enemies of the Umayyads forever for this outrage. The story is repeated in the account of Ibn al-Athīr, who, after all, can find no moment of unity to highlight in the desecration of al-Ḥusayn's corpse. Ibn Kathīr leaves the entire episode out but mentions, along with the others, that the head was then brought to Yazīd, whom he reports wept at al-Ḥusayn's death and was furious at the mutilation. However, al-Ṭabarī reports that when al-Ḥusayn's surviving family members are brought before Yazīd, they hurl mutual accusations of apostasy at each other. That, at least, is left out of the later retellings of Ibn al-Athīr and Ibn Kathīr.

3 Conclusion

Ibn al-Athīr, as we will see in the next chapter, has done everything he can to demonstrate the overall unity of Islam and the Muslims during the episodes of the *fitna* prior to Karbalāʾ. But he cannot avoid what is before his very eyes: Islam does find itself disunited and, in Ibn al-Athīr's time, at a most inconvenient moment, with the Mongols at the doorstep. Unable to pretend that such disunity does not exist, he finally allows it to appear, but only when the exigencies of the narrative render it absolutely necessary. The ultimate result of his narrative choices is that the disunity that plagues the Muslims of his day is presented as the result of the exaggeration and magnification of the wicked acts of a few evil men, rather than the natural outcome of inherent and deep-seated division. He has already worked very hard to rehabilitate the opponents of ʿAlī ibn Abī Ṭālib at Ṣiffīn, as well as the electors of ʿUthmān, despite the fact that it was their misdeeds that drove the *fitna* forward to this point. If his narrative is to be believed, it did not have to be that way; perhaps, with this new understanding of their history, Muslims could become united again.

---

15 Ibn Kathīr, *Bidāya* viii, 195–196.

Ibn Kathīr, a century later, has no message of unity to offer his contemporaries; the *fitna* is, to him, nothing but a story of Shīʿī duplicity, compounded honest error, and exaggeration—not the exaggeration, by posterity, of the deeds of a few evil opponents of ʿAlī and his descendants, as Ibn al-Athīr perceives, but rather the overveneration, and perhaps unmonotheistic behavior, of the mass of Shīʿa who hold ʿAlī and his descendants in too high esteem. The death of al-Ḥusayn itself, however, is not the narrative junction he chooses to emphasize that claim. The description of the slaughtering of the beloved grandson of the Prophet remains a raw moment, even for Ibn Kathīr. However, he has much to say about al-Ḥusayn's death, which, by the time the story of his death is related, he has already set down before the battle. That set-up helps to contextualize the painful moment of al-Ḥusayn's death and subsequent desecration. As we will see, both Ibn Kathīr and Ibn al-Athīr see the prologue to the battle, rather than the battle itself, to be far more fertile ground to advance their narrative agendas.

CHAPTER 4

Approaching Karbalāʾ

1 Towards Karbalāʾ

Before the battle itself, the historians are unified in their assertion that its participants seemed to sense its inevitability. In the section that begins with the heading "On the killing of al-Ḥusayn" in Ibn al-Athīr,[1] and "Account of the Year 61" in Ibn Kathīr[2] and al-Ṭabarī,[3] our historians all relate a set-up story with a foreboding tone. Al-Ḥusayn, on his way to Kūfa to join his followers, is intercepted by an Umayyad cavalry force of about 1,000 men. It is under the command of al-Ḥurr ibn Yazīd al-Tamīmī, who would later become famous for his heroic death fighting alongside al-Ḥusayn, but at this point is acting as a representative of Yazīd's governor of Iraq, ʿUbayd Allāh ibn Ziyād. His sympathy for al-Ḥusayn's plight is clear in each of the sources—more so in Ibn al-Athīr's account than in al-Ṭabarī's, as we will see—but he strictly adheres to his orders to make sure that al-Ḥusayn makes it all the way to Kūfa (then to be brought before ʿUbayd Allāh). Al-Ḥusayn, naturally opposed to going to Kūfa into the hands of one of his enemies, curses al-Ḥurr, who, seeking a way to discharge his duty without getting directly involved, tells al-Ḥusayn in an off-the-record tone, "I have not been ordered to fight you. I have only been ordered not to part from you until I bring you to Kūfa. Choose any road that will take you neither to Kūfa or Medina […]. Perhaps God will cause something to happen that will relieve me from being troubled in your affair."[4]

The narrative lingers on the various exchanges between al-Ḥusayn and al-Ḥurr for what might seem an inordinate amount of time, were there no pressing need to demonstrate al-Ḥurr's reticence to fight al-Ḥusayn before the heroic turn he takes, fighting alongside him once the battle is joined. At this point in the narrative, however, he continues to represent the Umayyad side, and as such, offers Ibn al-Athīr his typical challenge/opportunity: to emphasize the unity of the community, even as it is approaching its moment of greatest schism.

1 Ibn al-Athīr, *Kāmil* iii, 405.
2 Ibn Kathīr, *Bidāya* viii, 179.
3 Al-Ṭabarī, *Taʾrīkh* iii, 305.
4 Ibn al-Athīr, *Kāmil* iii, 405.

 | DOI:10.1163/9789004524255_006

2 Umayyad Representatives, Softened and Erased

The first exchange between al-Ḥusayn and al-Ḥurr is when the former orders his men to provide water for al-Ḥurr, his men, and their mounts. In al-Ṭabarī's account, and in Ibn al-Athīr's and Ibn Kathīr's as well, al-Ḥurr is presented as polite and courteous. When al-Ḥusayn asks him if he would care to lead his men in the midday prayers, he demurs and defers to al-Ḥusayn, who leads both his men, on their way to Kūfa to answer the call of the reputedly imam-less town, and al-Ḥurr's in prayer. When al-Ḥusayn seizes upon the platform he has been given to assert his rights—"fear God and recognize the rights of those of the family who are most pleasing to God; we are the *ahl al-bayt*, and as such we are more entitled to the authority of this government over you than these pretenders!"[5]—al-Ḥurr doggedly insists that he has only been sent to bring al-Ḥusayn to ʿUbayd Allāh ibn Ziyād, seemingly wanting no part of defending the Umayyad party line. When al-Ḥurr, immediately thereafter, prevents al-Ḥusayn and his men from leaving, al-Ḥusayn curses him—"May God deprive your mother of you!"—but al-Ḥurr refuses to take the bait, replying with "By God, there is no way for me to mention your mother [Fāṭima, the daughter of the Prophet Muḥammad] without saying only the best things possible."[6] It is at this point that al-Ḥurr suggests the loophole already mentioned: namely, that al-Ḥusayn pick a road that leads neither to Kūfa (where he is bound, and where al-Ḥurr is meant to usher him to ʿUbayd Allāh) nor to Medina (back from whence he came).

The two men, followed by their armies, travel alongside each other, and repeatedly, al-Ḥusayn's truculence is answered with al-Ḥurr's forbearance. Another call-to-loyalty speech by al-Ḥusayn follows, where he tells all those present: "In me you have an ideal model (*uswa*). However, if you will not act, but rather break your word and shirk your responsibility in the matter of the *bayʿa* that you have given, then you have not done so ignorantly […]. Thus you have mistaken your fortune and lost your destiny."[7] Ibn al-Athīr's account begins to differ from al-Ṭabarī's in that he omits a particularly vitriolic conclusion to al-Ḥusayn's speech—"I can only regard death as martyrdom, and life with these

5 Ibid. iii, 408; al-Ṭabarī, *Taʾrīkh* iii, 306; Cf. Ibn Kathīr, *Bidāya* viii, 180, who glosses over this pro-Shīʿī quote with a grudging *fa-khaṭabahum* (and then he gave a sermon to them).

6 Ibn al-Athīr, *Kāmil* iii, 408; al-Ṭabarī, *Taʾrīkh* iii, 306; Ibn Kathīr, *Bidāya* viii, 180, seems to have no compunction about including this interchange, which shows al-Ḥusayn as provocative and uncouth when contrasted to the courteous representative of the Umayyads, al-Ḥurr.

7 Ibn al-Athīr, *Kāmil* iii, 409; al-Ṭabarī, *Taʾrīkh* iii, 306; Ibn Kathīr, *Bidāya* viii, 180.

oppressors as a real hardship!"[8]—and a response by the galvanized Zuhayr ibn al-Qayn al-Bajalī, who exclaims his preference for "going with you [al-Ḥusayn] rather than staying in the world!"[9] While one must never discount a desire for greater brevity whenever a section from al-Ṭabarī's narrative is missing in Ibn al-Athīr's, the fact that, once again, the material that has been removed is an expression of the depth of the schism that is underway demonstrates Ibn al-Athīr's narrative priorities. In this section, the omission is certainly not increasing the drama.

Across all the narratives, at this juncture Al-Ḥusayn implicitly accuses al-Ḥurr of obedience to Satan. When al-Ḥurr cautions al-Ḥusayn against fighting when the odds are so stacked against him—"If you fight you will be fought, and the way I see it, if you are fought you will be killed"—al-Ḥusayn takes immediate umbrage and accuses al-Ḥurr of threatening to kill him: "Do you mean to frighten me with death? What worse disaster could befall you than if you killed me?"[10] Even the heretofore patient al-Ḥurr, evidently, has his limits, and so when al-Ḥusayn yet again calls him cursed (this time in verse), the conversation ends. In al-Ṭabarī's narrative, al-Ḥurr "drew away from him. He and his followers traveled on one side while al-Ḥusayn traveled on the other until they reached ʿUdhayb al-Hujānāt."[11] According to Ibn al-Athīr, however, even this is not enough to dissuade al-Ḥurr from his polite respect for al-Ḥusayn, who, at the same exact moment of the narrative, simply "traveled alongside [al-Ḥusayn] until they reached ʿUdhayb al-Hujānāt"[12] (with the separation of the two armies onto the opposite sides of the road purposefully omitted). This is another of Ibn al-Athīr's small performances of communal unity, inserted at a moment in the narrative when al-Ṭabarī's script bespeaks disunity, without changing the fundamental facts of the story.

At this point in the narrative, four men from Kūfa approach, and al-Ḥusayn (upon identifying them) declares that they are his supporters. When al-Ḥurr objects that they did not come with his original party, and that he intends to either detain them or send them back, al-Ḥusayn asserts, "I will defend them the way I would defend myself. These men are my supporters."[13] Al-Ṭabarī includes the following from al-Ḥusayn, which is omitted by Ibn al-Athīr: " 'They

8 Al-Ṭabarī, *Taʾrīkh* iii, 307.

9 Ibid. iii, 307.

10 Ibn al-Athīr, *Kāmil* iii, 409; al-Ṭabarī, *Taʾrīkh* iii, 307; Ibn Kathīr, *Bidāya* viii, 180.

11 Al-Ṭabarī, *Taʾrīkh* iii, 307.

12 Ibn al-Athīr, *Kāmil* iii, 409.

13 Ibn al-Athīr, *Kāmil* iii, 409; al-Ṭabarī, *Taʾrīkh* iii, 308. Ibn Kathīr simply paraphrases this exchange; see *Bidāya* viii, 181.

are just like those who came with me. Keep your faith regarding the agreement we have made [and let them stay]. Otherwise, I will have to do battle with you.' At that, al-Ḥurr desisted."[14] Ibn al-Athīr's performance of al-Ṭabarī's narrative, through just this type of omission, is a riff on the narrative that effaces as much effrontery, conflict, and discord as he reasonably can.

The narration continues when the four men arrive before al-Ḥusayn, who asks about the fate of the people of Kūfa under the governorship of ʿUbayd Allāh ibn Ziyād, al-Ḥurr's commander. Ibn al-Athīr presents the conversation as follows:

> Al-Ḥusayn said to them, "Tell the news of the people you have left behind you." Mujammiʿ ibn ʿAbd Allāh al-ʿĀʾidhī—he was one of them—said, "There has been much bribery among the nobles. Their coffers have been filled, and they are united against you. As for the rest of the people, their hearts are with you, but [against their will] soon their swords will be drawn against you."
>
> He then asked them about his messenger [whom al-Ḥusayn had sent to Kūfa], Qays ibn Mushir, and they told him of his death. The eyes of al-Ḥusayn glistened with moisture and he could not hold back the tears.[15]

Ibn al-Athīr's presentation of this moment seems unremarkable until compared with his source, al-Ṭabarī. Here is al-Ṭabarī's presentation of the moment:

> Mujammiʿ ibn ʿAbd Allāh al-ʿĀʾidhī, who was one of the group of four that had come to him, said, "There has been much bribery among the notables, and their coffers have been filled. Their support has been assured [through this bribery], and their loyalty [to Ibn Ziyād] is now certain. As for the rest of the people, their hearts are with you, but soon their swords will be drawn against you." Al-Ḥusayn then said, "Tell me, do you have any news of the messenger I sent to you?" They asked, "Who is it?" He told them it was Qays ibn Mushir al-Ṣaydāwī. They said, "Yes. Al-Ḥuṣayn ibn Tamīm captured him and sent him to [ʿUbayd Allāh] Ibn Ziyād. Ibn Ziyād ordered him to curse you and your father; instead, he called for God to bless you and your father while cursing Ibn Ziyād and his father. Then he called on the people to support you, and told them you were on

14 Al-Ṭabarī, *Taʾrīkh* iii, 308.

15 Ibn al-Athīr, *Kāmil* iii, 409.

> the way. Ibn Ziyād ordered him thrown from the wall of the palace." The eyes of al-Ḥusayn glistened with moisture and he could not hold back the tears.[16]

Ibn al-Athīr's performance, once again, omits the problematic narrative evidence of true discord while maintaining the integrity of the narrative. He presents a more bare-bones version of the story; sometimes the changes are for the sake of brevity, as with Ibn al-Athīr's decision to skip the meaningless back-and-forth in which al-Ḥusayn tells Mujammiʿ ibn ʿAbd Allāh the name of Qays ibn Mushir. But, while Ibn al-Athīr cannot leave out the bribery of the notables of Kūfa—it is too critical to the narrative—he leaves out the explicit charge that their loyalty to Ibn Ziyād was the benefit the bribery bought. Ibn al-Athīr also omits the entire narrative of Qays' death: a heroic death from the pro-Shīʿī perspective, as Qays dies for his loyalty to al-Ḥusayn and his father ʿAlī while under clear threat of capital punishment from the Umayyad governor Ibn Ziyād. Both crimes—bribery and murder—remain in Ibn al-Athīr's narrative, but he performs this moment without any incriminating details about the perpetrators. Even if one might argue that the guilt of the Umayyads could be inferred, the removal of those details remains consistent with Ibn al-Athīr's performative tactics elsewhere: whatever elements of the narrative that bespoke discord could be removed were removed.

Ibn Kathīr performs al-Ṭabarī's account more or less to the letter; a few changes to the syntax streamline the storytelling, but they constitute nothing of substance.[17] Ibn Kathīr will wait for a higher-stakes moment to challenge al-Ṭabarī's authority in any way, but when he does so, he will do so with flair (as we have already seen, and will see again).

The changes Ibn al-Athīr makes to this section of the narrative have little to do with setting up al-Ḥurr's character for his change of heart. The narrative utility of a character like al-Ḥurr ibn Yazīd at this juncture is not the same as his narrative utility once the battle is joined, which was discussed in the previous chapter. To be sure, all versions of the story foreshadow his defection to al-Ḥusayn's side. His sympathy for al-Ḥusayn, and his unflappable politeness in the face of al-Ḥusayn's belligerence, not to mention his eager exploitation (indeed, his suggestion) of loopholes that would infuriate Ibn Ziyād, are clearly designed to contextualize his fateful decision at Karbalāʾ within his character's established personality and preferences. Al-Ḥurr's utility for Ibn al-Athīr,

---

16 Al-Ṭabarī, *Taʾrīkh* iii, 308.

17 Ibn Kathīr, *Bidāya* viii, 181.

at least in terms of Ibn al-Athīr's conscious riffing on al-Ṭabarī's account, lies only in his role as an Umayyad representative. Without effacing the character entirely, Ibn al-Athīr performs a carefully curated version of the interaction between al-Ḥusayn and al-Ḥurr to try to erase the details of Umayyad misdeeds from collective memory, thus serving his largest objective: the enhancement of the memory of Islam's early unity.

Al-Ḥurr's and al-Ḥusayn's men are intercepted by a messenger from al-Kūfa bearing a letter from ʿUbayd Allāh ibn Ziyād. The message reads: "When my letter reaches you and my messenger reaches you, make al-Ḥusayn come to a halt. Let him stop in an open place, with no protection and no water. I have commanded my messenger to remain with you and compel you to do this, until he can bring me news of your compliance with my orders. Peace be with you."[18] The letter is identical in the accounts of al-Ṭabarī and Ibn al-Athīr, while Ibn Kathīr summarizes its contents. The messenger is described somewhat differently. Al-Ṭabarī writes: "Suddenly, a rider on a fast mount coming from al-Kūfa appeared. He was armed, and had a bow upon his shoulder. They all stopped and watched him. When he reached them, he greeted al-Ḥurr and his companions, but he did not greet al-Ḥusayn and his companions."[19] Ibn al-Athīr's performance of this moment omits both the speed of the Umayyad rider and, more relevantly, his armaments: "When they stopped, suddenly a rider from al-Kūfa came towards them. They stopped and watched him. He greeted al-Ḥurr, but he did not greet al-Ḥusayn and his companions."[20] It is almost as if Ibn al-Athīr is reluctant to suggest that an armed conflict is nigh until the fighting actually breaks out.

Immediately thereafter, al-Ḥurr is compelled to inform al-Ḥusayn and his men about this letter, and he does so reluctantly. Having already disarmed (by narrative omission) the messenger, Ibn al-Athīr now elides his identity, and a rather sharp retort from one of al-Ḥusayn's supporters. The following exchange is reported in al-Ṭabarī's narrative:

> Yazīd ibn Ziyād ibn al-Muhāṣir Abū al-Shaʿthāʾ al-Kindī al-Bahdalī, who was with al-Ḥusayn, looked at [ʿUbayd Allāh] ibn Ziyād's messenger and recognized him. He asked him, "Are you Mālik ibn Nusayr al-Baddī?" He said "Yes." [Mālik ibn Nusayr] was [like Yazīd ibn Ziyād] a member of the Tribe of Kinda. [Yazīd ibn Ziyād] said, "May your mother be deprived of you! What are you doing here?" [Mālik] replied, "What am I doing here?

18 Ibn al-Athīr, *Kāmil* iii, 411; al-Ṭabarī, *Taʾrīkh* iii, 309. Ibn Kathīr, *Bidāya* viii, 182.

19 Al-Ṭabarī, *Taʾrīkh* iii, 309.

20 Ibn al-Athīr, *Kāmil* iii, 411.

> I obeyed my imām and fulfilled my oath of allegiance." [Yazīd ibn Ziyād] Abū al-Sha'thā' said, "You have thereby disobeyed your God, and assisted your imām in destroying your own soul. You have earned shame and hell-fire! Indeed, God has said, 'We have made some of them imams, who summon people to hellfire, and on the Day of Resurrection they will not be helped.'[21] Your imam is one of those."[22]

The notion that the Umayyads were destined for eternal punishment for their sins is, for Ibn al-Athīr, an inconvenient notion present in al-Ṭabarī's writing, and so he eliminates it. This exchange is completely omitted from Ibn al-Athīr's version, and he simply skips straight to al-Ṭabarī's next sentence: "Al-Ḥurr ibn Yazīd began to make them stop in a place that was without water and where there was no village."[23] The two participants in this exchange, al-Ḥusayn's supporter Yazīd ibn Ziyād (not to be confused with Yazīd ibn Mu'āwiya or 'Ubayd Allāh ibn Ziyād, this episode's chief "villains") and the Umayyad messenger Mālik ibn Nusayr al-Baddī, do not play almost any role in the remainder of the story. This Yazīd, the supporter of al-Ḥusayn, is making his first appearance in the narrative (hence al-Ṭabarī's need to introduce him by his full name, including his *kunya* and his tribe, and his careful specification that he was a supporter of al-Ḥusayn), as is the Umayyad messenger Mālik, who is similarly introduced as a fellow member of the Kinda tribe. Yazīd ibn Ziyād dies in defense of al-Ḥusayn when the actual fighting breaks out; Mālik, for his part, wounds al-Ḥusayn's head during the battle and steals his cloak. Al-Ṭabarī mentions that this earned him the enmity of his own wife and lifelong poverty.

So much of al-Ṭabarī's script seems designed to criticize the Umayyad camp as aggressors, the first to introduce arms to the conflict, and a group of hell-bound usurpers. Ibn al-Athīr emphasizes the solidarity of some of their representatives, like al-Ḥurr, with al-Ḥusayn; he removes the implication that the Umayyads were the first ones to bear their weapons by removing any mention of the weapons themselves; and he even erases the notion that they are hell-bound by removing the interaction between the two rival Kindī tribesmen, Yazīd and Mālik. Ibn Kathīr speeds by this section as fast as he can. What is, for Ibn al-Athīr, a fertile opportunity to emphasize the unity even of the adversaries is, for Ibn Kathīr, an obstacle on the way to the main story.

---

21 Qur'ān 28:41. Arthur J. Arberry (trans.), *The Koran Interpreted* (New York: Macmillan, 1955). All Qur'ān citations are from this translation unless otherwise noted.

22 Al-Ṭabarī, *Ta'rīkh* iii, 309.

23 Ibid. iii, 310; Ibn al-Athīr, *Kāmil* iii, 411. Ibn Kathīr continues to offer only a summary account of this moment; see Ibn Kaṭhīr, *Bidāya* viii, 182.

3 Al-Ḥusayn is Detained and Denied Water

Regardless of how much Ibn al-Athīr might wish to present a version of the narrative that eliminates any hint of disunity, there are some Umayyad actions within the narrative that even the friendliest performance cannot erase. The denial of water to al-Ḥusayn is one of those.

The denial of water to the heroes of the narrative is by this point in the narrative a recurring trope. The readers of the narratives have seen this same situation play out before, and we will therefore see it in subsequent chapters. In fact, at Ṣiffīn, Muʿāwiya's army's attempt to deny ʿAlī and his followers access to the water of the Euphrates is explicitly tied to two prior denials of water: the Prophet's denial of water to the Meccans at Badr, and the conspirators' denial of water to the besieged ʿUthmān ibn ʿAffān. Here, we see it again, for a fourth time. In a desert environment like Arabia, the importance of water as a cultural symbol (not to mention a scarce necessity) needs little elucidation. The fact that al-Ḥusayn not only dies, but does so while thirsty, abets an emerging Shīʿī grudge that gets brought up as an almost formulaic element of any recounting of the Karbalāʾ narrative. Because it is so indelible a part of the narrative, Ibn al-Athīr is constrained to retain it; he is not free to omit it or change it. While he is able to alter the Umayyad approach to al-Ḥusayn's insurrection by softening al-Ḥurr's initial interaction with al-Ḥusayn, or narratively disarm the messenger who brings the command to prevent al-Ḥusayn from any water, some aspects of the story are too important and well-known to alter. A performance, after all, is always still anchored in its script.

Once water is denied, even the most conflict-averse character will have no choice but to fight.

4 Conclusion

The Battle of Karbalāʾ, on one level, was naught but a minor skirmish, the predictable conclusion to the ill-advised rebellion of al-Ḥusayn ibn ʿAlī ibn Abī Ṭālib against the current patriarch of the family that first had opposed the Prophet Muḥammad himself and then ʿAlī. This, most likely, is what it was in reality, and how it would have been perceived at the time. Indeed, it is absent from most of the early Muslim chronicles and from all of the extant non-Muslim histories that discuss the goings-on of the Near East's newest empire. Whether this is due to the insignificance of the event or the overwhelming pain it is said to have engendered cannot be surmised from our current vantage point. Regardless of whichever it was—an event either unmentioned or unmentionable—Karbalāʾ evolved into the most important moment in Islamic history, the site of memory that marshalled all events preceding it in the service of providing its proper context and meaning, and also the site of memory that colored all events subsequent to it with a sectarian glaze.

The event itself—the actual fight—engendered little disagreement among the three men examined in this study, first al-Ṭabarī and later Ibn al-Athīr and Ibn Kathīr. What they sought to do with Karbalāʾ was not to challenge the event but rather to give it its proper meaning. For al-Ṭabarī—certainly pro-ʿAlī and pro-ʿAlīd, but not a Shīʿī—the event was the quintessential tragedy of early Islam. Already middle-aged by the time of his death, the continuous reminders, often voiced in al-Ṭabarī's account by al-Ḥusayn himself, of the fact that he was the Prophet's grandson, the repeated callbacks to the Prophet bouncing al-Ḥusayn, then a young boy, on his knee, bespeak his innocence and his nobility at once. Al-Ḥusayn's death was the moment that, at the very least, the memory of the Umayyad dynasty became unsalvageable. It should be remembered that al-Ṭabarī was writing some decades after the ʿAbbāsids had overthrown the Umayyads, who survived for the moment as the overlords of al-Andalus, the Iberian Peninsula. The betrayal and murder of al-Ḥusayn, and then the desecration of his body, also serve to provide the seminal moment for the Shīʿī narrative of history.

Ibn al-Athīr and Ibn Kathīr both wrote at a time when that Shīʿī narrative of history was well-established, and both sought, in different ways, to undermine it. Ibn al-Athīr sought to emphasize unity, and while his presentation of the horrors of Karbalāʾ does not differ greatly from that of al-Ṭabarī, he avoids discussing or emphasizing disunity for as long as he could—basically until the moment the battle was joined. Ibn Kathīr had no intention of lending any credence to the Shīʿī story, and so—while he, too, presented a narrative of the fight itself that emphasized al-Ḥusayn's nobility—in the run up to the battle he was still shooting holes in the Shīʿī narrative, emphasizing the overveneration and exaggeration inherent therein.

Emphasizing unity and discrediting the Shīʿī narrative, however, are meaningless exercises if they are confined only to the episode of the narrative that had the greatest amount of staying power. The case had to be made from the very beginning. In order to give Karbalāʾ its proper context, one needed to return to a prior moment of similar narrative importance.

The standard narrative asserts that al-Ḥusayn was killed while rebelling against an unjust and illegitimate government. Had they been legitimate, al-Ḥusayn's role in the story would be fundamentally different. The question that arises relates to how we know the Umayyad kings were not caliphs. The answer, at first glance, would seem to be the succession of Muʿāwiya by Yazīd—it was the first example of hereditary rule, which Islam did not seem to sanction. However, as the narrative goes, that succession was merely one illegitimate act of an already-illegitimate regime. The Umayyads, according to the narrative, were illegitimate rulers right from the beginning of their dynasty. Their dynasty did not begin with the assassination of ʿAlī and the general acceptance of Muʿāwiya, perhaps by default, as the leader of the *umma*.

5 Next Stop

With the Karbalāʾ narrative thus discussed, the obvious question before us is what piece of the wider narrative must be our next stop. The most tempting next stop on the present narrative exploration in reverse is the career of Yazīd ibn Muʿāwiya himself: his conflict with the people of Medina and his appointment by his father, Muʿāwiya, as his successor make a kind of intuitive sense. Yazīd is, after all, the villain of this particular story; with apologies to Ibn Ziyād, who is presented as quite cruel, the buck stops with Yazīd. The Umayyads themselves, rather than their henchmen and functionaries, are the true villains of the Shīʿī story and the rehabilitative project for its detractors. But it turns out that the narrative of Yazīd's appointment as Muʿāwiya's successor and his time as caliph offers us little opportunity for insight. In fact, like many villains in many literary genres, Yazīd's character is generally underdeveloped. Even the most ardent defenders of the Sunnī version of the narrative display little interest in attempting to rehabilitate Yazīd. It took a particular project like Ibn ʿAsākir's *Taʾrīkh madīnat Dimashq*, whose goal was to rehabilitate the Umayyad dynasty in general and Sunnī Umayyad-era transmitters in particular, to present anything like a sympathetic version of Yazīd.[24] Even then, the portrayal is of "a valid and reliable transmitter of ḥadīths and an intelligent son, who is worthy of the caliphate (at least in his father's eyes), [who is] virtuous […] by reason of his connection to the age of the Prophet […] [and] a legitimate caliph to whom Muslims owed their obedience."[25] However, "even Yazīd's most ardent supporters could not very well hope to deny that he was given to wine, women, and song; nor could they pretend that there was no controversy about his succession; and they certainly could not avoid the reality that al-Ḥusayn's death took place at the hands of Yazīd's representatives. Ibn

24 James E. Lindsay, "Caliphal and Moral Exemplar? ʿAlī ibn ʿAsākir's Portrait of Yazīd b. Muʿāwiya," in *Der Islam* 74 (1997), 250–278.

25 Ibid. 253.

ʿAsākir attempts to deny none of these."[26] Of course, as Lindsay points out, Ibn ʿAsākir is not a world chronicler like al-Ṭabarī or Ibn al-Athīr. So, with a different goal, and a different audience, Ibn ʿAsākir is uniquely situated to say nice things about Yazīd, and even he limits himself to the precise task of establishing his reliability as a transmitter of tradition. Indeed, Ibn ʿAsākir gives only a cursory account of Yazīd's brief time as caliph and otherwise "walks [a] tightrope" between Yazīd's reliability and his moral failings, which he is clearly disinclined to mention too much. But such failings are too well-known for al-Ṭabarī and Ibn al-Athīr to avoid. For them, Yazīd is *the* villain of the Karbalāʾ story. While Ibn ʿAsākir may be able to salvage a piece of Umayyad memory with a selective focus on only certain aspects of Yazīd's life and reign, and thus gives only scanty coverage to Yazīd's more unsavory moments, there is no such prize awaiting al-Ṭabarī and Ibn al-Athīr for any massaging or refocusing of Yazīd's story. In many ways, Yazīd is not actually much of an actor in the story, but more of a symbol of the Umayyad dynasty's enduring illegitimacy. Possessed of all the moral failings for which the dynasty is infamous in a way that is almost metonymic, al-Ṭabarī's presentation of Yazīd is not meaningfully softened by Ibn al-Athīr. His appointment by his father Muʿāwiya as his designated successor was distasteful to Sunnīs and Shīʿa alike.

Furthermore, as Liew examines, Yazīd was a caliph whose reputation was so ghastly that the permissibility of his public cursing was a matter for scholarly debate, on which no less a scholar than the Ḥanbalī Ibn al-Jawzī (b. ca. 508/1114)—no Shīʿī sympathizer by any means—concluded that al-Ḥusayn's rebellion had been justified in that he had "rebelled to resist falsehood and establish what is lawful."[27] Now, it should be acknowledged that, as Liew points out, Ibn al-Jawzī's assertion was not meant to be taken as precedent or justification for other rebellions, a fact that did not save Ibn al-Jawzī's reputation from the wrecking balls of later prominent Ḥanbalīs like Ibn Taymiyya and Ibn Mufliḥ.[28] It must be said that they, too, took no issue with Ibn al-Jawzī's damning position on Yazīd, but rather with a misrepresentation of Ibn al-Jawzī's perspective on rebellion against any caliph, moral or otherwise. Pithily, Yazīd is potentially a Sunnī reclamation project whom Ibn al-Jawzī saw fit to curse publicly, and which Ibn Taymiyya wanted no part of. When such a particularly

26 Ibid. 253.

27 Abū al-Farāj ʿAbd al-Raḥmān ibn al-Jawzī, *al-Radd ʿalā l-mutaʿaṣṣib al-ʿanīd al-māniʿ min dhamm Yazīd*, ed. H. ʿA. Muḥammad (Beirut: Dār al-Kutub al-ʿIlmiyya, 2005), 63–64, cited in Han Hsien Liew, "Ibn al-Jawzī and the Cursing of Yazīd b. Muʿāwiya: A Debate on Rebellion and Legitimate Rulership," in *JAOS* 139 (2019), 642.

28 Liew, "Ibn al-Jawzī" 645.

Sunnī problem has lost the endeavor of Ibn Taymiyya, it has lost everyone. There is, consequently, no reason for us to stop and examine that point in the narrative. Sometimes a villain is just a villain.

Furthermore, inasmuch as the historians were ill-equipped to recast Yazīd as anything but a villain, none of them, even the most anti-Shīʿī among them, could stomach vilifying al-Ḥusayn. One well-known episode was recounted by al-Ṭabarī. When Yazīd first acceded to rulership, he summoned those parties whose loyalty caused him the most concern with regard to the giving of the *bayʿa*. These included ʿAbd Allāh ibn ʿUmar, ʿAbd al-Raḥmān ibn Abī Bakr, ʿAbd Allāh ibn al-Zubayr, and al-Ḥusayn. It was the last two that concerned him the most. Muʿāwiya, on his deathbed, had warned his son that he should deal first with Ibn al-Zubayr, who was raring for a fight. Al-Ḥusayn, Muʿāwiya counseled, could be handled more gently. When summoned, Ibn al-Zubayr did not come to Muʿāwiya and instead fled to Mecca; al-Ḥusayn, by contrast, did come (although not alone—he had a band of supporters with him, just in case). When al-Ḥusayn is confronted with Yazīd's demand for his oath of allegiance, delivered by Yazīd's henchmen al-Walīd ibn ʿUtba and Marwān ibn al-Ḥakam, he asserts that a *bayʿa* given in secret has no validity; the oath must be taken publicly. His pious excuse to leave the palace, and the clutches of his rival, thus made, al-Ḥusayn got up to go. At this point, Marwān says to al-Walīd, "If you let al-Ḥusayn leave without making the oath right now, you will never get it from him. So arrest him and do not free him until he takes the *bayʿa*, or else behead him." Al-Walīd, horrified, retorts that doing so would bring about "the utter destruction and ruin of my religion" and vows that "if the riches of the world were offered to me, I would not kill al-Ḥusayn," fearing "total destruction on the Day of Judgement, for in God's view there can be nothing more valuable than al-Ḥusayn's blood."[29] If anything, this section demonstrates that there were certainly limits to the amount of reframing renarration in which the historians could reasonably engage. It would undoubtedly be better for the cause of Syrian/Umayyad narrative redemption if Yazīd's moral failings were mitigated; likewise, if presenting al-Ḥusayn as even somewhat more unreasonable, more belligerent (towards Yazīd, that is; Ibn Kathīr presented him as plenty belligerent to al-Ḥurr), or simply more complex was an option available to Ibn Kathīr, there is no doubt he would have taken the opportunity to emphasize those moral failings. That he did not, and that he reserved his criticism for those

29 Al-Ṭabarī, *Taʾrīkh* iii, 270. The same exchange, with no meaningful alteration, occurs in Ibn al-Athīr, *Kāmil* iii, 378. Ibn Kathīr leaves out the bit about the value of al-Ḥusayn's blood, but nonetheless has al-Walīd aver "whoever kills al-Ḥusayn will be totally destroyed on the Day of Judgment," as recorded in *Bidāya* viii, 154–155.

he perceived as overzealous fools who venerated ʿAlī and the Ṭālibids excessively, is noteworthy. Clearly, whatever narrative wiggle room the historians possessed, it did not extend to al-Ḥusayn's character. It is impossible to discern whether their preservation of al-Ḥusayn's and Yazīd's characters was due their genuine belief in the one's virtue and the other's wickedness or due to their perceptions of what specific liberties they were free to take with their source material in al-Ṭabarī, or whether they feared scholarly or personal backlash for any assault on a piece of the narrative that, for some of their colleagues, readers, and neighbors, would have bordered on the sacred. So, while al-Ḥusayn's and Yazīd's actions and interactions may be recontextualized, reordered, or omitted as Ibn al-Athīr and Ibn Kathīr saw fit, their essential natures and roles in the story were unalterable. This is a strategy that, as we will see in the next section, they maintain with controversial figures like Muʿāwiya and ʿAmr ibn al-ʿĀṣ. The character traits of well-known personages—almost archetypal characters by the time Ibn al-Athīr and Ibn Kathīr were writing—merited little discussion for them, for there was nothing to be gained by presenting as green someone commonly understood as red.

The Umayyad dynasty, and all its many perceived moral failings, on the other hand, does merit their discussion. Ibn Taymiyya, for one, would argue—as just mentioned—that rebellion against any caliph, moral or otherwise, competent or otherwise, beloved or otherwise, was illegal, but only so long as the leader against whom the rebellion is directed was legitimate. The question of Yazīd's legitimacy, rather than his morality or his character, was thus the central question for Sunnī narrative reclaimers; and Yazīd's legitimacy was not his own, and had nothing to do with his character or his actions once in office, or even the manner of his appointment as his father's successor. That appointment, after all, had been Muʿāwiya's doing, not his, and if Muʿāwiya was a legitimate caliph, then so was Yazīd. So Yazīd's legitimacy is tied to his father's legitimacy (and the entire question of Umayyad legitimacy is tacked onto the question as well). The question of Umayyad legitimacy begins with the first claim of Muʿāwiya ibn Abī Sufyān to the rulership. As the dynasty is so often presented, Muʿāwiya's claim to leadership of the *umma* was cynical, opportunistic, of dubious legality, politically and religiously illegitimate, clever, and worldly. This claim was first pressed at the Battle of Ṣiffīn, and so that is where we must go next.

PART 2

The Betrayal at Ṣiffīn

CHAPTER 5

The Ṣiffīn Narrative

It is counterintuitive to skip over so much important material as we travel backward through the Islamic narrative. The Battle of Ṣiffīn, our next stop, is, after all, 19 years before Karbalāʾ. ʿAlī ibn Abī Ṭālib, al-Ḥusayn's father, was still alive, and generally (though, critically, not universally) acknowledged as the caliph of Islam. So, too, was Muʿāwiya ibn Abī Sufyān,[1] the father of Yazīd. Between the conclusion of Ṣiffīn and the commencement of hostilities at Karbalāʾ, ʿAlī would be assassinated, Muʿāwiya would become caliph and then die of old age, and his son Yazīd would become caliph after him in a controversial succession (it would be the first dynastic succession in Islamic history). ʿAlī's eldest son, al-Ḥasan, would abdicate any claims he had to leadership, perhaps under coercion. Finally, al-Ḥusayn would rise up against the Umayyads, beginning the sequence of events that would lead to the Karbalāʾ moment.

If the narrative is meant to explain and properly contextualize the evolution of Sunnī and Shīʿī identities, ʿAlī's death would seem to be the most intuitive site of memory to discuss next. After all, al-Ḥusayn's death at Karbalāʾ was (so the present argument goes) the most important event of the Islamic narrative. All the other events before Karbalāʾ gave it its meaning and context, and all the events after it occurred, in one form or another, in its shadow. Furthermore, the subsequent deaths of the lines of Imams—the descendants of ʿAlī, beginning with al-Ḥasan and al-Ḥusayn, and then (although their numbers and identities are disputed) a line of Ḥusaynids—are the signposts that mark the progress of at least the Shīʿī understanding of the course of their history. The assassination of the Imams by iniquitous usurpers is not only a trope; it is the recurring motif that gives the Shīʿī narrative its organizational structure. So why is ʿAlī's death not included in this analysis?

The simplest answer is that the importance of the deaths of all of those other Imams, from al-Ḥusayn onward, lies not in the actual death of the ʿAlīd scions but in the identities of their killers. In each case, it was a representative of the Sunnī caliphal administration—except for the death of ʿAlī. To be sure, ʿAlī was betrayed, his position was usurped, and he was murdered just like the rest of them, but when he was murdered it was by a Khārijī named Ibn

1 For a survey of the literature on Muʿāwiya, see R. Stephen Humphreys, *Muʿawiya ibn Abi Sufyan: From Arabia to Empire* (Oxford: Oneworld, 2006), esp. 1–22.

 | DOI:10.1163/9789004524255_007

Muljam. The murder of ʿAlī made narrative sense, even to the Shīʿa, given Khārijī positions. Both the Sunnīs and the Shīʿa agreed that the Khawārij officially left Islam behind when they left ʿAlī's service at Ṣiffīn.[2] They would become enemies of both the Sunnīs and the Shīʿa, both of whom, by the time any confirmable written sources survived, would see themselves on the same side in the Battle of Ṣiffīn, namely ʿAlī's. As such the Khawārij sent assassins to kill not only ʿAlī but his chief adversaries at Ṣiffīn, Muʿāwiya and ʿAmr ibn al-ʿĀṣ. The would-be assassins of ʿAmr and Muʿāwiya both failed. ʿAlī's life and career, and their meanings, are disputed, but his death was by no means a controversial moment; he was simply murdered by a villain of the narrative. Ibn al-Athīr and Ibn Kathīr, in other words, had no axe to grind with the standard narrative of ʿAlī's murder; he was, after all, the fourth of the *rāshidūn* caliphs, a legitimate Sunnī leader, and his killer was neither a Syrian, nor (in their view) even a Muslim when the act was done.

In any event, the story of ʿAlī's murder, because of the culprit's politics and theology, began at Ṣiffīn. Ṣiffīn was also more fertile ground for the two later historians to advance their narrative agendas, and an easier venue to work out the proper role of ʿAlī in the narrative. Perhaps more to the point, the Umayyad dynasty—the villains of the Karbalāʾ narrative, despite Yazīd ibn Muʿāwiya's apparent horror at the death of al-Ḥusayn—had its beginnings at Ṣiffīn as well. What makes a narrative venue like Ṣiffīn difficult to categorize is its multifaceted role in the larger story. It is not an end in and of itself, one that explains and contextualizes why and how sects developed in Islam (nor, even more importantly, does it offer an opportunity for historians to establish which sect is "correct"); that is essentially the goal of the Karbalāʾ narrative, and the various narratives that provide its context. Nor does Ṣiffīn begin to generate the cracks in the community that ultimately led there; that is arguably the moment of the election of ʿUthmān.[3] The Ṣiffīn episode is firmly in the middle of the critical narrative, and so its communicated meaning is, at one and the same time, the result of prior narrative choices and a contextualizer of later choices. But it is a particular middle that could be presented and understood in any number of

2 The word *Khārijī* (pl. *Khawārij*) has at its root the letters kh-r-j and literally means "those who exit."

3 A case could be made for any number of other venues for when the initial divide between Sunnīs and Shīʿa "began," or—more accurately—came to be remembered by later historians to have begun. Other obvious examples include the selections of Abū Bakr and ʿUmar as the first and second caliphs, respectively. As discussed in the introduction, perhaps the Ghadīr Khumm *ḥadīth*, or, rather, the argument over its veracity, would be a more appropriate place to start.

ways, depending on how the narrative is performed. The assassination of ʿUthmān, which was the catalyst for Ṣiffīn (and the Battle of the Camel in 36/656, the same year—a battle of perhaps equal intensity, but of less narrative consequence), was either justified or not. This critical question will be undertaken in the next section of this book, which discusses ʿUthmān directly, but we cannot ignore it here, largely because it is the question that drives the action at Ṣiffīn forward. Bearing this question in mind, therefore, we may proceed to a discussion of the event itself, particularly its conclusion.

The ultimate conclusion of Ṣiffīn had far-reaching consequences for the Islamic community and, obviously, for the narrative of its birth, beginnings, and growth. Despite what appears to be something just short of a rout of Muʿāwiya's forces by ʿAlī's, the battle ended in what initially appeared to be a political stalemate, but which was ultimately a victory for Muʿāwiya. At the end of the episode, ʿAlī's camp was split into his loyal followers on the one hand and the Khawārij on the other (their departure ostensibly due to their umbrage at ʿAlī's acceptance of a call for a cease-fire and arbitration, although al-Ṭabarī, Ibn al-Athīr, and Ibn Kathīr all tell you that they were naught but a bunch of cowardly hypocrites). This is critical because it provides context for ʿAlī's assassination; his assassin, Ibn Muljam, was one of the Khawārij. The stalemate at the end of the arbitration agreement also ended any pretensions ʿAlī may have had to unchallenged leadership over the entirety of the burgeoning caliphate. In truth, he never had it. Syria, under the governorship of Muʿāwiya, had never pledged allegiance to ʿAlī's rule. For the few years between the conclusion of Ṣiffīn and ʿAlī's murder, there was no question that the leadership was divided. Meanwhile, there is a compelling argument to be made that the conclusion of Ṣiffīn, while not definitively the end of ʿAlī's reign as caliph, could certainly be designated the beginning of Muʿāwiya's, and thus, the beginning of the Umayyad dynasty. While Muʿāwiya's own period of generally acknowledged rulership[4] is typically dated from ʿAlī's death, it is at the very last moment of the Ṣiffīn narrative that anyone—in this case, his advisor, ʿAmr ibn al-ʿĀṣ—first calls Muʿāwiya caliph. This represented a political victory for Muʿāwiya, who had entered the battle as a governor and a relative seeking justice for the slain Caliph ʿUthmān, refusing to pledge allegiance to ʿAlī unless ʿUthmān's killers (supporters of ʿAlī) would be delivered to him. Although he did not get what he initially claimed to have wanted—he was never able to compel ʿAlī to turn over ʿUth-

4 Though not, of course, universally acknowledged. ʿAlī's family and their supporters, obviously, never accepted the son of Abū Sufyān and his descendants and cousins as their rulers, even if some grudgingly bore the burden of living under usurpation for practical and self-preservatory reasons.

mān's killers—he did leave the battle as, at worst, one of two potential caliphs. This was a marked promotion from his original position, merely governor of Syria.

If Muʿāwiya's reign, albeit contested, began at the announcement of the arbitration agreement at Dūmat al-Jandal, and if Muʿāwiya's reign marks the commencement of the Umayyad dynasty, as it is generally considered to do, then under what circumstances was the dynasty founded? Was it legitimate or not? Critically, was al-Ḥusayn's later rebellion, as discussed in the first section, a justified rebellion against an illegitimate regime? If Karbalāʾ carried with it the narrative weight of Sunnīsm and Shīʿism, Ṣiffīn carried the weight of the Umayyads as a dynasty. The Umayyads emerged from the historical Ṣiffīn as Islam's first dynasty; they emerged from the Ṣiffīn narrative as Islam's first internal villains. Al-Ṭabarī had no problem with this presentation; as might be surmised, Ibn al-Athīr and Ibn Kathīr had different ideas.

1 Sourcing Ṣiffīn

As is the case with Karbalāʾ, many of the accounts of Ṣiffīn, which would certainly have served to diversify the perspectives on the battle, are now lost.[5] However, the sheer proliferation of perspectives is telling; Ṣiffīn was obviously an event that was considered by early Muslim historians to be of high importance. Fuat Sezgin's magnum opus, *Geschichte des arabischen Schrifttums*, lists a number of works under the title "Kitāb Ṣiffīn," which we unfortunately possess only in the form of scattered later quotations, if at all, and almost all of them exclusively in al-Ṭabarī's *Taʾrīkh*. Sezgin mentions a *Kitāb Ṣiffīn* of Abū Hudhayfa Isḥāq ibn Bishr ibn Muḥammad al-Bukhārī (d. 206/821), referenced in the *Fihrist* of Ibn al-Nadīm; however, the only extant quotations from this work are from the author's other works, which are not explored here.[6] Abū Isḥāq Ibrāhīm ibn al-Ḥusayn ibn Dayzīl al-Kisāʾī (d. 281/894) wrote a *Kitāb Ṣiffīn*, fragments of which are related in the works of Ibn Abī al-Ḥadīd[7] and Ibn

5 There does exist an anonymous *Akhbār Ṣiffīn* of unknown date and provenance. This *Akhbār Ṣiffīn* was edited as a PhD dissertation by ʿAbd al-ʿAzīz Ṣāliḥ al-Helabi, University of St. Andrews, 1974. Hinds describes this work in "The Banners and Battle Cries at Ṣiffīn (657 AD)," in *al-Abḥāth* (American University of Beirut) 24 (1971), 3–42.

6 Fuat Sezgin, *Geschicte des arabischen Schrifttums, Band 1* (Leiden: Brill, 1967), 293–294.

7 See ʿAbd al-Ḥamīd ibn Hibat Allāh ibn Abī al-Ḥadīd, *Sharḥ nahj al-balāgha* (Cairo: Dār Iḥyāʾ al-Kutub al-ʿArabīyah, 1964). Ibn Dayzīl is also sometimes called Ibn Dīzīl. See Sezgin, *GAS* i, 321.

Maʿṣūm,[8] as well as in Ibn Diḥya (d. 633/1235),[9] who quotes at length from him in his monograph *Iʿlam al-Naṣr al-Mubīn fī al-Mufāḍala bayn Ahlay Ṣiffīn*. Ibn Dayzīl also employed quotations from both al-Wāqidī's (d. 207/823)[10] *Kitāb Ṣiffīn* and that of Abū Mikhnaf, though Sezgin argues that this was probably based more upon his Iraqi tribal loyalties than on any sectarian bent.[11] Abū al-Qāsim al-Mundhīr ibn Muḥammad ibn al-Mundhīr ibn Saʿīd al-Qābūsī (d. fourth/tenth century), also composed a *Kitāb Ṣiffīn*, which may have been among the sources for Abū al-Faraj al-Iṣfahānī's small section on the Battle of Ṣiffīn in his *Kitāb Maqātil al-ṭalibīyyīn*.[12] It should be repeated that the surviving quotations from these works are extremely fragmentary and scattered—this is nothing like the situation with Naṣr ibn Muzāḥim, whose entire *Waqʿat Ṣiffīn* (or at least, something approximating it) was reconstructable from the works of al-Ṭabarī, as well as a few others, thus testifying to its enduring value as a foundational original source for al-Ṭabarī, although he clearly relies on his usual stable of tradents in addition to Naṣr ibn Muzāḥim. Jābir ibn Yazīd ibn al-Ḥārith al-Juʿfī (d. ca. 128/746) was mentioned by the Shīʿī scholar al-Najāshī (d. 450/1058) as having composed, among other works, a *Kitāb Ṣiffīn*.[13] Jābir's increasingly radical Shīʿī perspective caused his reliability to be questioned by Sunnī scholars like Abū Ḥanīfa (who accused him of having a *ḥadīth* for every legal question), and ultimately caused his exclusion from the *ḥadīth* collections of Bukhārī and Muslim. In all, Chase Robinson points out that fourteen separate monographs were composed on the Battle of Ṣiffīn in the century between 750 and 850, and another seven were composed by the year 950;[14] ʿAbd al-ʿAzīz Ṣāliḥ al-Helabi adds four to this number, citing twenty-five individual works on Ṣiffīn. Besides those works already mentioned, these include the lost works of Abān ibn Taghlib al-Bakrī (d. 141/758), Hishām ibn Muḥammad al-Kalbī (d. 204/809),[15] al-Wāqidī (d. 207/822), Abū ʿUbayda Muʿmar ibn al-Muthannā (d. 208/823), al-Madāʾinī (d. 225/839), Ibn

8 Sezgin, *GAS* i, 321.
9 Brockelmann, *GALS* i, 310–312, S i, 544–545.
10 For more on al-Wāqidī, see Brockelmann, *GALS* i, 141–142; Sezgin, *GAS* i, 294–297; Dūrī, *Rise of Historical Writing* 37–40.
11 Ursula Sezgin, *Abū Miḥnaf: ein Beitrag zur Historiographie der umayadischen Zeit* (Leiden: Brill, 1971).
12 Abū al-Farāj al-Iṣfahānī, *Kitāb Maqātil al-ṭālibiyyīn*, ed. Sayyid Ahmad Saqar (Beirut: Dār al-Maʿrifa, 1982).
13 Sezgin, *GAS* i, 307.
14 Robinson, *Islamic Historiography* 34.
15 For more on this Ibn al-Kalbī, see Yāqūt al-Rūmī, *Irshād* ii, 187–188, 219, 504; Ignaz Goldziher, *Muslim Sudies*, ed. S.M. Stern, i (Albany: SUNY Press, 1967), 185–187.

Abī Shayba (d. 235/849),[16] Ismāʿīl ibn ʿĪsā al-ʿAṭṭār (d. 232/857), Muḥammad ibn Zakariya al-Ghalābī (d. 298/910),[17] Ibrāhīm ibn Muḥammad al-Thaqafī (d. 283/896),[18] Hishām ibn al-Ḥakam al-Shaybānī (d. 199/815), ʿAbd al-ʿAzīz ibn Yaḥya al-Jallūdī (d. 322/944), and the anonymous *Akhbār Ṣiffīn* that is the focus of al-Helabi's dissertation.[19] He singles out Ibn al-Muthannā as an author who agreed with the Khārijī position. Sezgin also identifies an *Akhbar Ṣiffīn* by Ibn ʿUthmān al-Kalbī, who copied material from al-Haytham ibn ʿAdī.[20] This proliferation of Ṣiffīn texts is clear evidence of the importance of the story to Muslim writers. This could have been motivated by any number of factors, including a pious interest in *fitna*, or geography, or the political history of the early community in addition to the formation of sectarian identities. Still, the existence of (for one) Ibn al-Muthannā's Khāriji perspective on Ṣiffīn confirms that, even at this early stage, there were perspectives beyond the pro-ʿAlīd assessments of the earlier historians whose work has managed to survive.

2 The Elements of the Story

In 36/656, the armies of ʿAlī ibn Abī Ṭālib, then acknowledged by most of the Muslim world as the fourth caliph, and Muʿāwiya ibn Abī Sufyān, at the time the governor of al-Shām, met near the city of Raqqa on the banks of the Euphrates River. The confrontation had been brewing, and might well have been inevitable. ʿAlī's relationship with the killers of ʿUthmān, the previous caliph and a cousin of Muʿāwiya, was too close for political expediency. There were consequently those within the community who immediately saw ʿAlī as tainted with the murder of his predecessor. After dispatch-

16 See Ibn al-Nadīm, *Fihrist* 229; Aḥmad ibn ʿAlī al-Khaṭīb al-Baghdādī, *Taʾrīkh Baghdād*, ed. Muṣṭafā ʿAbd al-Qādir ʿAṭā', x (Beirut: Dār al-Kutub al-ʿIlmiyya, 1997) 66–71; Brockelmann, GALS i, 215.

17 Al-Ghalābī was one of the authorities most often quoted by Abū Bakr Muḥammad al-Ṣūlī (d. 335/947), a prolific author, collector of poetry, and oft-quoted authority for reports on caliphs and poets.

18 See Ibn al-Nadīm, *Fihrist* 279; Yāqūt al-Rūmī, *Irshād* i, 294–295; Brockelmann, GALS i, 225; Sezgin, GAS i, 321.

19 Abdul-Aziz Saleh Helabi, *A Critical Edition of* Akhbār Ṣiffīn (PhD diss., University of St. Andrews), 11–33.

20 Sezgin, GAS i, 314. See s.v. Al-Haytham ibn ʿAdī (d. 206 or 207/821 or 822) in Brockelmann, GALS i, 213. See also Stefan Leder, *Das Korpus al-Haiṯam ibn ʿAdī (st. 207/822): Herkunft, Überlieferung, Gestalt früher Texte der aḫbār Literatur* (Frankfurt: Vittorio Klosterman, 1991).

ing Ṭalḥā ibn ʿUbayd Allāh and al-Zubayr ibn al-ʿAwwām at the Battle of the Camel (see Chapter 9), the showdown between the two most powerful men in the Muslim world at the time was on. What follows are the elements of the story:

2.1 *The Journey of ʿAlī from Baṣra to Kūfa to Ṣiffīn and Muʿāwiya's Journey to Ṣiffīn*

In Rajab 36/December 656, following the Battle of the Camel at Baṣra, ʿAlī and his followers begin their journey past Kūfa to meet Muʿāwiya's army at Ṣiffīn. During this journey, one of the most important events is the dispatch of an emissary, Jarīr ibn ʿAbd Allāh al-Bajalī, to Muʿāwiya in an attempt to convince him and his followers to take the *bayʿa* (oath of allegiance) and pledge their allegiance to ʿAlī.

As ʿAlī makes the journey to the banks of the Euphrates, he interacts with the locals in a variety of ways. Sometimes he is forced to confront them, to demand their quarter; sometimes, he takes on new supporters. One important anecdote is ʿAlī's reluctant enlistment of the foolish and fickle (and equally reluctant) governor of Kūfa, Abū Mūsā al-Ashʿarī. Abū Mūsā is later appointed as ʿAlī's representative in the arbitration.

Meanwhile, Muʿāwiya comes to Ṣiffīn as well, gathering support along the way. His most notable recruit is ʿAmr ibn al-ʿĀṣ. He arrives at the Euphrates River before ʿAlī.

Eventually, ʿAlī and his followers get to the Euphrates to find that Muʿāwiya controls the drinking water supply.

2.2 *The Battle by the Water*

Thirsty after their long journey, ʿAlī and his men ask Muʿāwiya for access to water to slake their thirst, but are denied. ʿAlī's army attacks and conquers both banks of the Euphrates and magnanimously distributes water to both sides.

2.3 *The Makeup of the Armies and the Early Skirmishes*

Most of the accounts include, in varying degrees of detail, a discussion of the makeup of both ʿAlī's army and Muʿāwiya's army. In addition to numbering the soldiers, usually classified as *muhājirūn* and *anṣār* or by city of origin, these discussions mostly concern which Companions of the Prophet were on which side. ʿAmmār ibn Yāsir, an elderly Companion of the Prophet, is among those prominently mentioned as a supporter of ʿAlī.

The Battle of Ṣiffīn, following the skirmishes by the water, was actually a series of small *mano a mano* duels, followed by one major pitched battle.

2.4 *Laylat al-Harīr—the Main Battle*

There is a large battle between ʿAlī's soldiers and Muʿāwiya's. This main battle is remembered by the name *laylat al-harīr*—the "night of clamor."

2.5 *Call for Arbitration; Appointment of Arbiters; Withdrawal of the Armies*

By far the most famous and complex episode of the story of Ṣiffīn is the call for arbitration by Muʿāwiya's camp and ʿAlī's grudging acquiescence. Seeing that the fighting favors ʿAlī, Muʿāwiya's shrewd general, ʿAmr ibn al-ʿĀṣ, comes up with a plan either to provide his men with respite, capitalize on the existing divisions within ʿAlī's camp, or, ideally, both. By raising copies of the Qurʾān upon their lances, the Syrians appeal to the religious instincts of ʿAlī's men and provide an alternative means of ending the conflict to those soldiers who were appalled that the struggle over ʿUthmān's blood had engendered a necessity for Muslims to fight other Muslims.

The cease-fire agreement requires both camps to nominate an arbiter to negotiate and agree upon a ruling that would settle the affair in a just manner. Muʿāwiya immediately, and without resistance from his followers, appoints ʿAmr ibn al-ʿĀṣ. ʿĀlī, plagued by the divisions within his ranks, is blocked from sending his first choice, ʿAbd Allāh ibn ʿAbbās, because of objections to the nepotism implicit in ʿAlī's appointment of his cousin. ʿAlī's second choice for representation in the arbitration, al-Ashtar, is similarly rejected on the grounds that the latter was one of ʿUthmān's attackers and would thus be an unacceptable negotiating counterpart to ʿAlī's Umayyad adversaries. So he is forced to send Abū Mūsā al-Ashʿarī, a late-comer to his cause, having joined up in support of ʿAlī under some duress while ʿAlī was in Kūfa, making his way towards the Euphrates. Abū Mūsā is presented in the sources as a fickle, weak-willed, and gullible member of the Arab elite.

At this point in the narratives, there is a discussion of the terms of the arbitration. One important episode revolves around the way in which the document of agreement refers to ʿAlī. ʿAmr refuses to allow ʿAlī to be referred to in the document by the title *amīr al-muʾminīn* (Commander of the Faithful), and his refusal becomes a sticking point. ʿAlī acquiesces on the grounds that the Prophet had allowed himself to be designated simply as Muḥammad ibn ʿAbd Allāh, rather than *Rasūl Allāh* (Messenger of God), during his negotiations with his Meccan adversaries at Ḥudaybiyya. It was Abū Sufyān, the father of Muʿāwiya, who had objected to Muḥammad's claim to divine prophethood on that earlier occasion. It is agreed that both armies should withdraw, to reassemble only when ʿAmr ibn al-ʿĀṣ and Abū Mūsā have made their decision.

When the terms of the arbitration are settled, ʿAlī and his men retire to Kūfa, while Muʿāwiya returns to Damascus. At this point, the divisions in ʿAlī's camp that ʿAmr had hoped to exploit are realized; a group of soldiers, asserting that "there is no judgment but that of God" (*lā ḥukmā illā lillāh*), object both to the decision to cease fighting when the battle was so clearly proceeding in their favor, and to ʿAlī's apparent use of the leadership of the Muslim community as a bargaining chip (and, even worse, his willingness to forfeit it), and rebel against him, ultimately forming the nucleus of the Khārijī sect. As we have seen, the decision to accede to Muʿāwiya's call for arbitration would have fateful consequences for ʿAlī, as a member of this splinter group would later be responsible for his assassination. Khārijīs would also make unsuccessful attempts on the lives of Muʿāwiya and ʿAmr ibn al-ʿĀṣ.

2.6 *Negotiation, Ruling, and Reneging*

The two arbiters discuss the matter before them, evidently searching for common ground to solve the division plaguing the Islamic community. The specifics of the discussion between ʿAmr ibn al-ʿĀṣ and Abū Mūsā al-Ashʿarī are recounted. Several possible solutions to the stalemate are discussed, including a number of potential third-party replacements for ʿAlī as caliph, but in the end it is ʿAmr who suggests the idea that, for immersing the community in strife, ʿAlī and Muʿāwiya both should be deposed, and the Muslims should select a new caliph for themselves. Given Abū Mūsā's strong antipathy towards *fitna*—in fact, it is his most defining characteristic—ʿAmr sets out the perfect bait to entice the other to abandon his cause. Abū Mūsā's agreement to the ouster of both men is already a major victory for Muʿāwiya. Coming into the conflict, he had been a governor of Syria and claimant on his kinsman's blood but had no claim to the rulership of the entire community. Thus, when ʿAmr agrees on Muʿāwiya's behalf to remove him from the position of caliph, and not the governorship of Syria, Muʿāwiya relinquished nothing; indeed, he was elevated to legitimate potential claimant. ʿAlī, by contrast, had been almost universally acknowledged as the caliph following the Battle of the Camel, even by Muʿāwiya, who had made his *bayʿa* conditional upon justice for ʿUthmān, but, with that condition met, presumably would have been willing to acquiesce to ʿAlī's caliphate and content himself with ruling Syria (or so Muʿāwiya's stated position suggests). Now, having foolishly allowed Muʿāwiya to appear as ʿAlī's equal on the document regarding the terms of the negotiation, with the title *amīr al-muʾminīn* removed, Abū Mūsā has agreed to the abdication of ʿAlī. This sequence of events beneficial to Muʿāwiya comes, of course, after the call for arbitration, which had been an act of desperation.

The two armies reconvene at Dūmat al-Jandal. Abū Mūsā, flattered by ʿAmr in the latter's invitation to address those assembled first, foolishly declares the sovereignty of ʿAlī at an end, rejects any sovereignty for Muʿāwiya, and calls for elections, as he and ʿAmr ibn al-ʿĀṣ had agreed. ʿAmr likewise deposes ʿAlī in front of the masses but reneges on his promise and declares Muʿāwiya caliph, causing a scuffle to break out.

The outcome of the arbitration was a crushing blow to ʿAlī's prestige, and a significant enhancement of Muʿāwiya's. With the latter's political star in ascendance, the general acceptance of his sovereignty when a Khārijite assassinates ʿAlī is a *fait accompli*. The subsequent course of events provides ample testimony to the battle's critical position in the sectarian theater of the early Islamic narrative.

3 The Stakes

While not of such grand importance to the authors as the meaning of Karbalāʾ, Ṣiffīn represents a bottleneck of the narrative through which all the major characters who were active at the time were compelled to pass. Its stakes were greater than those of the Battle of the Camel, an event of the same year and comprising many of the same themes that drive the Ṣiffīn narrative: loyalty, rebellion, and legitimacy of rule. However, the Battle of the Camel provides little more than an entrée to Ṣiffīn. While its themes are important, and continue, its major antagonists, Ṭalḥā ibn ʿUbayd Allāh and al-Zubayr ibn al-ʿAwwām, are simply killed, and with the exception of al-Zubayr's son ʿAbd Allāh, who will play an important role in later *fitna*, their lives are relegated to two-dimensionality.

The stakes for the Ṣiffīn narrative are as follows:

1. *The meaning of ʿAlī's death:* At stake in the Battle of Ṣiffīn is the assassination of ʿAlī, obviously one of the most important moments in terms of establishing the recurring Shīʿī theme of the martyrdom of the ʿAlīds. It also builds upon, and culminates, the narrative of ʿAlī's hard political luck. He was never able to establish himself as the rightful, unquestioned, and unopposed leader of the community, and his assassination is the emphatic conclusion to his efforts to do so.
2. *The reputation and legitimacy of the Umayyads:* In many ways, Muʿāwiya was precisely the leader the Islamic world needed at the time he became its leader, just after the assassination of ʿAlī. Acknowledged even by his detractors as generous, wise, and capable, it was under Muʿāwiya that the nascent Muslim polity achieved a stable administrative and finan-

cial equilibrium. Nonetheless, later historians (writing, it must be remembered, under the ʿAbbāsids) were compelled by questions of both ideology and patronage to remember the Umayyads in a negative light. Muʿāwiya, as the founder of the dynasty, becomes narratively metonymic for it. As we will see with the character of ʿUthmān in the next section, the nature of the character and the meaning of his life are established at the end of the reign of his immediate successor and focus on the means by which he achieved power. In Muʿāwiya's case, the apparently underhanded tactics of his army at Ṣiffīn set the tone for the entire period of Umayyad rule. The discussion of just how contemptible those tactics actually were provides an opportunity to characterize Muʿāwiya and his successors.

CHAPTER 6

The Battle of Ṣiffīn: Fight and Conclusion

1 Introduction

That ʿAlī and Muʿāwiya would come to battle feels, in retrospect, like an inevitability. The third caliph, ʿUthmān ibn ʿAffān, had been murdered by some of ʿAlī's supporters. ʿAlī demanded the loyalty, in the form of an oath known as *bayʿa*, from the potentates of the empire; many acquiesced, but some, such as Ṭalḥa ibn ʿUbayd Allāh and al-Zubayr ibn al-Awwām, refused. Those two were vanquished shortly thereafter at the Battle of the Camel (36/656). The most important holdout, however, was Muʿāwiya ibn Abī Sufyān, the governor of Syria. Muʿāwiya had been appointed governor of Syria by ʿUmar ibn al-Khaṭṭāb and confirmed in his position by ʿUthmān. The second son of Abū Sufyān, the Prophet's first adversary, Muʿāwiya was by this time the patriarch of the Umayyad branch of the Quraysh (his elder brother Yazīd had died, perhaps of plague, some years before). From Muʿāwiya's perspective, ʿAlī's accession to the caliphate was suspect. The murderers of ʿUthmān, Muʿāwiya's cousin, remained unpunished, and support for ʿAlī was lukewarm and intermittent. The approach to the battle will be discussed in Chapter 7; for now, we pick up the action *in medias res*, with the fighting already begun.

The battle had been going poorly for Muʿāwiya's camp, so ʿAmr ibn al-ʿĀṣ hit upon a strategy that brilliantly exploited the existing divisions within ʿAlī's camp. There were some who fought for ʿAlī out of true loyalty to his cause. Others were there under duress. Muʿāwiya's camp, while clearly the militarily weaker party, was unified in purpose. The diversity of conflicting interests within ʿAlī's camp were critical not only to ʿAlī but also to the rest of the narrative treated in this book. The fault lines within ʿAlī's camp, already fracturing because of earlier strife (like the Battle of the Camel) and the means by which they were enlisted (some were compelled to join), would, over time, combine with the reactions to Karbalāʾ and evolve into the large splits and communal divisions that came to be called "Sunnī" and "Shīʿī." There is not a one-to-one correlation between the perspectives of ʿAlī's supporters at Ṣiffīn and their later theological positions, nor is this the only factor that contributed to the emergence of Sunnī and Shīʿī ideologies and communities.[1] It is, however, an indelible piece of the sectarian narrative.

---

1 Martin Hinds, "Kufan Political Alignments and their Background in the mid-7th Century A.D.,"

 | DOI:10.1163/9789004524255_008

The confusing end to the Battle of Ṣiffīn is one of the more important battlegrounds of the narrative for Ibn al-Athīr and Ibn Kathīr. Much of the criticism directed at the Umayyads over the centuries centered upon their opposition to ʿAlī and their guilt (or at least complicity—but mostly guilt) in the murders of ʿAlī and his line of descendants known to Shīʿī history as the Imams. For historians less concerned with the Umayyad reputation, Ṣiffīn's denouement is just exhibit a of Umayyad duplicity. But for those men who are the focus of this study, the first acts of the dynasty—though it may be still a few years in the future relative to Ṣiffīn—provide a critical opportunity to rescue an important piece of the Umayyad reputation. The Umayyad family were after all the pre-Islamic Meccan elite. The arbitration that concluded the Ṣiffīn event was another example of that elite's use of devious methods to keep ʿAlī from power. He had similarly been duped at the time of the accessions of each of his three predecessors, but especially at the appointment of ʿUthmān ibn ʿAffān.

The stakes of the moment, therefore, are high, but only for historians like Ibn al-Athīr and Ibn Kathīr. The standard version of the story, which is very well-known, naturally favors the anti-Umayyad perspective: Muʿāwiya's army was losing the fight, so ʿAmr disingenuously called for arbitration based upon the Qurʾān. The call for arbitration divided ʿAlī's camp. Some felt the battle itself was an expression of God's will and therefore wanted to continue fighting at all costs, and some were in favor of any resolution that would end the inter-Muslim fighting. The confusion stopped the fighting, and while Muʿāwiya could simply appoint his self-interested but committed supporter, ʿAmr ibn al-ʿĀṣ, as his representative at the arbitration, ʿAlī's divided camp limited his political options and forced him to appoint the tepid anti-*fitna* activist Abū Mūsā al-Ashʿarī to argue his case. This created a fraught situation for ʿAlī. While ʿAmr would negotiate on behalf of his patron Muʿāwiya, Abū Mūsā would negotiate with the exigent goal of ending the fighting at whatever political cost to ʿAlī. ʿAmr then tricks Abū Mūsā into deposing ʿAlī while he himself confirms Muʿāwiya as his legitimate successor—a stunt that ʿAlī's side straightforwardly rejects, but which divides the loyalties of the believers. Whether ʿAmr's stunt constitutes a legitimate legal action is fundamental to one's opinion of the Umayyad dynasty's genesis, as both its supporters and its detractors would agree that this was its beginning.

---

in *IJMES* 2 (1971), 348. Hinds points to Ḥujr ibn ʿAdī al-Kindī, who was eclipsed by his relative al-Ashʿath ibn Qays al-Kindī, newcomer tribesmen who arrived after ʿAlī's death who resisted established political power for the sake of their own independence, and so on. Essentially, early membership in proto-Shīʿī movements was not necessarily tied to an ancestor's position in ʿAlī's camp at Ṣiffīn, but the narrative relevance of the call for arbitration is evident.

The fight at Ṣiffīn itself receives far less narrative treatment than either the aftermath (which will be discussed in this chapter) or the prebattle maneuvering. The arbitration scene and its aftermath set the stage for ʿAlī's assassination; the battle itself is little more than an action sequence. In the orbit of that action sequence, however, there is one genuine curiosity: the death of one of the participants—ʿAmmār ibn Yāsir—comes during the battle ("the night of clamor", or *laylat al-harīr*) in the narratives of al-Ṭabarī and Ibn al-Athīr, but Ibn Kathīr suggests it may have come only after the fighting had largely ceased. Because of ʿAmmār's relationship to the Prophet Muḥammad, and especially because of the Prophet's unnervingly apropos prediction about ʿAmmār's eventual killers, he becomes a site of memory in and of himself. It is not only the authors, but even the characters within the story, who struggle to commandeer the meaning of his death—even in the midst of the battle.

2 A Broken Link to the Prophet: The Battlefield Death of the Elderly ʿAmmār ibn Yāsir

Abū al-Yaqẓān ʿAmmār ibn Yāsir ibn ʿĀmir ibn Mālik was one of the earliest converts to Islam and had fought at the battles of Badr, Uḥud, and the rest of the battles of the Prophet, as well as at the Battle of Yamāma under Abū Bakr, where he is said to have lost an ear. Having served as governor of Kūfa under ʿUmar ibn al-Khaṭṭāb, he had always been a strong supporter of ʿAlī and outspoken opponent of ʿUthmān. His most important characteristic to the Islamic community at the time of the composition of these histories was his closeness to the Prophet, his piety, and his devotion to Islam, all of which represented a link to Islam's holiest times and period of remembered unity. ʿAmmār, despite his advanced age (he was, according to the standard narrative, at least ninety years old at the time of Ṣiffīn), takes part in the battle, and ultimately dies in it. This is significant for a number of reasons, preeminent among them a well-known *ḥadīth* in which the Prophet predicts to ʿAmmār that he will be killed by the "rebel band" (*al-fiʿa al-bāghiya*).[2] His death becomes a representative for the real tragedy of the *fitna* and highlights the trauma for those generations that did not experience it. ʿAmmār ibn Yāsir serves as a place-holder for all the Companions of the Prophet, and

2 *ʿAmmār taqtuluhu al-fiʿa al-bāghiya*. See A.J. Wensinck, *Concordance Et Indices De La Tradition Musulmane: Les Six Livres, Le Musnad D'Al-Darimi, Le Muwatta'De Malik, Le Musnad De Ahmad Ibn Hanbal*, i (Leiden: E.J. Brill, 1936), 204. According to Wensinck this *ḥadīth* appears in the *Musnad* of Aḥmad ibn Ḥanbal and the collections of Muslim and al-Tirmidhī.

even for the whole generation of the early community that was destroyed by the *fitna*. His death, perhaps more even than ʿAlī's, marks the end of the remembered age of righteousness and unity that would be eclipsed by the subsequent rise to power of the Umayyads and the emergence of Islam's sectarian divisions—a negative development by all surviving standards. The Syrians were, according to some historians, aware even before the battle that fighting against ʿAmmār would put the legitimacy of their cause on shaky ground because of the *ḥadīth* relating the Prophet's pronouncement. Although this exchange does not appear in any of the three narrative sources most closely examined in this book, the biographical dictionary *Taʾrīkh madīnat Dimashq* of ʿAlī ibn ʿAsākir relates the following exchange between a supporter of Muʿāwiya and a cousin of his in ʿAlī's army, which illustrates the stakes of ʿAmmār's personal support:

> [*Dhū al-Kalāʿ al-Ḥimyarī*]: When the day began, that Tuesday, the people went out in their ranks, and Abū Nūḥ al-Ḥimyarī said, "I was in ʿAlī's cavalry, and I realized that one of the Syrians was calling out for Abū Nūḥ al-Ḥimyarī." Abū Nūḥ said, "Which of you wants him?" And he said, "Al-Kalāʿī," so I said, "You've found him. Who are you?" He said, "I am Dhū al-Kalāʿ, so come to me." He said, "God forbid I come to you any way but here in my ranks." He said, "Come to me, and you will have the protection of God, the protection of his Messenger, and the protection of Dhū al-Kalāʿ until you return. I just want to ask you about something relating to your opinion of this matter." So Abū Nūḥ went to him, and Dhū al-Kalāʿ went to him until the two of them met. Then Dhū al-Kalāʿ said to him, "Seeing as how I called you here, I want to relate to you a Ḥadīth which ʿAmr ibn al-ʿĀṣ related to him about the reign of ʿUmar." Abū Nūḥ said, "What is it?" Dhū al-Kalāʿ said, "ʿAmr ibn al-ʿĀṣ said to us that the Messenger of God (may God's prayers and peace be upon him) said, 'The people of Iraq and the people of al-Shām will meet in two ranks, one of which will be right.'" He said, 'The right one will have ʿAmmār ibn Yāsir.' Abū Nūḥ said, "Yes, by God, for ʿAmmār is with us and here in our ranks." He said, "Has he come here to fight us?" Abū Nūḥ said, "Yes, by the Lord of the Kaʿba, he is here with me to fight against you."[3]

3 ʿAlī ibn ʿAsākir, *Taʾrīkh madinat Dimashq*, eds. ʿUmar al-Amrawī and ʿAlī Shīrī, xvii (Beirut: Dār al-Fikr, 1995–2001), 393. This story first appeared in *Waqʿat Ṣiffīn* and *Kitāb al-Futūḥ*; the version in *Taʾrīkh madinat Dimashq* is repeated almost verbatim by Ibn al-ʿAdīm for inclusion in *Bughyat al-ṭalab fī taʾrīkh Ḥalab*.

Dhū al-Kalāʿ is obviously troubled by the notion of having to fight against ʿAmmār, and not just because of the latter's age; he is concerned ʿAmmār's support of ʿAlī makes Muʿāwiya's supporters rebels. The killing of the very elderly ʿAmmār in a battle with mostly of men six and seven decades his junior was not a surprise. As the story appears in both al-Ṭabarī's and Ibn al-Athīr's accounts: "ʿAmmār said, 'Onward, Hāshim![4] Paradise lies beneath the shadows of the swords, and death lies in the tips of the spears! The gates of heaven have been opened, and the houris have adorned themselves. Today I shall meet the beloved ones, Muḥammad and his party.'"[5] Ibn al-Athīr then relates the following rebuke by ʿAmmār to ʿAmr ibn al-ʿĀṣ, which al-Ṭabarī had placed slightly earlier, part of which (in al-Ṭabarī's account) had been directed not towards ʿAmr but towards ʿUbayd Allāh ibn ʿUmar ibn al-Khaṭṭāb: "'ʿAmr, you have sold your soul [*dīnaka*] for Egypt, damn you!' [ʿAmr][6] replied, 'No, I only seek vengeance for the blood of ʿUthmān ibn ʿAffān.' [ʿAmmār] replied, 'I bear witness, from what I know of you, that you seek the face of God in nothing that you do. If you are not killed today, you will die tomorrow. Since men are rewarded according to their intentions, consider what it is that you intend.'"[7] ʿAmmār ibn Yāsir's death is related factually, but without details, in both of these accounts.

ʿAmmār's death is where the authorial debate about the nature of rebellion begins, even within the story. ʿAmr's son ʿAbd Allāh is understandably concerned, given that men from their army have just killed ʿAmmār, which implicitly makes them "the rebel band" the Prophet Muḥammad had cursed:

> ʿAbd Allāh said to his father, "Father, have you killed this man in your fighting here, despite what the Messenger of God said about him?" [ʿAmr] replied, "What did he say?" [ʿAbd Allāh] said, "Were you not with us when we were building the Mosque [in Medina], and all the people were bringing one stone and one brick at a time, but ʿAmmār brought two bricks and two stones at a time? He fainted from the exertion, and the Messenger of God came, and wiped the dust off his face, saying, 'Woe to you, Ibn Sumayya [ʿAmmār]! Everyone moves one brick and stone at a time, and you move two bricks and two stones at a time, desiring a divine reward! Despite this, the rebel band will kill you, woe to you!'" At this, [ʿAmr] pushed his son's horse away, and pulled Muʿāwiya towards him. He cried,

4 That is, Hāshim ibn ʿUtba, known as al-Mirqal (the "swift she-camel"), ʿAmmār's companion at the moment and a protagonist of *laylat al-harīr*.

5 Al-Ṭabarī, *Taʾrīkh* iii, 99; Ibn al-Athīr, *Kāmil* iii, 187.

6 In al-Ṭabarī's version, it is ʿUbayd Allāh, and it follows a different accusation.

7 Ibn al-Athīr, *Kāmil* iii, 187.

> "Muʿāwiya, did you hear what ʿAbd Allāh has just said?" [Muʿāwiya] asked, "What did he say?" So he related to him the report, and Muʿāwiya sneered, "You are a stupid old dotard. You keep on telling your tales while you splash around in your own piss. Was it we who killed ʿAmmār? No! Rather, those who killed ʿAmmār are the ones who brought him here!"[8]

In most accounts of ʿAmmār ibn Yāsir's death, loaded with meaning as it is, it occurs during *laylat al-harīr*, the main battle itself. The death of the venerable old man, a link to the age of the Prophet, seems narratively tailored to provoke the arbitration. The motivation for prompting a negotiated settlement on Muʿāwiya's side was obvious: the alternative was clearly military defeat. But how is an army on the verge of achieving a rout of its enemy convinced to cease pressing the fight? In this case, the narratives of al-Ṭabarī and Ibn al-Athīr suggest that it was a death so traumatizing that it made the cost of continuing the fight seem so high as to make any victory Pyrrhic.

Yet, somehow, Ibn Kathīr's narrative includes a version of ʿAmmār ibn Yāsir who survives *laylat al-harīr* unscathed. To be more accurate, Ibn Kathīr relates all the same information included in al-Ṭabarī,[9] including his death during *laylat al-harīr*, but includes the following when discussing the call for arbitration:

> Al-Haytham ibn ʿAdī, in his book that he composed about the Khawārij,[10] said that Ibn ʿAbbās reported that Muḥammad ibn al-Muntashir al-Hamadānī cited on the authority of some of the participants of Ṣiffīn, and some of the people who were the leaders of the Khawārij whom ʿAlī did not consider liars, that ʿAmmār ibn Yāsir found this repugnant, and denounced it, and told ʿAlī the extent to which it disgusted him. Then he said, "Who shall look to God before seeking the wisdom of those other than He?"[11] Then he fought until he was killed, may God have mercy upon him.[12]

The admission that this anecdote is sourced from trustworthy Khawārij is probably enough to call it into question for most people (Ibn Kathīr, who holds no love for the Khawārij, included), so he clearly intends for the readers to take

8 Al-Ṭabarī, *Taʾrīkh* iii, 99; Ibn Kathīr, *Kāmil* iii, 188–189.

9 Ibn Kathīr, *Bidāya* vii, 258–259.

10 For ʿAbd Allāh ibn ʿAbbās in the work of al-Haytham ibn ʿAdi, see Stefan Leder, *Das Korpus al-Hayṯam ibn ʿAdī* (Frankfurt am Main: Klostermann, 1991), 237.

11 This is an attempt to spur Companions to action in battle, rather than relying on a political process fraught with human frailty and chicanery.

12 Ibn Kathīr, *Bidāya* vii, 260.

the story with a grain of salt. However, keeping ʿAmmār alive until this juncture allows Ibn Kathīr to portray ʿAmmār's opinion on the arbitration—and to have ʿAmmār's last act be a suicidal charge prompted by disgust directed at ʿAlī and those who were accepting the arbitration. Whether he believes this to have actually happened is immaterial; by including it (where al-Ṭabarī and Ibn al-Athīr did not), Ibn Kathīr manages to plant in the minds of his readers at least the suggestion of what ʿAmmār—perhaps the last surviving, universally admired Companion of the Prophet—thought of what was coming next. He chose death over supporting ʿAlī. That Ibn Kathīr would assassinate the character of such a figure by including the suggestion that he was at least partially aligned with the Khawārij demonstrates the lengths to which he was prepared to go to imply ʿAlī's error to his readers.

3 Arbitration, Negotiation, and a Portentous Stalemate

The stray *khabar* in Kathīr's work notwithstanding, across most accounts of the battle, when ʿAmmār dies, ʿAlī issues a challenge of single combat to Muʿāwiya, which al-Ṭabarī's ʿAmr urges Muʿāwiya to accept (Muʿāwiya accuses his henchman of being impatient for his death so that he can gain in power, a statement that at once derides ʿAmr for his ambition and Muʿāwiya himself for his cowardice in the face of a fair challenge). After Muʿāwiya's refusal, each historian spends some time describing the military maneuvers that constitute the battle. Al-Ṭabarī reports that the battle was going poorly for the Syrians, and ʿAmr came up with a desperate ploy to save his side.

> When ʿAmr ibn al-Āṣ saw that the circumstances of the battle had gone in the Iraqis' favor, he feared destruction. He said to Muʿāwiya, "What do you think if I suggest something to you that can only increase our unity, and that can only divide them?" [Muʿāwiya] said, "Yes," and [ʿAmr] said, "We shall raise the copies of the Qurʾān[13] and then we will say: 'Their con-

13 Hawting, in his translation of this section of al-Ṭabarī's history, points out that the term *maṣāḥif*, the plural of *muṣḥaf*, traditionally means copies of the Qurʾān, but that it is unlikely that Muʿāwiya's army would have had enough copies of the Qurʾān (still relatively newly standardized by ʿUthmān) to have been useful as a call for cease-fire up and down the lines of a clangorous battle. His translation simply retains the term *maṣāḥif* in deference to the controversy. However, it is clear from later in the narrative—specifically, ʿAlī's army's answer that "we respond to the book of God" when "the men saw that the *maṣāḥif* had been raised," and given the Qurʾān's obvious role in the subsequent discussion between ʿAmr ibn al-ʿĀṣ and Abū Mūsā al-Ashʿarī—that al-Ṭabarī thought that the

> tents are authoritative between us and you.' Even if some of them refuse to accept it, you will find that there are those among them who will say, 'On the contrary, we must accept it,' a there will be a schism among them. On the other hand, if they all say, 'Indeed, we will accept what is in it' [as authoritative in our dispute], then we will have extricated ourselves from this battle and this war until an appointed time, or a later occasion." So they raised the copies of the Qur'ān on their lances, and they said, "This is the Book of God, great and mighty, between us and you! Who shall defend the borders of al-Shām after the people of al-Shām [have all died here]! And who shall defend the borders of Iraq after the people of Iraq [have all died here]!" When the people [in 'Alī's army] saw that the copies of the Qur'ān had been raised, they said, "We answer to the Book of God, great and mighty, and we turn in repentance to it."[14]

Neither Ibn al-Athīr nor Ibn Kathīr disputes this fundamental fact of the narrative, although both do shorten this conversation into a single monologue by 'Amr (and, as we will discuss shortly, Ibn Kathīr has some specific historiographical criticism to offer). Of course, the schism "predicted" by 'Amr does indeed occur in 'Alī's camp. Both Ibn al-Athīr and Ibn Kathīr repeat al-Ṭabarī's claim that the most forceful of the men who demanded that 'Alī accept the arbitration "afterward became Khawārij," and they demanded that he put a stop to the fighting. A tense exchange follows:

> 'Alī sent Yazīd ibn Hāni' to al-Ashtar, demanding that he come to him. Al-Ashtar protested, "This is not the hour that you wish to come to me to tell me to abandon my position, for God will deliver his victory to me anon!" Yazīd returned and reported this to him, and the voices screamed out and the dust rose from al-Ashtar's direction. The people said [to 'Alī], "By God, we believe you commanded him to keep fighting!" 'Alī retorted, "Did you see me whisper a secret to him? My words are upon your heads, and you all heard them!" They demanded, "Then command him to come to you, and if you do not, then we are leaving you!" 'Alī said, "Woe, O Yazīd! Say to him, 'Come to me, for the *fitna* has taken hold.'" Then this news came to al-Ashtar, and he said, "[Is this about] the raising of the *maṣāḥif*?" He

---

items raised upon the lances of Mu'āwiya's army were indeed copies of the Qur'ān itself, however unlikely that may have been. See G.R. Hawting (trans.), *The History of al-Ṭabarī. Vol. 17: The First Civil War* (Albany: SUNY Press, 1996), 78, n. 319; and Martin Hinds, "The Siffin Arbitration Agreement," in *JSS* 17 (1972), 93–113.

14 Al-Ṭabarī, *Ta'rīkh* iii, 101.

> said, "Yes." He said, "By God, we thought this might engender difference and division [in our camp]! This is a stratagem of Ibn al-ʿĀṣ! Do you not see how close we are to victory? Do you not see what God has given us?" And he withdrew back to them. Yazīd said to him, "Is it your wish to be victorious when the Commander of the Faithful must make peace with his enemies or be killed?" He said, "By God, no. God forbid!" Then he told them what they had said [to ʿAlī], so al-Ashtar came to them and said, "O people of Iraq! O people of disgrace and weakness! Now you have betrayed the people. They knew that you were to be victorious over them, and raised the *maṣāḥif* and called for arbitration based upon what is in the Qurʾān—how have you been taken in by those who, by God, have already left behind that which God commanded them to do, and the Sunna of he to whom it was revealed? Grant me some time (to finish what I started), for I was at the cusp of conquest." They said, "No." He said, "Grant me some time, for I have already tasted victory!"[15]

This is more or less identical to both Ibn Kathīr's version and al-Ṭabarī's version (the differences are stylistic, not substantive): al-Ashtar, the great warrior, is appalled at being recalled just as he is on the brink of victory. How different history could be had al-Ashtar been allowed to press his insurmountable advantage! Alas, ʿAlī's freedom of action becomes constrained by the fact that, evidently, egregious hypocrites comprise a significant portion of his army.

Ibn Kathīr's performance of the installment of the Ṣiffīn narrative in which ʿAmr calls for arbitration based upon the Qurʾān, and in which ʿAlī's men react to that call, is expanded from what appears in al-Ṭabarī's or Ibn al-Athīr's accounts. He relates the call for arbitration itself but does not immediately attribute the idea to ʿAmr; initially, the moment reads like a grassroots event: "ʿAlī and his followers were on the verge of slaughtering them, and at that point the people of Syria raised the copies of the Qurʾān on their lances and called out, 'This is between us and you! For if all the people die, who shall guard the frontiers? Who shall wage Jihad against the pagans and the heathens?' "[16] Both al-Ṭabarī and Ibn al-Athīr preceded this call for ʿAlī's army to accept the "judgment of the Qurʾān" with the scene cited above, in which ʿAmr slyly plots to use the Qurʾān to drive a wedge into the existing schisms in ʿAlī's army. Ibn Kathīr, mentioning al-Ṭabarī by name—for him, a clear sign that he is about to disagree

15 Ibn al-Athīr, *Kāmil* iii, 193.
16 Ibn Kathīr, *Bidāya* iii, 261.

with al-Ṭabarī—relates the following, which calls into question the notion that this had been either a purposeful side effect or the purpose itself of the call for arbitration.

> Ibn Jarīr [al-Ṭabarī] and other historians have mentioned that the one who came up with that idea was ʿAmr ibn al-ʿĀṣ, when he saw that the Iraqis were on the verge breaking through at that place. [They claim that ʿAmr] wanted to disrupt the flow of the situation and delay the matter, so that both the contending parties would hold its own against the other, while the people were killing each other. So he said to Muʿāwiya, "I have just come upon something right now, something that can contribute to us nothing but unity, and can contribute to them nothing but division. I believe that if we raise the copies of the Qurʾān and call them to arbitration based upon the Qurʾān, either they will all agree and it will end the killing, or they will differ, and some will say, 'let us answer them,' and some will say, 'no, let us not answer them.' It shall paralyze them and bring about their woe." Imām Aḥmad [ibn Ḥanbal] said that he was told by Yaʿlā ibn ʿUbayd, on the authority of ʿAbd al-ʿAzīz ibn Siyāh, on the authority of Ḥabīb ibn Abī Thābit that [Habīb] came to Abū Wāʾil in his family's mosque. "I asked about the people whom ʿAlī killed at Nahrawān, regarding what requests of ʿAlī's they complied with, and what requests they did not, and what they regarded as permissible in battle." Then he said, "We were at Ṣiffīn, and when the fighting was going against the Syrians, they stopped the fighting out of desperation. It was only then that ʿAmr ibn al-ʿĀṣ said to Muʿāwiya, 'Send word to ʿAlī with a copy of the Qurʾān, and call him to the book of God. He shall not reject you.'" A man came to him and said, "The book of God between us and you!" Then he quoted: "Have you not regarded those who were given a portion of the Book, being called to the Book of God, that it might decide between them, and then a party of them turned away, swerving aside?"[17] And ʿAlī said, "Yes! I accept that, the book of God between us and you." And the Khawārij came to him, as did we of the *qurrāʾ*,[18] that day, with their swords upon their shoulders, and they said, "O Commander of the

17 Qurʾān 3:23.

18 This (infamous, to historians of early Islam) term is often translated as "Qurʾān reciters," but given the context, this is not a particularly satisfying interpretation of this appearance of it. See G.H.A. Juynboll, "The Qurrāʾ in Early Islamic History," in *JESHO* 16 (1972), 113–129. The term is almost certainly what Hodgson means by "piety-minded," and may refer to those Muslims who had memorized some portion of the Qurʾān.

> Faithful, what can these cowards intend other than to prevent us from charging them with our swords, and letting God judge the matter between us and them?" Then Sahl ibn Ḥanīf spoke, saying, "O you people! You are deluding yourselves. For you know what happened to us at the battle of Ḥudaybiyya—that is the peace that was made between the Messenger of God and the pagans, and even as we were fighting ʿUmar came to the Messenger of God and said, 'O Messenger of God, are we not in the right, and are they not manifestly mistaken?' and then he told the remainder of that *ḥadīth*."[19]

This is part of what appears to be a relatively important reclamation project for Ibn Kathīr: the character of ʿAmr ibn al-ʿĀṣ. The important moment for Ibn Kathīr's ʿAmr, however, is not here: it is coming shortly, at the denouement of the Ṣiffīn episode. ʿAmr is going to make an unprecedented claim in Ibn Kathīr's version of that moment, and it is the need to maintain at least the possibility of ʿAmr's credibility that motivates Ibn Kathīr to call into question al-Ṭabarī's attribution of the idea of arbitration to ʿAmr. His source for challenging al-Ṭabarī on this point is also interesting in that it gives voice to the otherwise-reviled Khārijī perspective (just as the alternative version of ʿAmmār ibn Yāsir's death relied on a Khārijī source), albeit in the form of a *khabar* that is authorized by Aḥmad ibn Ḥanbal, whose view of history dovetailed nicely with Ibn Kathīr's. Ibn Ḥanbal makes explicit statements that ʿAlī was the fourth caliph and the fourth best, but this ardently Sunnī perspective never contradicts the fact that ʿAlī was a legitimate and righteous caliph, certainly worthy of the term *rāshid*.[20] Ibn Kathīr, like Ibn Ḥanbal, is not interested in arguing against ʿAlī's legitimacy as caliph but rather against the Shīʿa's reverential recollection of him. Ibn Kathīr's focus is on the necessity of an imam for the community's health and salvation, a priority that Ibn Ḥanbal would share. With no assertion that Muʿāwiya was *more* valid than ʿAlī, but an argument that an imam at all times is essential, he is able to legitimize Muʿāwiya's subsequent supremacy over the Islamic Empire from the moment of ʿAmr's deception of Abū Mūsā, while avoiding any controversial disavowal of ʿAlī's validity as one of the *rāshidūn*. As far as ʿAmr ibn al-ʿĀṣ goes, the call for arbitration is one of the key moments that earns him the nickname "the sly fox" and a reputation as a devious schemer. Removing the idea from ʿAmr

---

19 Ibn Kathīr, *Bidāya* vii, 261–262. The conclusion of the story of the *ḥadīth* referenced here is that Muḥammad, secure in his faith and the righteousness of his cause, continued the fight and earned a great victory.

20 Christopher Melchert, *Ahmad ibn Hanbal* (Oxford: Oneworld, 2006), 95.

and placing it upon "the people" is a way for Ibn Kathīr to erode some of the slyness away from ʿAmr, increasing his credibility for the critical moment to come.

ʿAmr ibn al-ʿĀṣ is chosen to represent Muʿāwiya at the arbitration, and Abū Mūsā al-Ashʿarī is forced upon ʿAlī. Abū Mūsā was far from ʿAlī's first choice. The historians record ʿAlī's attempts to choose his arbiters, both of which are rejected. ʿAlī first proposed ʿAbd Allāh ibn ʿAbbās, who was rejected by ʿAlī's disgruntled men because of his close relation to ʿAlī. The goal, as far as they were concerned, was to appoint someone to find a way out of the *fitna*, not somebody to represent ʿAlī's interests. ʿAlī then tries to appoint his staunch supporter and best fighter, al-Ashtar, whom the mutineers (which is not too strong a word) reject even more forcefully. They reject all representatives other than Abū Mūsā al-Ashʿarī: the man who had warned against the evils of the *fitna*. He had deserted ʿAlī's army rather than be caught up in the *fitna* and so was an ideal choice to end the *fitna*—always assuming the good faith of the other side.

Unsurprisingly, in al-Ṭabarī's and Ibn al-Athīr's narratives, there is not much good faith recorded coming from the Syrian side. There is a callback to the Battle of Ḥudaybiyya at the outset. ʿAmr objects to the recording of ʿAlī's title in the document they are producing as *amīr al-muʾminīn*, and ʿAlī agrees to allow it to be omitted, because the Prophet had done so (thus allowing a not-so-subtle identification of this Umayyad army with the Umayyad army that had opposed the Prophet Muḥammad, and an identification of ʿAlī with the Prophet). ʿAmr objects to the comparison; ʿAlī insults his mother as a whore (he calls her "famous"). The Khawārij leave at this point in the narrative, and there is an interlude while ʿAlī deals with them at Nahrawān. The Ṣiffīn narrative picks up a couple of weeks later, as Abū Mūsā and ʿAmr meet at the town of Dūmat al-Jandal. They argue over the rightness of Muʿāwiya's cause to seek vengeance for ʿUthmān, over ʿAlī's rights to protect his killers, and over the justice of ʿUthmān's death and the circumstances of his assassination. Finally, they come to the question of how to move forward, and Abū Mūsā suggests deposing both men (there is some evidence that Muʿāwiya may have already claimed the caliphate,[21] but none of the narratives say that explicitly) and put the matter to an election of the people, and his counterpart agrees. ʿAmr flatters Abū Mūsā into speaking first when the armies have reassembled; he predictably and honestly reports this decision, which ʿAmr immediately disavows. He proclaims Muʿāwiya as the caliph; a scuffle breaks out, and the armies withdraw, leaving neither man clearly in charge and the community in turmoil.

21 Khaled Keshk, "When did Muʿāwiya Become Caliph?," in *JNES* 69 (2010), 31–42.

Ibn Kathīr's biggest change at Ṣiffīn is the last moment in the narrative: when the two arbiters, Abū Mūsā al-Ashʿarī (representing ʿAlī) and ʿAmr ibn al-ʿĀṣ (representing Muʿāwiya), come to announce the results of their arbitration to the assembled armies at Dūmat al-Jandal:

> [T]hey agreed that the two of them would depose both Muʿāwiya and ʿAlī, and they would put the matter to a *shūrā* amongst the people, who would agree on someone they would select for themselves. Then they came before the crowd where the people were gathered. ʿAmr did not go before Abū Mūsā in anything, but on the contrary deferred to him in all matters, politely and reverentially. He said to him, "O Abū Mūsā, get up and inform the people what we have both agreed upon." So Abū Mūsā stood up and spoke in front of the people, praised God and extolled him, and then the Messenger of God, and then he said, "O you people! We have just looked into the matter facing this *umma*, and we did not see any option better than the one agreed upon by ʿAmr and me. That is, that we depose ʿAlī and Muʿāwiya, and put the matter to a *shūrā*, for which the people will take responsibility to appoint over themselves whom they choose. I hereby depose ʿAlī and Muʿāwiya." Then he stepped aside, and ʿAmr climbed up to the stage. He praised God and extolled him, and then he said, "Indeed, this one has just said what you have all heard, and deposed his master! I, likewise, depose him, just as he has. But I confirm my master, Muʿāwiya, for he is the *walī* of ʿUthmān ibn ʿAffān, the claimant of his blood, and the most righteous of the people in his position!" For ʿAmr ibn al-ʿĀṣ had seen that the people had been left without an imam, and this situation would lead to a long period of corruption (*kāna ʿAmr ibn al-ʿĀṣ raʾa anna taraka al-nās bi-lā imāma wa-l-ḥāla hadhihi yuʾadī ilā mafsada tawīla*), exceeding the disagreements that the people had just experienced. He thus confirmed Muʿāwiya out of necessity. His *ijtiḥād* [independent reasoning] was in error, but he was still correct in his action [given his fundamental assumption] (*faʾaqarra Muʿāwiya lamā rāʾa dhālika min al-maṣlaḥa, wa-al-ijtiḥād yukhṭiʾ wa-yuṣīb*).[22] It is said that Abū Mūsā spoke to him uncouthly, and that ʿAmr ibn al-ʿĀṣ answered in kind.[23]

---

22 Cf. Aaron Hagler, "Repurposed Narratives, Repurposed Narratives: The Battle of Ṣiffīn and the Historical Memory of the Umayyad Dynasty," in *Journal of Islamic and Middle Eastern Multidisciplinary Studies* 3 (2013), 1–27, which offers a slight mistranslation of this sentence.

23 Ibn Kathīr, *Bidāya* vii, 272.

At the last moment, Ibn Kathīr jumps to a qualified defense of ʿAmr ibn al-ʿĀṣ, who he has spent some significant effort rehabilitating, as we have already seen in the case of the attribution of the idea to raise the *maṣāḥif* to others (and as we will see later, as Ibn Kathīr largely eliminates ʿAmr from the *shūrā* narrative, in which he traditionally played a small but no less duplicitous role). Ibn Kathīr is not prepared to take ʿAmr's side—after all, this is a case of one Companion unseating another Companion who is a legitimate ruler—but he is consistent in that he gives ʿAmr the benefit of the doubt he affords to all of the *aṣḥāb*, including Ṭalḥa and al-Zubayr in the case of the Battle of the Camel. Ibn Kathīr agrees with Ibn Taymiyya that the Companions were not immune from error, but that they were (as the Qurʾān repeatedly emphasized) the very best of men. He therefore must navigate a very narrow narrative course: one that sees ʿAmr's apparently duplicitous chicanery not as a sin but as an error committed for an honest, and even praiseworthy, motive.

Given Ṣiffīn's central place in the narrative of the *fitna*—and given this moment's import to the Ṣiffīn episode—Ibn Kathīr accomplishes his narrative task with the simple qualification that ʿAmr, in accordance with his rights as a Companion, acted appropriately. If ʿAlī was, indeed, officially out of power and no longer the caliph—as ʿAlī's own arbiter, Abū Mūsā, had publicly affirmed a few seconds prior—then at that moment, there was no possibility of *khurūj* (defined as disobedience to proper authority). ʿAlī, at that moment, *was no proper authority*, as the people had "been left without an imām," and the community was, in fact, leaderless. He therefore put forward Muʿāwiya as a candidate to a vacant position.

Given ʿAmr's evident manipulation of the entire arbitration agreement in the other accounts, and the way he craftily maneuvered Abū Mūsā into creating exactly the kind of situation that would allow ʿAmr to win the arbitration so entirely, Ibn Kathīr's defense of him is remarkable. In the end, Ibn Kathīr was loyal to his Companion-centered approach. In one sentence, Ibn Kathīr changes the entire meaning of the Ṣiffīn story within the wider narrative. Rather than the most prominent of early Umayyad ignominies before Karbalāʾ, Ṣiffīn becomes a venue for the defense of Ibn Kathīr's two most important messages: first, that Shīʿa are wrong about the Companions, who could be neither rebels nor apostates (a claim supported by the Qurʾān); and second, Syria's place in the early Islamic narrative is unfairly maligned. More especially, Ibn Kathīr utilizes the Ṣiffīn story as a venue to defend his presentation of Karbalāʾ. By legitimizing Muʿāwiya's accession through his defense of ʿAmr's proclamation of him as caliph, he thus legitimizes the dynasty. The narrative butterfly effect of this performance means that, later, when Muʿāwiya appoints

Yazīd as his successor, he has the legal grounding to do so; and, thus, when al-Ḥusayn revolts against Yazīd, he is rebelling against a similarly legitimate ruler.

This is not to say that Ibn Kathīr wishes to align himself with the Umayyads; he still asserts that ʿAmr was mistaken in his fundamental assumption, and he still expresses his grief at al-Ḥusayn's death. He does not sing Yazīd's virtues either. But he does make room for the notion that the Shīʿī narrative is wrong; it is a result that he has in mind not only when discussing Karbalāʾ but the rest of the narrative as well.

CHAPTER 7

Preparing the Battle

1 Introduction

Before the Battle of Ṣiffīn could take place, the stage had to be set. ʿUthmān's assassination had sent the community into paroxysms of uncertainty and unease, centered around some troubling questions. How closely was ʿAlī tied to ʿUthmān's killers? What was the proper response to his death? Should the community follow ʿAlī while he lay under the cloud of suspicion? Naturally, there were those who answered that final question about following ʿAlī in the negative. Muslim historians often classified the opposition to ʿAlī in venal terms. But that need not detain us here: what matters here is that setting the scene for the events of Ṣiffīn had certain requirements. The opposition to ʿAlī had to be branded. While there is broad agreement on the players and course of events, the meaning of the characters' actions, and the motives that directed them, differed from narrative performance to narrative performance.

We begin, as always, with the broad outlines that constitute the episode's consensus framework. ʿUthmān has just been assassinated; as the next chapter will demonstrate, the figure of ʿUthmān was a critical historiographical reclamation project for Ibn al-Athīr and Ibn Kathīr. There were those in the community—in particular Muʿāwiya, but not forgetting Ṭalḥā ibn ʿUbayd Allāh and al-Zubayr ibn al-ʿAwwām—who took up arms against ʿAlī for the cause of seeing ʿUthmān's killers destroyed. The latter, along with ʿAlī's longtime rival, the Prophet's widow ʿĀʾisha bint Abī Bakr, opposed ʿAlī at the Battle of the Camel (36/656) and were defeated. Then, ʿAlī's army marched towards Ṣiffīn for the confrontation with Muʿāwiya's army.

2 The Battle of the Camel

Like the appointment and succession of Yazīd ibn Muʿāwiya, we here come upon an episode that is indispensable to the wider narrative but unprofitable to explore deeply in the present study. The Battle of the Camel is an event whose theme is similar to Ṣiffīn's, but which possesses significantly lower narrative stakes. This is largely because of the fate of its two antagonists, Ṭalḥā ibn ʿUbayd Allāh and al-Zubayr ibn al-ʿAwwām. According to al-Ṭabarī, the two men were not only early supporters of ʿAlī but were among the group of muhājirūn and

 | DOI:10.1163/9789004524255_009

anṣār who gathered around ʿAlī, giving him their *bayʿa* when news of ʿUthmān's death came.[1] There was some grumbling among the people in Medina that day; Saʿd ibn Abī Waqqās, the governor of Kūfa, refrained from giving the *bayʿa* "until the people have,"[2] and ʿAbd Allāh ibn ʿUmar ibn al-Khaṭṭāb expressed similar reservations. The fiery al-Ashtar offered to cut off ʿAbd Allāh's head for his rudeness,[3] but ʿAlī restrained him. Al-Ṭabarī specifically mentioned Ṭalḥā and al-Zubayr, however, as being the first to give allegiance, a fact that bespeaks their eager support for the man they would later fight. Al-Ṭabarī has Ḥabīb ibn Dhuʾayb note Ṭalḥā's crippled hand, whereupon Ḥabīb laments that "the first hand that gives the *bayʿa* is deformed; this does not bode well."[4] Ibn al-Athīr repeats the anecdote, which obviously serves to establish the earliness of their allegiance and to foreshadow its defective nature. But interesting symbolism aside, the Battle of the Camel is ultimately a narrative dead end. While it ends the stories of Ṭalḥā and al-Zubayr (although not the stories of al-Zubayr's descendants), managing to take a few shots at them for their hypocrisy, the real conflict the authors must tend to is the one that is concurrently taking place further north. Muʿāwiya ibn Abī Sufyān is determined to seize power for himself and to gain vengeance for his murdered cousin. In order to achieve this, he must first solidify his support and seek wise counsel. In this case, the counsel is that of ʿAmr ibn al-ʿĀṣ. Meanwhile, ʿAlī does the same, and he negotiates with the fickle governor of Kūfa, Abū Mūsā al-Ashʿarī.

3 The Allegiances of ʿAmr ibn al-ʿĀṣ and Abū Mūsā al-Ashʿarī

The two men who will be most responsible for concluding the Ṣiffīn narrative, as discussed in Chapter 6, are the two men who kick off this section of the narrative: ʿAmr ibn al-ʿĀṣ and Abū Mūsā al-Ashʿarī.

Al-Ṭabarī's account of Ṣiffīn opens with the story of ʿAmr ibn al-ʿĀṣ consulting his two sons on which side to join. Given ʿAmr's decisive role at Ṣiffīn, this is a natural place to begin. ʿAmr's choice is by no means a foregone conclusion; readers have already been introduced to him as the conqueror of Egypt, but also in the context of a pesky act of political chicanery during the *shūrā* of ʿUthmān, as related in the accounts of al-Ṭabarī and Ibn al-Athīr. When ʿAmr reenters the

1 Al-Ṭabarī, *Taʾrīkh* ii, 696.
2 Ibid. ii, 697.
3 Ibid. ii, 697.
4 Ibid. ii, 697. The Arabic reads *La yatimmu hadha al-am*, which literally means "this matter will not finish well."

narrative, al-Ṭabarī gives us the scene in which he is informed of the assassination of the man whom he helped elect caliph. According to a bizarre story transmitted on the authority of Ṣayf ibn ʿUmar, ʿAmr hears about the story in stages while encamped with his two sons at ʿAjlan. A succession of messengers bring him the latest news, each of them bearing an uncannily appropriate name: in order, Hasīra, Qattāl, and Ḥarb, whose names mean "Besieged," "Killed," and "War," a reasonable three-word summary of the evolving state of the Caliph ʿUthmān and of the capital of Medina. Al-Ṭabarī then flashes back to a scene from ʿAmr's time in ʿUmān, where he had been sent by the Prophet. There, a Jewish scholar predicted, with similarly uncanny accuracy, the natures and fates of the first four caliphs. The Jewish scholar probably did not have Muʿāwiya in mind when he prophesied that the fifth ruler of the community would be "the ruler of the Holy Land [*al-arḍ al-muqaddasa*] [whose] kingdom would last a long time," and about whom "those who formerly differed would agree,"[5] but the description seems to fit nonetheless.

Confronted with the news of the caliph's death, and then with the news that ʿAlī had received the allegiance of the people of Medina and subsequently defeated Ṭalḥā and al-Zubayr at the Battle of the Camel, ʿAmr calls on his two sons, ʿAbd Allāh and Muḥammad, to seek their advice. "Someone," according to al-Ṭabarī (he does not specify who), told ʿAmr of Muʿāwiya's opposition to ʿAlī. ʿAlī was already ʿAmr's political opponent, if not his enemy, owing to ʿAmr's earlier opposition to ʿAlī at the time of the *shūrā*, so this was a dire situation indeed for ʿAmr. ʿAmr says to his sons, "There is no benefit to me with ʿAlī [as caliph]. He is a man who takes full advantage of his *sābiqa*, and he will share none of his authority with me."[6] His sons reply: "ʿAbd Allāh said, 'The Prophet died pleased with you; Abū Bakr died pleased with you; ʿUmar died pleased with you. I believe you should stay your hand and sit in your house until the people agree on a leader, and then you should pledge your allegiance to him.' Muḥammad said to ʿAmr, 'You are one of the most important of all the Arab chiefs, and I do not think this matter should be settled without your voice or vote.' "[7] Al-Ṭabarī's ʿAmr then sums it up for the reader, in case he was not clear on the stakes: "ʿAbd Allāh, you have given me advice that is better for me in the hereafter, and safer for my religion. Muḥammad, you have given me advice that is more beneficial for my worldly life, but worse for me in the hereafter."[8] There is no doubt, in other words, that we are meant to understand that ʿAmr, true to

5 Al-Ṭabarī, *Taʾrīkh* iii, 69. The scholar was probably making a reference to the Messiah.
6 Ibid. iii, 69–70.
7 Ibid. iii, 70.
8 Ibid. iii, 70.

the character that was already established in the *shūrā* episode, has decided to act through cynical politicking rather than spiritual righteousness. This cynic's close association with Muʿāwiya's cause, and then with his ascendancy and his dynasty, cast a disparaging light on the dynasty as a whole.

Al-Ṭabarī stops short of accusing ʿAmr of literally selling his allegiance; al-Ṭabarī's contemporary, Aḥmad ibn Dāʾūd al-Dīnawarī, records the following conversation in his *al-Akhbār al-ṭiwāl*:

> [ʿAmr] said, "As for ʿAlī ibn Abī Ṭālib, truly the Muslims do not consider you two equals." Muʿāwiya said, "He is complicit in the murder of ʿUthmān, in the appearance of *fitna*, and in the division of the community." ʿAmr said, "Even if that were true, you do not have either his precedence in Islam (*sābiqatihi*) or his close relation (to the Prophet), but I will help your faction if you give me what I want." He said, "Name your price." ʿAmr said, "Make me your governor of Egypt for as long as you rule."[9]

Indeed, ʿAmr is later rewarded with the governorship of Egypt, a land he had conquered as a younger man. Petersen believes that al-Dīnawarī's point of view and purpose was to take "the legality of ʿAlī's election as his foundation, and his object is to prove that the Caliph had a clear right to fight down the three rebellious movements, first and foremost that of Muʿāwiya, by military means, seeing that they are without legal justification and breaking down the unity of Islam which the caliph represents."[10] He also denies "the Syrian governor's action its tinge of legality."[11] Perhaps that is the reason he takes the extra step to make ʿAmr's unscrupulousness explicit. Al-Yaʿqūbī, another contemporary, records that ʿAmr is equally speculative in his motives, but less specific as to the price of his allegiance: "No, by the eternal God, I will not give you my *dīn* until I have taken something from your [Muʿāwiya's] possessions."[12] The fact that al-Ṭabarī does not record such a statement by ʿAmr indicates that he likely thought it spurious; al-Dīnawarī and al-Yaʿqūbī, by contrast, were more fiercely partisan, anti-Umayyad if not necessarily Shīʿī.

Ibn al-Athīr presents the same story with more concise language.[13] Ibn Kathīr leaves it out entirely; by the time ʿAmr rejoins his narrative, he is already in Muʿāwiya's camp and serving as his chief advisor.

---

9 Aḥmad ibn Dāwūd al-Dīnawarī, *Al-Akhbār al-ṭiwāl* (Leiden: E.J. Brill, 1888), 167–168.
10 Ibid. 167.
11 Ibid. 167.
12 Aḥmad ibn Abī Yaʿqūb ibn Wadih al-Yaʿqūbī, *Taʾrīkh* (Leiden Brill, 1883), 186.
13 Ibn al-Athīr, *Kāmil* iii, 158.

As for Abū Mūsā al-Ashʿarī, his first appearance in the narrative arrives before the Battle of the Camel, in which he warns ʿAlī to avoid *fitna* at all costs. Abū Mūsā's character is obviously quite important, but also relatively simple, without any of the nuance that comes to accompany the character of ʿAmr ibn al-Āṣ. Abū Mūsā is presented as profoundly opposed to all forms of *fitna* and uses his status as a companion of the Prophet to advance his position to the Kūfans, whom he governs. This section from al-Ṭabarī's history is a speech that more than adequately describes his position: the less part one takes in *fitna*, the better for his eternal soul.

> [Abū Mūsā said]: "This *fitna* is blind and deaf. It is trampling on its halter. The sleeper in it is better off than the sitter. The sitter in it is better off than the stander; the stander, better off than the walker. The walker in it is better off than the runner; the runner, better off than the rider. It is a *fitna* that rips [the community] apart like a stomach ulcer. It has come at you from the place where you were safe and leaves the wise man bewildered like someone without experience. We, the congregation of the Companions of Muḥammad, are better able to understand the *fitna*—when it approaches it confuses and when it retreats it discloses."[14]

This perspective helps give the reader insight into why Abū Mūsā is so eager to end the *fitna*, and then so gullible at the conclusion of the Ṣiffīn narrative, in the negotiation with ʿAmr.

Of course, it is another Companion of the Prophet, the venerable ʿAmmār ibn Yāsir, who heckles Abū Mūsā and goads him into supporting ʿAlī in al-Ṭabarī's version. But like Jarīr ibn ʿAbd Allāh and al-Ashʿath ibn Qays, and despite his apparent conscientious objection to *fitna* in all its forms, Abū Mūsā's main motivation for joining ʿAlī's march to Ṣiffīn seems to be for reasons of personal expediency; he faced the loss of his governorship of Kūfa as punishment for his continued neutrality. The reader was not expected to confuse his enlistment in the cause with his unwavering support of it. Nor, indeed, would such a supposition have been made for most of ʿAlī's apparent supporters. Abū Mūsā is something of a stock character in all three accounts, and in many other accounts. He is not the subject of a great deal of character development. Rather, his main narrative purpose is to be gullible enough to get trampled by ʿAmr ibn al-ʿĀṣ in the arbitration discussion, and so giving him a simple, one-note motiv-

14 Al-Ṭabarī, *Taʾrīkh* xvi, 94.

ation is sufficient. He is so opposed to *fitna*, we are meant to understand, that he will leap at any opportunity to end it, regardless of the cost to his rightful ruler.

4 The Correspondence between ʿAlī and Muʿāwiya

In this section, ʿAlī dispatches an emissary, Jarīr ibn ʿAbd Allāh al-Bajalī, to Muʿāwiya, against the better judgment of Mālik al-Ashtar, who is among the most vocal of his own supporters. Emissaries are exchanged between the two parties, while Muʿāwiya wins the support of the clever and ambitious ʿAmr ibn al-ʿĀṣ. The contours of the dispute between ʿAlī and Muʿāwiya are made clear.

One of the main issues treated by al-Ṭabarī's story of the emissaries is the *bayʿa*, the pledge of allegiance. Since the *bayʿa*, and specifically Muʿāwiya's refusal to take the *bayʿa*, is at the very heart of the Ṣiffīn story, it deserves some discussion. It is not entirely clear whether the term was used in the sense of "pledge of allegiance" at the time of Ṣiffīn: in the Qurʾān, it appears as a commercial term (as in *Barāʿa*, 9:111), in which a bargain (*bayʿ*) is made between God and the Muslims, namely that they fight for Him and He rewards them with paradise; in *al-Fatḥ* (specifically 48:10 and 48:18), those who pledge allegiance to Muḥammad (*yubāyiʿūnaka*) implicitly pledge allegiance to God, and once again are rewarded for the bargain; and in *al-Mumtaḥana* (60:12), in which women (and, later tradition adds, noncombatant men) wish to pledge themselves to the Prophet and to God (*yubāyiʿnaka*), the Prophet is instructed to accept the pledge from them (*fa-bāyiʿhunna*) and ask forgiveness for them from God. It should also be noted that, in early Islamic times, the gesture associated with a *bayʿa*—that is, a handclasp—was identical to the gesture associated with concluding a business arrangement:[15] "In the Qurʾānic *bayʿa* we have a ritual that combines ancient Arabian ideas of covenant before a patron deity, confirmed by a handclasp, with genetically related ideas about covenant found in late antique Christianity. The *bayʿa* also unites the pre-Islamic rhetoric of unity for success in war (God, it is worth remembering is *khayr al-nāṣirīn*, 'the best of allies in war' [Q 3.150]) with parallel monotheist ideas about martyrdom and pious self-sacrifice in God's cause."[16] In this context, and in light of its appearance (and the appearance of its related verb) in the Qurʾān, the *bayʿa* must be understood in terms of exchange, as a mutually beneficial arrange-

15 See Marsham, *Rituals* esp. 40–57.
16 Ibid. 57.

ment. One gives the *bayʿa* to another, be it to God, a caliph, or a military leader (often all three at the same time), in return for victory, booty, justice, and salvation. This certainly does something to contextualize the implication that ʿAmr requested a form of recompense for his allegiance to Muʿāwiya.

During the three decades of conquest following the death of the Prophet Muḥammad, a number of religiopolitical institutions came into being, including the caliphate and the *bayʿa*, through which the incumbent caliph was recognized as *amīr al-muʾminīn*, Commander of the Faithful. Marsham concludes that "these pledges were a fusion of long-standing, pre-Islamic religio-political custom with late antique monotheist ideas about leadership and authority."[17] Muḥammad accepted the *bayʿa* from the Meccans when he entered the town,[18] and Abū Bakr accepted it, sometimes through his commanders, during the *ridda* wars.[19] It was a natural outgrowth of its role as an exchange of loyalty for rewards that it grew, with the first caliphs, to become not just an affirmation of loyalty but the standard accession ritual for a new caliph. What is clear from the literature is that it was a bidirectional oath; ʿUthmān, according a tradition related by Sayf ibn ʿUmar, "led the people in prayer [and] increased [their stipends]" upon his accession.[20]

The *bayʿa*'s role in the Ṣiffīn story, therefore, has bearing far beyond Muʿāwiya's reluctance to give ʿAlī his allegiance. ʿAmr ibn al-ʿĀṣ, who becomes Muʿāwiya's most key advisor and general, is also faced with the choice of to whom to pledge allegiance. As cynically as pro-ʿAlīd sources may view ʿAmr ibn al-ʿĀṣ for his allegiance to Muʿāwiya, whom they consider (at best) in error, there is no reason, given the Qurʾānic and early Islamic context for allegiance, to single him out for denigration for expecting something in return for his loyalty and council.

Another concept that appears in this section is that of *ṭulaqāʾ*. The *ṭulaqāʾ* (singular, *ṭalīq*) referred to the Meccan Qurashīs who, according to Islamic law, technically became the Prophet's lawful property when he conquered Mecca in 8/630. However, instead of retaining them as captives, the Prophet released them as freedmen (*ṭulaqāʾ*). The notion of the *ṭulaqāʾ* presented in this section is noteworthy, since mention of the concept occurs in the narrative before it becomes relevant to the story.

This reference to Muʿāwiya's ineligibility, the predictive denial of any right Muʿāwiya has to be caliph, premature at this juncture of the narrative, consti-

17 Ibid. 60.
18 The account of this is included in almost all chronicles of the time.
19 Marsham, *Rituals* 66.
20 See Ibid. 70.

tutes an ahistorical utterance, and it is one that will be repeated in different forms and at different points in the various Ṣiffīn narratives.

In this section, we also see the first instance among the works examined in this study of the idea of the *walī*, a term of ambiguous meaning whose role in the Ṣiffīn story helps shape its development in the works of subsequent historians. The word *walī* comes from the root w-l-y, meaning "to be close to," or "to be friends with," and can possess any number of meanings, including: helper or supporter; benefactor; patron; relative; owner; or legally responsible person. This ambiguity of meaning becomes important in the story, as the concept of *walāya* comes to be at the heart of the disagreement between ʿAlī and Muʿāwiya. In Naṣr ibn Muzāḥim's *Waqʿat Ṣiffīn*, as recorded by al-Ṭabarī, Muʿāwiya himself makes the claim that he is ʿUthmān's *walī* (although for the most part, in the Ṣiffīn story, it will be ʿAmr ibn al-ʿĀṣ making the claim about Muʿāwiya during the arbitration with Abū Mūsā al-Ashʿarī). But what precisely is meant by this? In this case, Muʿāwiya is arguing both that he is ʿUthmān's relative and, most of all, the legally responsible person, in the sense meant in the Qurʾān;[21] that is, legally entitled to seek revenge on ʿUthmān's killers. The Shīʿī concept of *walāya* that would develop thereafter has decidedly different implications; it can mean, in addition to the more earthly meanings listed above, spiritual inheritance of esoteric knowledge and divine proximity and sanctity (these are, in part, what modern Shīʿa mean when they term ʿAlī ibn Abī Ṭālib as *walī Allāh*).[22] The spiritual senses of the term have their basis in the Qurʾān; however, in the Ṣiffīn story, the term *walī* is never used in a spiritual sense but rather is always employed with reference to a kind of limited worldly authority. It is certainly not demonstrably incorrect for Muʿāwiya to claim to be ʿUthmān's *walī*, and later for ʿAmr to make the same claim about Muʿāwiya. From a literalist standpoint, the Qurʾān says that the *walī* of an unjustly slain man will be given power; technically, Muʿāwiya *is* ʿUthmān's *walī*, at least in the one sense of the word. To ʿAlī, naturally, the meaning of *walī* suggested by the Qurʾān implies "closest relative," which, as a nephew of ʿUthmān, Muʿāwiya was emphatically not. Like the concept of the *bayʿa*, the proper use of the term *walī* is presented as one of the fundamental disagreements between ʿAlī and his supporters on the one hand and Muʿāwiya and his supporters on the other.

Ibn al-Athīr, as is his standard practice, carefully recycles al-Ṭabarī's material for this section of his presentation of the Ṣiffīn narrative, but makes sure to omit anything problematic. For example, he chooses simply not to mention

21 *Al-Isrāʾ*, Qurʾān 17:33.

22 See Dakake, *Charismatic Community* 23–31.

Muʿāwiya's status as a *ṭalīq*. While the point of Muʿāwiya's ineligibility to lead the community had been mentioned (at this early juncture in the story) by al-Ṭabarī, Ibn al-Athīr's main source of information, and had even been highlighted and emphasized by the Shīʿī *muʾarrikhī*s, al-Masʿūdī and al-Maqdisī, Ibn al-Athīr steers his account clear of such dangerous waters and avoids the issue altogether: "ʿAlī said, 'Go to him and invite him to find common ground with us, that he might return to us.' So he sent him with a letter he had written to Muʿāwiya, informing him of the agreement of the muhājirūn and the anṣār in taking the *bayʿa* for him, as well as of the demise of Ṭalḥā and al-Zubayr, and his war against them, and inviting him to enter into obedience to him, as the muhājirūn and the anṣār had already done."[23] This section is precisely where the first references to the *ṭulaqāʾ* appeared in al-Ṭabarī's account. It is possible that Ibn al-Athīr thought the point somewhat too arcane for his readership and glossed over it for the sake of readability, as he was known to do. It was also possible that he felt that the term's appearance at this point in the narrative would be out of place (although the fact that he also did not include any mention of Muʿāwiya being a *ṭalīq* when the issue would have come up—during the negotiation between Abū Mūsā and ʿAmr ibn al-ʿĀṣ—suggests that this was not the case). The pro-ʿAlīd authors' references to the *ṭulaqāʾ* stand as some of their most persuasive arguments about the iniquity of the sequence of events, culminating in the rise of the Umayyad dynasty, that is a direct result of the battle's outcome; when Ibn al-Athīr omits it, he implicitly moves his account away from the vehemently pro-ʿAlīd perspective and subtly defends Muʿāwiya by overlooking this strong argument against him. The other authors who omit the point about the *ṭulaqāʾ*, including the vehemently pro-ʿAlīd al-Yaʿqūbī, do so because it makes no real dramatic sense to express it *at this point* in the narrative when Muʿāwiya, called upon to pledge his allegiance to ʿAlī in a ritual act of obedience, refuses until he achieves justice for his murdered kinsman, ʿUthmān.

As far as Ibn Kathīr goes, there is nothing unfamiliar in this section. It is clear that Ibn Kathīr draws heavily from the nearly identical accounts of Naṣr ibn Muzāḥim—al-Ṭabarī—and Ibn al-Athīr (it hardly matters which one was his source, although of course it was al-Ṭabarī). There is nothing novel in this section relative to those earlier, "standard" accounts. Long gone by the time of Ibn Kathīr are the days when the lists of names of muhājirūn and anṣār would carry weight as implicit arguments for ʿAlī's legitimacy; those lists seem to have

---

23 ʿIzz al-Dīn Abū al-Ḥasan ibn al-Athīr al-Jazarī, *al-Kāmil fī al-Taʾrīkh* ii (Beirut: Dār al-Kitāb al-ʿArabī, 1998), 628–630.

disappeared by the tenth century, when the *mu'arrikhī* historians wrote in the dominant historiographical genre, whose focus on readability rendered those lists vestigial. Naturally, Ibn Kathīr never mentions the notion that Muʿāwiya is a *ṭalīq* due to the circumstances of his father's forced conversion at all.

5 The Battle by the Water: Softening Umayyad Villainy at Ṣiffīn

This question is an example of a smaller issue that was nonetheless worthy of editorial effort on the part of Ibn Kathīr and Ibn al-Athīr. In al-Ṭabarī's version of the story, there was no shortage of examples of Umayyads behaving badly during the Ṣiffīn narrative. The first such opportunity was at the juncture of the initial encounter between ʿAlī's army and Muʿāwiya's at Ṣiffīn. Muʿāwiya's troops had arrived first, and had taken up a defensive position, blocking ʿAlī's thirsty men from the waters of the Euphrates. Al-Ṭabarī relates the following:

> According to Abū Mikhnaf—Yūsuf b. Yazīd—ʿAbdallāh b. ʿAwf b. al-Aḥmar: When we reached Muʿāwiyah and the Syrians at Ṣiffīn, we found that they had chosen an even, wide, and spacious position. They had seized the watering place, and it was in their possession. Abū al-Aʿwar al-Sulamī had lined up horsemen and foot soldiers by it, and he had placed the archers in front of his men. He had formed a row with spears and shields, and helmets on their heads, and they had resolved not to let us reach the water.
>
> In alarm we went to the Commander of the Faithful and told him about that, and he summoned Ṣaʿṣaʿah b. Ṣūḥān. He told him, "Go to Muʿāwiyah and say this: 'We have come to you like this but are reluctant to fight you before exhorting you by all possible means. But you have advanced your horsemen and foot soldiers against us and have attacked us before we attacked you. You began the fighting against us while we considered that we should hold back from fighting you until we had appealed to you and put before you our arguments. And this is another thing that you have done—you have barred our men from the water, and they will not stop fighting unless they have drunk. So send your men to allow mine access to the water and hold off from fighting until we consider our dispute and what we have come for and what you have come for. But, if you prefer that we should give up what we came for and leave the men to fight at the water, so that only the victors drink, we will do so.' "[24]

---

24 Hawting (trans.), *History of al-Ṭabarī* 14–15.

> [...] By God, the next thing we knew, Muʿāwiyah was sending troops of horsemen to Abū al-Aʿwar to stop our men from getting to the water. ʿAlī sent us against them, and we fired arrows and thrust with spears and then gave blows with the swords. We were granted victory over them, and the water came into our hands. We said, "By God we will not allow them to drink from it," but ʿAlī sent to us, saying, "Take what water you need and return to your camp. Leave them alone, for God has given you victory over them because of their evil and oppression."[25]

Ibn al-Athīr's version of the story is, as expected, appropriated almost entirely from al-Ṭabarī; he includes a much longer description of the fighting itself than al-Ṭabarī and, at the end of the battle, an interchange between ʿAlī's emissary and Muʿāwiya, wherein the former calls Muʿāwiya to pledge allegiance to ʿAlī based upon his excellence, precedence, and *dīn.*

Ibn Kathīr's account contains the story of Ṣaʿṣaʿa ibn Ṣūḥān, whom ʿAlī sends to Muʿāwiya as an emissary, which originally appeared in the account of Naṣr ibn Muzāḥim as retold in al-Ṭabarī:

> ʿAlī's companions came to him and told him this, and he sent Ṣaʿṣaʿa ibn Ṣūḥān to Muʿāwiya, and he said to him, "We have come prepared to fight you until we achieve our objectives, but you have still made war upon us before we began with you, and now, finally, you have prevented us from the water!" When this came to Muʿāwiya, he said to the people, "What should we do?" ʿAmr said, "Release it, for it is neither just nor seemly that we should be well-watered and they should be thirsty." Al-Walīd said, "Rebuff them, let them taste of the thirst they gave to Commander of the Faithful ʿUthmān when they besieged him in his quarters, and they denied him food and water for forty mornings." ʿAbd Allāh ibn Saʿd ibn Abī Sarḥ said, "Deny them the water until the night. Perhaps they will return to their country." Muʿāwiya said nothing, so Ṣaʿṣaʿa ibn Ṣūḥān said to him, "What is your answer?" Muʿāwiya said to him, "My opinion will come to you hereafter." When Ṣaʿṣaʿa returned and informed his party of this news, the horses and men rode, and they did not stop until they had conquered the water decisively, agreed on arrangements for the path to the water, and nobody denied anybody any water thereafter.[26]

25 Ibid. 16.
26 Ibn Kathīr, *Bidāya* vii, 246–247.

While Ibn Kathīr's version of the exchange is recorded more or less as al-Ṭabarī recorded it, in this section his project of rehabilitating the character of ʿAmr ibn al-ʿĀṣ is quite evident. Not only does ʿAmr not come up with the idea of preventing ʿAlī and his men from drinking—just as he would not come up with the idea of raising the *maṣāḥif* at the story's climax—but he specifically denounces the wickedness of the act. One would expect such virtue, after all, from a Companion of the Prophet, whose well-meaning virtue is a key cog in Ibn Kathīr's historiographical discrediting of Shīʿī sources.

Given the perspectives sympathetic to the Umayyads that Ibn Kathīr brings to bear on later parts of the Ṣiffīn story, particularly on the subject of the arbitration and the reneging of ʿAmr ibn al-ʿĀṣ, it is noteworthy that Ibn Kathīr does not make use of other versions, including Ibn al-ʿAdīm's account of the battle by the water in *Bughyat al-ṭalab fī taʾrīkh Ḥalab*, which relieves Muʿāwiya from some—indeed, most—of the responsibility for the Syrians' cynical denial of the water of the Euphrates to ʿAlī and his men. However, either way, it is not Ibn Kathīr's intent to present Muʿāwiya as any kind of saint. Nor can he make additions or alterations to the story that, though casting the Syrian leader in a decidedly better light, undermine the literary verisimilitude of the narrative and its structure. Muʿāwiya, in order to emerge from this story in an orthodox fashion, must retain control over the actions of his men. As we have seen, particularly with Ibn Kathīr's explication of the permissibility, and indeed the propriety, of the deception played upon Abū Mūsā al-Ashʿarī, Ibn Kathīr is making certain to present Muʿāwiya (as a symbol for the Umayyad dynasty as a whole) as a legitimate caliph, whose assumption of power is both legal and right. There is no indication that he is trying to present Muʿāwiya as being on the right side of Ṣiffīn itself. This venture does not require that the Syrians be saints, nor, indeed, always right. However, to legitimize his authority, Muʿāwiya must *retain* authority throughout. This requires no change to the story on Ibn Kathīr's part. It only requires that he avoid the tempting slippery slope of weakening Muʿāwiya's authority, as Ibn al-ʿAdīm did in the *Bughya*, for the short-term payoff of increasing his perceived righteousness.

6 Conclusion

The Battle of Ṣiffīn is a transitional moment on the Islamic narrative. With Ṣiffīn, the narrative focus on the divisions plaguing the early community shifted to the emergence of crystallized sectarian divisions. By the time Ibn al-Athīr and Ibn Kathīr were writing, of course, the sects were theologically solvent and politically salient. But a cursory glance at the variety of important narrative moments that are contained within the Ṣiffīn narrative demonstrate its importance. In addition to all of the tropes, including the betrayal of ʿAlī and the political chicanery of the Umayyads, and the callbacks, including to Ḥudaybiyya, the Ṣiffīn story marks an important political transition. Specifically, although it does not officially end the reign of ʿAlī and the *rāshidūn*, it does end any pretense ʿAlī may have to rulership over a loyal, united empire. By the same token, while it does not officially kick off the Umayyad dynasty, it does establish the beginning of Muʿāwiya's claim to rulership over a united, if agitated, empire.

Ṣiffīn also marks the first moment the political divisions that plagued the *umma* after the Prophet's death officially gave birth to a new sectarian identity. This was not, of course, that of the Sunnīs or the Shīʿa—those would come later—but rather the Khawārij, whose defection from ʿAlī's camp over his (forced) acceptance of ʿAmr's arbitration proposal established the notion that a significant divergence from the general consensus of political mores constituted an act of apostasy. Of course, the Khawārij would claim that those who remained behind for the arbitration discussions were the ones who left Islam and that they, the Khawārij, were in fact the true Muslims.

The Sunnīs and Shīʿa of later generations both saw their own communities on ʿAlī's side of the Battle of Ṣiffīn. Later generations of Sunnīs and Shīʿa had good reasons to see themselves opposing the Umayyads, but not the same reasons. Sunnīs writing in the ʿAbbāsid milieu, like al-Ṭabarī and Ibn al-Athīr, opposed the Umayyads for political, rather than sectarian, reasons. Ibn Kathīr, writing in a post-ʿAbbāsid world, was less beholden to the dynasty that itself overthrew the Umayyads but was still subject to the historiographical picture that their reign generated. This was most unlike the Shīʿa, who saw the Umayyads as the chief villains in their central historical drama, and the ʿAbbāsids as the Umayyads' double-dealing successors.

Because Ṣiffīn, as a site of memory, offered Shīʿa the chance to advance that narrative, Ibn al-Athīr and Ibn Kathīr were forced to shape their narrative around it. As they would do with Karbalāʾ, Ṣiffīn, while not a battlefield of their choosing, was nonetheless an opportunity to highlight those aspects of the story they felt were most important to amend from their generally pro-ʿAlīd source material, like that of al-Ṭabarī. Once again, Ibn al-Athīr omitted the passages that heightened any sense of disunity. Ibn Kathīr bided his time on changes until the very end, when he dropped the narrative bombshell that, regardless of what had come before and regardless of whether or not he was correct in supporting him in the first place, ʿAmr ibn al-ʿĀṣ's confirmation of Muʿāwiya as his caliph was a legal act.

If Muʿāwiya's accession was legal, then his caliphate was legal, and then his son Yazīd's accession was also legal. If that is the case, then al-Ḥusayn's death at

Karbalāʾ, while horrifying and regrettable, was not the eschatological calamity that the Shīʿa of his time and before made it out be. Rather, it was the predictable death of a pious rebel against an undesirable, but legal, government, and the natural conclusion to an act of an imprudent political insurgency.

The only element that could derail this narrative of Karbalāʾ is if Muʿāwiya himself had been a rebel, or even perhaps an apostate, when he fought against ʿAlī at Ṣiffīn. This brings up the question of whether ʿAlī deserved the *bayʿa* from Muʿāwiya or not, which can only be answered by reasoning out whether, first, Muʿāwiya had a legitimate grievance that ʿAlī protected the killers of ʿUthmān ibn ʿAffān, and second, whether Muʾāwiya was the appropriate man to demand that the killers be punished. The second was clearly a matter of opinion; the question of legitimate grievance, however, brings up a third key question. Was the death of ʿUthmān justified or not? This can only be answered if a fourth question is answered: was ʿUthmān a legitimate ruler? The search for the answer to this question takes us back to the beginning of ʿUthmān's reign. If his election was legitimate, then his assassins should be punished. If ʿAlī protected them, then Muʿāwiya was right to fight him. If Muʿāwiya was right, then his election was legal.

The meanings of every moment hinge upon the meanings of the critical moments that came before.

PART 3

The Election of ʿUthmān

CHAPTER 8

The Story of ʿUthmān

On the 18th of Muḥarram, in the Hijri year 36 (July 17, 656), the Egyptian, Kūfan, and Baṣran opponents of the Caliph ʿUthmān ibn ʿAffān grew impatient with their siege and burst into his home, killing him and severing the fingers of his wife, Nāʾila, who had raised her hand in defense of her husband. Only the third successor to the Prophet Muḥammad, ʿUthmān was not the first caliph to be assassinated; his predecessor, ʿUmar ibn al-Khaṭṭāb, had been attacked and mortally wounded by a slave twelve years earlier. The assassination of ʿUthmān, however, was a grimmer event for the nascent Islamic polity; unlike ʿUmar, ʿUthmān had been slain by fellow members of the Muslim Arab elite. ʿUthmān's bloody shirt and Nāʾila's fingertips were sent to Damascus, there to be used to incite the population against the forces that had dared to strike the caliph down. He was, after all, one of the Banū Umayya (Umayyads), the Meccan branch of the Quraysh tribe that had come to dominate Syrian political life.

So were planted the seeds of the first *fitna*, or period of inter-Muslim communal strife, in Islamic history. The mutineers who killed ʿUthmān were supporters of the man who would become his successor: ʿAlī ibn Abī Ṭālib, the Prophet Muḥammad's first cousin and son-in-law. Unlike ʿUthmān, who was from the powerful Banū Umayya, the Prophet and ʿAlī were both members of the Banū Hāshim during pre-Islamic days, the lesser branch of the Quraysh. The Banū Umayya had been early enemies of Islam, and late converts to it. Their power over the city of Mecca still afforded them great influence throughout the empire when ʿUthmān was murdered; Muʿāwiya ibn Abī Sufyān, a cousin of the slain caliph, administered al-Shām (Syria, more or less) as its governor.

When ʿUthmān was slain, the old Meccan rivalry between the Banū Umayya and the Banū Hāshim reared its head. ʿAlī, the story goes, had been recognized as the next caliph by most of the surviving muhājirūn (the group of 70 converts from Mecca who had emigrated with the Prophet from Mecca to Medina) and the anṣār (the Prophet's Medinan supporters), as well as most of the people in all lands of the empire, save Syria. However, the pro-Umayyad opposition from Syria was strong. It was unclear to the Syrian partisans and notables what role, if any, ʿAlī may have played in the assassination of ʿUthmān, and their suspicions were exacerbated by ʿAlī's protection of the assassins, who were among his strongest supporters. ʿAlī, in an attempt to shore up his support, set out against the rebellious Ṭalḥā and al-Zubayr, who were supported by the Prophet's widow

 | DOI:10.1163/9789004524255_010

ʿĀʾisha, and fought them at what became known as the Battle of the Camel (36/656). Ṭalḥā and al-Zubayr were killed at the battle, and ʿĀʾisha was captured and confined to house arrest in Mecca.

While he was campaigning against these two rebels in Baṣra, ʿAlī must have been aware of the storm brewing to the west, in Syria. It was to ʿUthmān's powerful kinsman Muʿāwiya ibn Abī Sufyān, the governor of Syria, that ʿUthmān's bloody shirt and Nāʾila's severed fingertips had come and were displayed for the people to see. In a state of righteous anger, Muʿāwiya's armed Syrian supporters vowed to seek revenge for the murdered caliph and agreed to withhold the *bayʿa*, or pledge of allegiance traditionally given to a new caliph, from ʿAlī until he turned the killers over to face their justice. They also vowed to abstain from ritual ablutions until the justice of the matter was served.

ʿAlī was unwilling to accept this state of affairs; convinced that his accession had been legal and binding, ʿAlī considered it Muʿāwiya's legal and religious duty to pledge allegiance to him as caliph. He set out in force for Syria, therefore, to get what he felt was his due obedience. Muʿāwiya had claimed the right of blood revenge for his murdered kinsman, ʿUthmān, and intimated that ʿAlī was complicit, if not actively involved, in his assassination; he set out from Syria with a force of his own. The two armies, sending envoys back and forth as they approached each other, met at the banks of the Euphrates River near the village of Ṣiffīn, which of course was discussed in the last chapter.

ʿUthmān's time in office is historiographically controversial, but like Ṣiffīn and Karbalāʾ, there are a few elements that always appear, a narrative scaffolding for his reign. What follows are the elements of the ʿUthmān story:

1 The *Shūrā*

When ʿUthmān's predecessor ʿUmar is mortally wounded (23/644), upon his death bed he orders six men to consultatively choose one from among their number to serve as his successor. Those six men include ʿUthmān and ʿAlī, along with ʿAbd al-Raḥmān ibn ʿAwf, Saʿd ibn Abī Waqqāṣ, al-Zubayr ibn al-ʿAwwām, and Ṭalḥa ibn Ubayd Allāh (the last two making a guest spot in the narrative before their decisive roles in the Battle of the Camel episode). Leder divides the *shūrā* story into further elements, which he calls "subnarrations."[1]

1 Stefan Leder, "The Paradigmatic Character of Madāʾinī's *shūrā*-Narration,'" in *SI* 88 (1998), 35–54.

Essentially, after the council is appointed, it deliberates and, through a series of political machinations, ʿUthmān and ʿAbd al-Raḥmān conspire (or collaborate, if you like) to see to it that the former is elected and that ʿAlī is once again shut out.

2 Six Good Years, Six Bad Years

A period of twelve years hardly constitutes a single conceptual episode; however, in most of the narratives it is afforded about the same amount of text as are very important discrete events, like Ṣiffīn and Karbalāʾ, and is thus treated only very generally. ʿUthmān's life, incidentally, may be treated in multiple ways in the sources, largely dependent on their genre. *Manāqib* and *faḍāʾil*, for example, tend to focus on his personal qualities that relate to his role as a Companion of the Prophet, while chronicles (such as those examined in this study) are more likely to devote attention to his tenure as caliph.[2] ʿUthmān is credited with centralizing power and establishing the definitive version of the Qurʾān. He also saw the continued expansion of the nascent Islamic polity into Nubia and North Africa in the west, and the effective subjugation of Iran in the east. In fact, some central players of the Ṣiffīn story, like Jarīr ibn ʿAbd Allāh al-Bajalī and al-Ashʿath ibn Qays al-Kindī, greatly improved their standing through their participation in the conquest of Persia.[3] Despite these early successes, ʿUthmān's fortunes (and the historical memory of his rule) turn in the year 30/650, traditionally when he lost a signet ring that the Prophet had gifted to him. Popular discontent grew, particularly in Kūfa, Egypt, and Medina, and a combination of ineffective appointed governors and poorly managed strife between preexisting factions led to a mutiny in Medina that ended with ʿUthmān's assassination. The narrative descriptions of the assassination (and the rising discontent that led to it) are much more abundant than the description of the rest of his reign. This fact offers credence to the notion that ʿUthmān's assassination was of greater narrative concern to the historians than the rest of his reign.

---

2 Keaney, *Medieval Islamic Historiography* 7–8.

3 Kennedy, *Prophet* 71.

3 Muʿāwiya on the Minbar

Muʿāwiya ibn Abī Sufyān, at this point the governor of al-Shām, was incensed by the death of his kinsman the caliph and appalled at his presumed successor ʿAlī's refusal to punish the assassins. While ʿAlī had managed to remove most of ʿUthmān's appointed governors, Muʿāwiya had a strong military at his disposal (situated, as he was, on the Byzantine frontier) and was not so easily neutralized.[4] Even had he wished to avoid conflict with ʿAlī (and there is scant evidence to suggest that he did), when ʿUthmān's wife Nā'ila sent Muʿāwiya his blood-stained shirt and, gruesomely, her own fingertips, sliced from the hand she lifted to defend her beset husband, he could not afford not to demand justice from ʿAlī. His display of the relics of ʿUthmān's grisly murder to the population of Damascus sent the Syrians, and the narrative, careening towards Ṣiffīn.

4 The Stakes

The story of ʿUthmān's assassination is critical to establishing the justification of both sides at Ṣiffīn (which, as we saw, was itself critical for establishing the legitimacy of the Umayyad forces at Karbalā'). What was the nature of ʿUthmān's assassination? Was it justified, or legal? Was it moral or immoral? And, perhaps most importantly, to what extent was ʿAlī involved in the assassination? The extant sources agree that he was not, but his close association with, and protection of, ʿUthmān's killers in what follows is the direct cause of both the Battle of the Camel and the Battle of Ṣiffīn—and, of course, for all that follows after those events.

In ʿUthmān's case, the authors have a positive wealth of information, anecdotes, *akhbār*, and *aḥādīth* from which to craft their presentations. In terms of the narrative, however, there are three key moments ("set-up stories," in Keshk's parlance) that serve to give the assassination its meaning. The first is, of course, the moment of ʿUthmān's election. Like Muʿāwiya's appointment of his son Yazīd, the meaning of the end of ʿUthmān's political career and life is most directly established by the nature of his election: the contentious *shūrā*. Next is the presentation of ʿUthmān's reign: the cliché that he had six good years followed by six bad years. Finally, there is a moment that comes after the assassination, and one which is most often appended to the Ṣiffīn episode: the display of ʿUthmān's bloody shirt and Nāʾila's severed fingers on the stage in Damascus as

4 Ibid. 76.

Muʿāwiya works the *ahl al-Shām* into a state of vengeful agitation. As always, we will examine these episodes in reverse chronological order.

The stakes for this moment are obviously high. They are:

1. *The meaning of ʿUthmān's death*: Although, from the standpoint of the linear narrative, the assassination of ʿUthmān may seem like the undercard to the main event between ʿAlī and Muʿāwiya, it should be borne in mind that his assassination was a far more jarring event for the early Islamic community than was the assassination of his predecessor, ʿUmar ibn al-Khaṭṭāb. ʿUmar's death was tragic for the community; deeply shocking and horrifying though it was, the community did not respond to it by descending into a civil war. The *shūrā* that ultimately elected ʿUthmān was more analogous to a minor constitutional procedural predicament than an existential crisis. ʿUthmān's death, on the other hand, was fraught with political peril. ʿUmar had been killed by the Persian slave Fīrūz; ʿUmar is even reported to have had the time, on his deathbed, to thank God that his killer was not a Muslim. ʿUthmān had no time to offer such a prayer, nor did he have occasion. The Muslims who killed him were close associates of ʿAlī, one of the two most powerful men in *dār al-islām*. The other most powerful man in the *umma*, of course, was ʿUthmān's cousin Muʿāwiya, who had the twin benefits of noble Meccan blood and the army of al-Shām. The assassination of ʿUthmān was the opening of a Pandora's box in more ways than one: beyond its role as a catalyst for the ʿAlī-Muʿāwiya *fitna*, ʿUthmān's death was the first political assassination in Islamic history. It would not be the last.
2. *The legitimacy of ʿAlī's reign:* ʿAlī's legitimacy is denied by neither Sunnīs nor, obviously, Shīʿa. To Shīʿa, ʿAlī was the first Imam and the rightful successor to the Prophet; to Sunnīs, ʿAlī was the fourth of the *rāshidūn*, the "rightly-guided" caliphs. He is therefore "claimed" by both communities, although there is a significant amount of disagreement over the nature and meaning of his career. The permissibility of ʿUthmān's death, and ʿAlī's relationship to it, provide the immediate context for his ascension.
3. *The legitimacy of Muʿāwiya's grievance:* Muʿāwiya is not exactly the most malevolent moustache-twirling stock villain of the early Islamic narrative—that dishonor probably goes either to his father Abū Sufyān or his son Yazīd—but he is a distinct and probably unchallenged third. As the patriarch of the Sufyānid line who happens to alive at the moment of the narrative when the *fitna* breaks out, he serves the primary antagonistic function within both the Sunnī and Shīʿī narratives, and is the best-developed character of the three. As the founder of the Umayyad dynasty,

he is almost a synecdoche for it; his grand entrance into the story's center ring carries with it the narrative opportunity to characterize the very dynasty itself.

4. *ʿUthmān:* The character of ʿUthmān ibn ʿAffān, for all his centrality in the *fitna* story and the overall narrative battleground aligned along Sunnī-Shīʿī fault lines, was the product of a series of significant historiographical projects in its own right. The assassination of ʿUthmān "marked the end of the religio-political balance established by Muhammad and inaugurated the debate over and quest for authentic Islamic government."[5] Keaney argues that "the two sides in the revolt [against ʿUthmān] came to represent in Islamic collective memory and political discourse some of the key tensions in the pursuit of Islamic government—namely, religious versus political authority and preserving unity versus preserving justice."[6] She explains, "medieval Muslim historians debated the tensions arising from competing religio-political ideals and the disparity between these ideals and contemporary realities by continually reinterpreting" the character of ʿUthmān.[7] Keaney's earlier monograph deftly traces ʿUthmān's character from the ninth through the fourteenth centuries CE and demonstrates how contemporary concerns influenced the extent to which the historians treated ʿUthmān sympathetically. Unsurprisingly, earlier sources like Ibn Saʿd focus on ʿUthmān's avarice and nepotism,[8] while later historians like Ibn Kathīr shift the blame for the troubles of his reign to the incompetence of his representatives and governors.[9] ʿUthmān, in other words, is a controversial figure in his own right, and a strong case can be made (as Keaney's study does) that the assassination of ʿUthmān, rather than the battle of Karbalāʾ, is the center of the historiographical body exerting its narrative gravitational pull both forward and backward chronologically. What makes Karbalāʾ a better choice for the present study is its decisiveness. Whether or not it is accurate to say that the historical Karbalāʾ was the sectarian Rubicon of Islamic history, Ibn al-Athīr and Ibn Kathīr understood it as such. ʿUthmān's career, for all its thematic resonance on the issues that would come to divide Sunnīs from Shīʿa, left

5 Keaney, *Medieval Islamic Historiography* 1.

6 Ibid. 1.

7 Ibid. 1.

8 Ibid. 29; see also Muḥammad ibn Saʿd, *Kitāb al-Ṭabaqāt al-kabīr*, eds. Joseph Horovitz and Edward Sachan (Leiden: E.J. Brill, 1904), 39.

9 Keaney, *Medieval Islamic Historiography* 123; see also Heather Keaney, *ʿUthman ibn ʿAffan: Legend Or Liability?* (London: OneWorld, 2021); and Ibn Kathīr, *Bidāya* vii, 196.

time in the narrative for those rifts to be healed. To be fair, for anyone reading one of these accounts with knowledge of what comes next, the narrative at this point generally feels like a runaway train: the *fitna* feels inevitable, as ʿAlī's dependence on ʿUthmān's killers and Muʿāwiya justifiable desire for justice are on a collision course. But the emergence of Shīʿism as a sect distinct from Sunnīsm was not centered around these events; the murder of ʿUthmān provides the "set-up" for the confrontation between ʿAlī and Muʿāwiya, and the subsequent betrayal of ʿAlī (and then his descendants). Karbalāʾ, not the assassination of ʿUthmān, is the "and now you know the rest of the story" moment. Even so, ʿUthmān is an important historiographical battleground, and "winning" the battle for his character is an indispensable piece of presenting Karbalāʾ's meaning properly.

5 Six Good Years and Six Bad Years: The Caliphate of ʿUthmān ibn ʿAffān

5.1 *The ʿUthmān Interlude*

Before Muʿāwiya could demand revenge for the murdered caliph, his kinsman, the assassination of ʿUthmān ibn ʿAffān, the third of the Sunnī *rāshidūn* caliphs, had to be contextualized. To some extent, what he did while in office—the key narrative site for creating a picture of ʿUthmān's character—is not as important as the means by which he got elected, which will be discussed in detail in the next section. The stakes for ʿUthmān's actual time in office, therefore, are low when compared to even moderately important sites of memory, namely any spot in which there is a transition from one leader to another. The elections and assumptions of the office of these caliphs brings up many more of the divisive communal issues, including political and spiritual legitimacy, than do the actual political careers of those in office. ʿUthmān's career is no exception.

That does not mean that Ibn al-Athīr's and Ibn Kathīr's performances of ʿUthmān's time in office were dull. Even with lower stakes relative to Karbalāʾ, ʿUthmān's character is every bit as contentious when it comes to Sunnī and Shīʿī narratives as is his election and his assassination. The lowered stakes, however, make the prize for "winning" the site of ʿUthmān's character decidedly more abstract than the prize for "winning" Ṣiffīn or, especially, Karbalāʾ. ʿUthmān could be a "good" leader without undermining the central Shīʿī claim that he had wrongfully usurped the leadership of the community from ʿAlī or, more accurately, that he had been just one of a series of usurpers. His contributions to the community could theoretically be ungrudgingly related without conceding the legitimacy of the very notion of the caliphate. On the flip side, ʿUthmān could be a "bad" caliph—and could be presented as such by a Sunnī historian—without casting any aspersions on his legitimacy, or asserting the righteousness of those who rebelled against him. Nonetheless, ʿUthmān's murder, and the questions surrounding his murderers, could not be presented without profound consequences for both ʿAlī's time as caliph and Muʿāwiya's actions against him. Neither, for that matter, can the episode of his election be related without the performance of that episode impacting the question of the rightness or wrongness of his murder. The twelve years of ʿUthmān's reign, therefore, are window dressing to the sites of memory that have a genuine impact on the narrative.

Perhaps nothing attests to the narrative inconsequentiality of ʿUthmān's actual career in office greater than the almost universal brevity of its treatment. After an introduction to ʿUthmān himself, a report of his speech and some of his significant appointments of governors, al-Ṭabarī spends about as much text on ʿUthmān's entire reign as he does on important singular events, like the Battle of Ṣiffīn. His presentation is interspersed with stories of various conquests and wars (against Adharbayjān and Armenia,[10] Ṭabaristān,[11] and Byzantium,[12] especially), and mostly seems concerned with moving characters around the expanding empire, placing them where they need to be for what follows. ʿUthmān's appointment of Abū Mūsā al-Ashʿarī, who will play such a decisive role (or perhaps it would be more apt to say that he will play such an *in*decisive role) at Ṣiffīn, as governor of Baṣra places him where he needs to be; his appointment of the inept Saʿd ibn Abī Waqqāṣ over Kūfa serves as a prologue to that city's role in the events that are to come. But there is no narrative battleground to be fought and won: no high-stakes moment, rife with narrative consequences, for al-Ṭabarī or his later colleagues to ensure conveys the proper meaning. This is not to say that the events of ʿUthmān's reign were inconsequential. Indeed, the list of conquests under his rule is impressive indeed, and the canonization of the Qurʾān (which is remembered to have been one of his primary contributions to Islamic civilization) is of unquestionable importance. Still, there is nothing to fight over. ʿUthmān's reign serves the narrative as naught but exposition.

It probably comes as no surprise that Ibn al-Athīr's account of his time as caliph is even more succinct, with Ibn Kathīr's account even briefer still. Al-

10 Al-Ṭabarī, *Taʾrīkh* ii, 591–593.

11 Ibid. ii, 607–608.

12 Ibid. ii, 618–626.

Ṭabarī, Ibn al-Athīr, and Ibn Kathīr are not alone in this narrative strategy related to ʿUthmān's time in office. As Keaney points out, silence is the general treatment ʿUthmān receives, as Ibn Khayyāt records only the conquests and Ibn Saʿd skips straight from the *shūrā* to the list of charges against ʿUthmān at the time of the revolt, eliding his caliphate entirely.[13] Al-Balādhūrī's *Ansāb al-Ashrāf* takes a different tactic, painstakingly detailing every single abuse.[14] However, al-Balādhūrī's narrative mission in compiling *The Genealogies of the Notables* was to catalog rather than narrate. The fact that the minutiae exist in *Ansāb al-Ashrāf*, but are omitted from the synthetic narratives we are discussing, demonstrates clearly that it was not for lack of knowledge of what happened that ʿUthmān's time as caliph is presented in such scanty terms.

5.2 *ʿUthmān's Alteration of the Pilgrimage Rites*

One anecdote may serve to demonstrate the modes of narrative performance undertaken by Ibn al-Athīr and Ibn Kathīr when confronted with an inconvenient script. As just described, ʿUthmān's entire executive career is essentially effaced by the later historians. In the year 29 AH, al-Ṭabarī tells us, ʿUthmān altered the pilgrimage rights. The originator of the report is al-Wāqidī:

> The people first spoke openly about ʿUthmān when he prayed two *rakʿa* prayers at Minā during his reign. During the sixth year of his reign he completed the prayers with an additional two prayers. More than one of the Prophet's companions took exception to that. This was discussed by those who wished to make trouble for him, until ʿAlī came to [ʿUthmān] with some others. [ʿAlī] said to him, "By God, there is no command, either new or old, to [say the *rakʿa* four times]. You have witnessed your Prophet pray only two *rakʿa* prayers. Then Abū Bakr and ʿUmar did the same, as did you at the beginning of your reign. I do not know upon what basis you have [added two extra prayers]!" [ʿUthmān] said, "It is my own personal opinion."[15]

There follows, in al-Ṭabarī's history, a similar interchange between ʿUthmān and ʿAbd al-Raḥmān ibn ʿAwf—who, as we will see in the next section, will be recognizable to the reader as the man most directly responsible for ensuring that ʿUthmān, rather than ʿAlī, would succeed the assassinated ʿUmar ibn

13 Keaney, *Medieval Islamic Historiography* 35.
14 Ibid. 36.
15 Al-Ṭabarī, *Taʾrīkh* ii, 606.

al-Khaṭṭāb as Islam's third caliph. It is noteworthy, in that regard, that ʿAbd al-Raḥmān would express any concern about what can only be described as ʿUthmān's ritual *bidʿa*:

> [When] someone came to ʿAbd al-Raḥmān ibn ʿAwf and said, "Have you heard about your brother [in-law]? He prayed four *rakʿa* prayers!" ʿAbd al-Raḥmān and his companions then prayed two *rakʿa* prayers, and then he set out to see ʿUthmān. He said to him, "Did you not pray [only] two *rakʿa* prayers in this very place with the Messenger of God?" He said, "Yes, I did." [ʿAbd al-Raḥmān] continued, "And did you not pray [only] two *rakʿa* prayers with Abū Bakr?" He said, "Yes, I did." [ʿAbd al-Raḥmān then] said, "And the same with ʿUmar?" Again, he answered "Yes." He said, "And did you not pray [only] two *rakʿa* prayers at the outset of your caliphate?" He said, "Yes." [Then ʿUthmān] said, "Abū Muḥammad, listen to me. I was told that some of the Yemenis and the poorly-educated pilgrims last year said, 'The proper prayer is two *rakʿa*s for the resident, and here is your imam ʿUthmān praying two *rakʿa*s.' In Mecca, I have family, and I decided it would be best to pray four *rakʿa*s because of my fear for the people. Also, I have taken a wife there, and I have some property in al-Ṭā'if, and sometimes I stay there after the day of return from the pilgrimage." ʿAbd al-Raḥmān ibn ʿAwf said, "None of this is any excuse. You say that you have family there, but your wife is in Medina, and she comes and goes as you wish. As for your property in al-Ṭā'if, it is a three-night journey [from Mecca], and you are not a resident of al-Ṭā'if."[16]

ʿAbd al-Raḥmān then reiterates the importance of following the precedent set by the Prophet, Abū Bakr, and ʿUmar, with ʿUthmān again replying, "It is my own personal opinion." Al-Ṭabarī continues:

> ʿAbd al-Raḥmān left and met up with Ibn Masʿūd, who said, "Abū Muḥammad, is what we have heard untrue?" [ʿAbd al-Raḥmān] said, "No." Then Ibn Masʿud said, "Then what should I do?" He answered, "You must do what you know [is right]." Ibn Masʿūd said, "Disagreement is evil. Word has reached me that he prayed four times, and so my companions and I prayed four times." Then ʿAbd al-Raḥmān said, "Word has reached me that he prayed four times, but my companions and I prayed two. But from now on I shall do as you say—that is, we, like him, shall pray four times."[17]

---

16 Ibid. ii, 606.
17 Ibid. ii, 606.

Ibn al-Athīr relates a summarized version of 'Uthmān's interaction with 'Abd al-Raḥmān. Ibn Kathīr presents an even more abbreviated account. For both, abbreviation seems to be the tactic of choice when it comes to 'Uthmān's time as caliph. This is because 'Uthmān is a character both Ibn al-Athīr and Ibn Kathīr would like to rehabilitate (and the details, such as they are, in al-Ṭabarī's narrative are inconvenient in that regard), and because the narrative stakes are so low. After all, as 'Abd al-Raḥmān's final reaction to 'Uthmān's four *rak'a* prayers shows, the important lesson of 'Uthmān's career is that a ruler—good or bad—must be obeyed. 'Abd al-Raḥmān even makes this point explicit, as his opinion changes from "do what you know is right" to "we must follow the leader, even if he is in error" at the conclusion of the *khabar*. The notion that 'Uthmān was actually a good and virtuous ruler seems to be unconquerable territory for Ibn al-Athīr and Ibn Kathīr, and irrelevant besides. The critical characteristic to establish for 'Uthmān's narrative is whether his assassination was or was not illegal. We explored the consequences of that question's answers in the previous chapter: the legality or illegality of 'Uthmān's assassination fundamentally changes the meaning of Ṣiffīn, the Umayyad dynasty, Karbalā', and Sunnīsm and Shī'ism themselves. For 'Uthmān's assassination to have the proper narrative function, it is not his time as caliph that plays any decisive role. Rather, it is his legitimacy to be in office in the first place that will dictate the legality of this assassination.

For that, the authors must establish the legality or illegality of his selection as caliph. Of course, the other candidate was none other than 'Alī ibn Abī Ṭālib, and the means of selection were reported by al-Ṭabarī to be irregular, both in the nature of the electoral process and in the way in which the process played itself out politically. 'Abd al-Raḥmān ibn 'Awf—seen here dreadfully concerned that 'Uthmān is leading the people down the wrong ritual path—plays a decisive role in the *shūrā*, or electoral council, charged by 'Umar with selecting from among its six members the second caliph's successor. The *shūrā* is territory whose capture carries with it critical narrative victories.

CHAPTER 9

The *Shūrā* of ʿUthmān

1 Introduction

The question of ʿUthmān's legitimacy clearly hung over his entire twelve-year reign like a storm cloud, and that uncertainty winds its way all the way through the remainder of the early Islamic narrative tapestry like a loose thread. If that thread is pulled out of the narrative, everything that follows loses its meaning. Since what follows is of such critical importance, establishing ʿUthmān's legitimacy or nonlegitimacy has profound consequences for the remainder of the story.

If ʿUthmān's reign was legitimate, then it follows that the readers were meant to consider the rebellion against him as unjustified, especially when one takes into account the ubiquitous Sunnī notion that "a bad leader is better than no leader," which, as we saw, served as the theoretical underpinnings of ʿAmr ibn al-ʿĀṣ' big moment at Ṣiffīn, in which he confirmed Muʿāwiya as caliph by default after tricking Abū Mūsa al-Ashʿarī into announcing ʿAlī's removal. ʿUthmān's murder becomes not a course correction for an errant community but rather another nail in the coffin of communal unity, leading to the *fitna* that is to come. Establishing ʿUthmān's legitimacy in office would also mean that Muʿāwiya would be justified in taking up arms against ʿAlī; it would follow that the Battle of Ṣiffīn, while regrettable, was a conflict between two "right" sides (though Sunnī and Shīʿa alike would assert that the Khawārij sealed their eternal damnation there). ʿAmr ibn al-ʿĀṣ appoints a reasonable candidate to a vacant post at the Dūmat al-Jandal arbitration scene, and while there remains a few years of cold conflict between the Dūmat al-Jandal and his generally accepted start as the first Umayyad caliph, it is eminently sensible that Muʿāwiya take over after ʿAlī's death. With Muʿāwiya's "rightness" established, his assumption of the caliphate, filling the power vacuum left when ʿAlī met his end at the hands of one of the Khawārij, becomes acceptable, and his appointment of his son as his successor becomes a rightfully legal, if distasteful, attempt to ensure the stability of the *umma* following his impending death. Yazīd almost becomes just another ruler instead of a villain; al-Ḥusayn becomes a rebel against a legitimate, if subpar, ruler; and Karbalāʾ, like Ṣiffīn, becomes a (very) regrettable conflict between two "rights." It follows, if that is the nature of Karbalāʾ, that the Shīʿī overvenerate ʿAlī and al-Ḥusayn both, and are manifestly wrong in their theology, *fiqh*, and practice.

 | DOI:10.1163/9789004524255_011

On the other hand, if ʿUthmān's reign was not legitimate, the very same events take on an entirely different cast. The rebellion against ʿUthmān becomes a course correction, and his murder, while regrettable, becomes justified. Muʿāwiya would not have been justified, therefore, in taking up arms against the rightful ruler, ʿAlī, and Ṣiffīn becomes a conflict where there is a right side (ʿAlī), a wrong side (Muʿāwiya), and a treacherous side (the Khawārij). ʿAmr ibn al-ʿĀṣ's tricky double-speak at the Dūmat al-Jandal arbitration scene is nothing but the cynical (and borderline sophomoric) exploitation of a problematic and dubious loophole, which does not thereby establish Muʿāwiya's legitimacy. ʿAlī's murder thereby becomes an extra-perfidious act, and Muʿāwiya's assumption of the duties of caliph becomes an act of outright usurpation. That act of usurpation colors the legitimacy of his entire dynasty (with ʿUmar ibn ʿAbd al-Azīz ever the pious exception that proves the impious Umayyad rule), including, especially, his son Yazīd. Yazīd, now an illegitimate ruler, illegally appointed by his equally illegitimate father, has al-Ḥusayn's small band of rebels snuffed out to eliminate the pious example that gives his regime out as unlawful and wicked. In this version of the narrative, ʿAlī and al-Ḥusayn are pious heroes and leaders, lighting the proper path for the *umma* to follow. Shīʿī veneration of those men (and their special descendants and relatives) becomes proper, and these narrative consequences make Shīʿī theology, *fiqh*, and practice manifestly right.

A lot, in other words, hinges on the question of whether ʿUthmān belonged in the executive role in the first place. This is not the only such moment with such high stakes. There are opportunities for course corrections later in the narrative, and we have already discussed these; they include Ṣiffīn and the Battle of Karbalāʾ itself (although by the time one gets to Karbalāʾ, its narrative meaning is more or less established by these events that came before it). In general, the question of legitimacy is settled by examining the means of selection, and the authors' opinions on those means determines the legitimacy of the elected ruler. Appointment by the previous rightful ruler is generally considered acceptable; therefore, if one accepts Abū Bakr as the rightful successor to the Prophet Muḥammad, Abū Bakr's appointment of ʿUmar raises no eyebrows. This is also why Sunnīs and Shīʿa argue so vociferously about Ghadīr Khumm, the famous *ḥadīth* in which the Prophet is said to have named ʿAlī as his successor.[1] Neither Sunnīs nor Shīʿa dispute the validity such an appointment

1 The Prophet is reputed to have said "man kuntu mawlahu fa-ʿAlī mawlahu," which means "he whose *mawla* I am, ʿAlī is [also] his *mawla*," which Shīʿa took to be a declaration of the Prophet's desire that ʿAlī succeed him. The Sunnīs obviously had different interpretations, including that this was a declaration of esteem and affection rather than a political appoint-

would have had if it were true; Sunnīs dispute the veracity of the *ḥadīth* itself, in full knowledge that its authentication, to oversimplify the matter, would verify the central Shīʿī claims about the succession, legitimacy, and the very course of early Islamic history. Acclamation by the community is accepted by Sunnīs, but not Shīʿa (this allows Sunnīs to consider Abū Bakr's reign legitimate, despite a lack of explicit Prophetic endorsement); on the other side, the Shīʿa maintain that descent from ʿAlī (and sometimes Fāṭima), and the spiritual qualities of *nass* and *ʿilm*, are the sole arbiters of proper rulership for all would-be imams after ʿAlī.

This makes ʿUthmān's election a vitally important narrative theater for Ibn al-Athīr and Ibn Kathīr. ʿUthmān was elected by a *shūrā*—an "electoral council" of six men appointed by ʿUmar ibn al-Khaṭṭāb as he lay mortally wounded, charged to select one from among their number to serve as caliph upon ʿUmar's looming death. Through a process we will explore shortly, two candidates emerge as the favorites, and the other four men become kingmakers. Of course, those two finalists are ʿAlī ibn Abī Ṭālib and ʿUthmān ibn ʿAffān. Ultimately, ʿUthmān is selected, and the rest is narrative.

A staunch Shīʿī would have no trouble rejecting ʿUthmān's selection as proper grounds for establishing his legitimacy. To the Shīʿa, ʿUthmān is ineligible for the office by virtue of his lack of Prophetic endorsement. He is also unsuited for the office by virtue of his more unsavory personal characteristics (which were highly developed aspects of his characterization) and improperly chosen through an illegitimate electoral process initiated by a usurper. In this context, the notion that ʿUthmān's successful manipulation of this situation grants him any legitimacy seems laughable. Had ʿAlī emerged from this process as the victor, and the community united behind his leadership, it is highly likely that Shīʿism as such would never have needed to develop. Historians would have presented ʿAlī's electoral victory in this process as the notables of the community wisely (finally) acknowledging his rightful authority, established at the time of the Prophet's death, and putting the errant community back on the right course. The narrative might have written Abū Bakr and ʿUmar off as the early (and perhaps understandable) missteps of a community struggling to live rightly in a post-Prophetic world. The rest of the narrative would have been indelibly changed.

---

ment. For a useful biography on Ghadīr Khumm, see Arzina Lalani, "Ghadir Khumm," *Oxford Bibliographies in Islamic Studies*, ed. Andrew Rippin, https://www.oxfordbibliographies.com/view/document/obo-9780195390155/obo-9780195390155-0105.xml (accessed June 5, 2022). For a Shīʿī perspective, see Hassan Abbas, *The Prophet's Heir: The Life of Ali ibn Abi Talib* (New Haven: Yale University Press, 2021), esp. 71–91.

Of course, that is not what is remembered to have happened. Ibn al-Athīr and Ibn Kathīr were compelled to find a way to make ʿUthmān's election legitimate; if they could not, the foundation for their entire narrative enterprise sinks. There is no opportunity to change the major facts of this narrative; it is far too famous. There is also no argument that they can make that will convince a Shīʿī-sympathizing reader that this process was appropriate (although they will of course maintain that position). To make this narrative serve their larger objective, Ibn al-Athīr and Ibn Kathīr must begin what they have already continued during the Ṣiffīn narrative: they must appropriate ʿAlī's character and make him speak for them. ʿAlī is like the king in a game of narrative chess: because so much of Shīʿī historical memory rests upon his character, cornering and manipulating his character itself becomes a cheap, though relatively effective, means of undercutting all the other Shīʿī narrative claims.

2 Narrating the *Shūrā*

The elements of the *shūrā* narrative have been explored elsewhere,[2] but bear repeating. The narrative begins with the mortal wounding of ʿUmar ibn al-Khaṭṭāb, who selects six men to choose from among themselves a worthy successor. They are ʿAlī ibn Abī Ṭālib, ʿUthmān ibn ʿAffān (who emerge as the two front-runners), Saʿd ibn Abī Waqqās, al-Zubayr ibn al-ʿAwwām, Ṭalḥa ibn ʿUbayd Allāh (these last two to be ʿAlī's opponents at the Battle of the Camel), and ʿAbd al-Raḥmān ibn ʿAwf. When it becomes clear that the choice will be between ʿAlī and ʿUthmān, the other members of the *shūrā* are divided. Al-Ṭabarī reports that al-Zubayr declared his support for ʿAlī, Ṭalḥā declared his support for ʿUthmān, and Saʿd declared his support for ʿAbd al-Raḥmān. ʿAbd al-Raḥmān, sensing an opportunity, withdrew from consideration and, with the assurance of Saʿd's support of whichever candidate he would choose, quickly positioned himself in the kingmaker role. Now, and for the duration of the affair, ʿAbd al-Raḥmān became the most powerful man in the Islamic world: he alone had the clout to select ʿUmar's successor. As we will see, ʿAbd al-Raḥmān's motives are not uniformly presented across the narratives but are critical to the story. If ʿUthmān's legitimacy or illegitimacy as a ruler is the foundation upon which the wars fought by and against ʿAlī and al-Ḥusayn acquire their meanings, and his election is the fundamental determinant of that legitimacy, that electoral process is immediately one of the higher-

2 Leder, "Paradigmatic Character"; see also Hagler, "Sapping the Narrative" esp. 307–309.

stakes moments of the entire narrative. Now, the entire procedure's legitimacy rests upon ʿAbd al-Raḥmān ibn ʿAwf's reasons for selecting ʿUthmān over ʿAlī.

Performing the narrative in such a way as to make it appear "above board" on its own terms—assuming, as any Sunnī would, that the process itself was not inherently corrupted—would still not win over a single Shīʿī reader. The establishment of ʿAbd al-Raḥmān's "appropriate" motives might only convince an ʿAlī-sympathizing Sunnī, at best. It will be in the treatment of ʿAlī, and especially his reaction to the disappointment of losing, that Ibn al-Athīr and Ibn Kathīr will be able to undermine the Shīʿī narrative. Al-Ṭabarī, their script's writer, is not a Shīʿī, but his vilification of the Umayyads means that he has no need to soften the ambiguity of ʿUthmān's election, ʿAbd al-Raḥmān's motives, or ʿAlī's reaction. This means that, while the elements of the *shūrā* narrative—what Leder calls "subnarrations," and which have been referred to in the present study, in other contexts, as sites of memory—must remain constant, Ibn al-Athīr's and Ibn Kathīr's performances of these elements of the story will directly challenge the meaning implied by al-Ṭabarī's version.

3 ʿAbd al-Raḥmān ibn ʿAwf: Cynical or Sincere?

Otherwise a relatively minor character in the narrative, the impact of ʿAbd al-Raḥmān ibn ʿAwf (d. 32/652–653) on the Islamic narrative might be less only than central characters, like the Prophet Muḥammad, ʿUthmān, ʿAlī, Muʿāwiya, and al-Ḥusayn. He was an early convert and Companion of the Prophet, taking part in the emigration of the earliest Muslims to Ethiopia, thereafter joining the Prophet in Medina and taking part in the Battles of Badr and Uḥud. He worked to convert the tribes of Dūmat al-Jandal to Islam, supported the reign of Abū Bakr, and expressed reticence about ʿUmar as Abū Bakr's successor, but still served him as a trusted advisor. Despite his appointment of ʿUthmān during the *shūrā* narrative, he is later supposed to have come to regret his choice. He was also one of the ten whom the Prophet Muḥammad predicted would join him in Paradise.[3]

When it became clear that ʿAlī, ʿUthmān, and ʿAbd al-Raḥmān each enjoyed the support of one of their fellow committee members, ʿAbd al-Raḥmān played his hand. The following is related in al-Ṭabarī's account:

---

3 Wilferd Madelung, "ʿAbd al-Raḥmān b. ʿAwf," in *EI*³, consulted online on October 31, 2017, http://dx.doi.org.du.idm.oclc.org/10.1163/1573-3912_ei3_COM_24664.

> ʿAbd al-Raḥmān said, "Which one of you will withdraw from this, and agree to appoint the best of you?" No one answered. So he said, "Then I withdraw." ʿUthmān said, "I am the first to accept [this]. I heard the Messenger of God say, '(ʿAbd al-Raḥmān) is trustworthy on earth and will be in heaven.'" The group said, "We agree to this," but ʿAlī remained silent. So (ʿAbd al-Raḥmān) said, "What do you say, Abū al-Ḥasan?" (ʿAlī) replied, "Give me your word you will consider truth paramount, you will not follow your whim, you will not show any preference for a relative, and you will not let the community down." (ʿAbd al-Raḥmān) said [to the others], "Give me your solemn promises that you will stand with me against anyone who reneges [on my final decision] and you will approve of anyone I choose for you. I impose a pact with God upon myself that I will show no preference for a relative, because he is a relative, nor shall I let down the Muslims."[4]

ʿAlī's rather pointed demand that ʿAbd al-Raḥmān foreswear any nepotism gets right to the heart of the matter when it comes to ʿAbd al-Raḥmān's motives. His connections to ʿUthmān and the Umayyads were many. His father, ʿAwf, had been a trading partner of ʿUthmān's father, ʿAffān; the two had even died together during a raid by the Banū Jasīma.[5] ʿAbd al-Raḥmān, not coincidentally, was also married to Umm Kulthūm bint ʿUtba, a half-sister of ʿUthmān.

Ibn al-Athīr carefully prunes al-Ṭabarī's narrative of any indication that ʿAbd al-Raḥmān was consciously aware of his familial connections to ʿUthmān. He cannot omit that element of the story from his narrative; it is too important. The selection from al-Ṭabarī, quoted above, is repeated by Ibn al-Athīr, with the exception of his omission of the line "I heard the Messenger of God say, '(ʿAbd al-Raḥmān) is trustworthy on earth and will be in heaven.'" One would almost think the two men had not known each other since childhood.

However, this change is a small one. Nowhere in Ibn al-Athīr's account of the *shūrā* is it ever made explicit that ʿUthmān and ʿAbd al-Raḥmān are relatives—or, incidentally, that Saʿd ibn Abī Waqqās is related to both of them, which he is. In fact, when the matter comes up, Ibn al-Athīr takes pains to erase it. *Al-Kāmil* continues in an identical manner to al-Ṭabarī's *Taʾrīkh*. The electoral preferences of each member of the council becomes clear; al-Zubayr is for ʿAlī, and Ṭalḥā is for ʿUthmān. Clearly learning in ʿUthmān's direction, ʿAbd al-Raḥmān has but one person to convince: the last member of the *shūrā*, Saʿd ibn

4 Al-Ṭabarī, *Taʾrīkh* ii, 582.
5 Madelung, "ʿAbd al-Raḥmān b. ʿAwf."

Abī Waqqāṣ, who is reticent about supporting ʿUthmān. ʿAbd al-Raḥmān was aware that Saʿd had the power to cancel out his vote for ʿUthmān and deadlock the council, so he worked to convince him. Al-Ṭabarī writes that moment as follows: "ʿAbd al-Raḥmān said to Saʿd [b. Abī Waqqāṣ], 'We are cousins [*anā wa-anta kalāla*]. Throw in your lot with me so that I can choose' [*ijʿal naṣībaka lī fa-khtārū*]. [Saʿd] replied, 'If you choose yourself, that is fine! But if you would choose ʿUthmān, then [know that] I prefer to support ʿAlī.'"[6] Here is Ibn al-Athīr's performance of that moment: "ʿAbd al-Raḥmān said to Saʿd [b. Abī Waqqāṣ], 'Throw in your lot with me' [*ijʿal naṣībaka lī*]. [Saʿd] replied, 'If you choose yourself, that is fine! But if you would choose ʿUthmān, then [know that] I prefer to support ʿAlī.'"[7] Ibn al-Athīr has removed a grand total of four Arabic words from the narrative: "We are cousins" [*anā wa-anta kalāla*] and "so that I can choose" [*fa-khtārū*]. By erasing these words, Ibn al-Athīr has not eliminated the notion that there was a concern about nepotism—after all, he let ʿAlī's demand for ʿAbd al-Raḥmān's oath to avoid a nepotistic decision stand. However, he has successfully eliminated the notion that ʿAbd al-Raḥmān himself was aware of any nepotism, or that he was using his family connections unduly to manipulate the electoral process. The omission of the word *fa-khtaru* (so that I can choose) means that, when Saʿd, shortly thereafter, consents to abide by ʿAbd al-Raḥmān's decision, he does so as an equal elector casting his own vote, and not as a man who has given his vote away to his cousin.

This is not the only omission Ibn al-Athīr makes from this section. He also omits any notion that ʿAbd al-Raḥmān had any ambition for power himself, thus allowing him to be presented as a kingmaker unsullied by personal ambition.[8] The cloud of nepotism continues to hang over the election of ʿUthmān. However, with these very subtly altered performances of al-Ṭabarī's narrative, Ibn al-Athīr has turned ʿAbd al-Raḥmān's selection of ʿUthmān from a cynical act of political opportunism into the sincere, if imperfect, selection of his preferred candidate.

---

6 Al-Ṭabarī, *Taʾrīkh* ii, 582.

7 Ibn al-Athīr, *Kāmil* ii, 463.

8 Ibn al-Athīr, *Kāmil* ii, 463; and al-Ṭabarī, *Taʾrīkh* ii, 582: Ibn al-Athīr omits a reply by Saʿd ibn Abī Waqqāṣ to ʿAbd al-Raḥmān ibn ʿAwf, where the former states: "I am afraid that weakness has overcome you. Do as you think best. You know what ʿUmar's death bed instructions were;" and Ibn al-Athīr, *Kāmil* v. 2, 463 and al-Ṭabarī, *Taʾrīkh* v. 2, 583, where Ibn al-Athīr omits a brief exchange between Saʿīd ibn Zayd and ʿAbd al-Raḥmān, in which Saʿīd asserts his preference for ʿAbd al-Raḥmān, who demurs. Both omissions reject the notion that ʿAbd al-Raḥmān himself had any support, or that he may have coveted personal power, thus eliminating from Ibn al-Athīr's narrative any hint of a potential ʿAbd al-Raḥmān caliphal term of office.

4 ʿAlī's Reactions: Playing the Wild Card

Al-Ṭabarī's description of the moment when ʿAbd al-Raḥmān establishes himself as the deciding vote is notable for ʿAlī's reticence. First, he remains silent when ʿAbd al-Raḥmān makes his proposal, despite the assent of the other four members of the *shūrā*; then, he extracts an oath from ʿAbd al-Raḥmān ibn ʿAwf to abstain from nepotism. While Ibn al-Athīr leaves this section alone and simply repeat's al-Ṭabarī's words (with the exception of omitting ʿUthmān's effusive statement of praise for ʿAbd al-Raḥmān) Ibn Kathīr changes the meaning by playing with the timing:

> The situation became such that three of [the members of the council] were responsible for choosing [the new caliph] from among the remaining three [members]. Al-Zubayr sought to empower ʿAlī; Saʿd [ibn Abī Waqqāṣ], who was not under consideration, sought to empower ʿAbd al-Raḥmān ibn ʿAwf; and Ṭalḥā supported ʿUthmān ibn ʿAffān, may God be pleased with him. So, ʿAbd al-Raḥmān said to ʿAlī and ʿUthmān, "Which of you will withdraw from the matter, and undertake to appoint the better of you?" Both ʿAli and ʿUthman remained silent, until ʿAbd al-Raḥmān said, "I renounce my claim in this matter, and by God I will appoint one of you two." Then, they both said yes! Then each one of them spoke, and each one made a case for his appointment by discussing his own virtues, and then they each took a vow to abide by [ʿAbd al-Raḥmān's] decision.[9]

Where al-Ṭabarī emphasized that ʿUthmān was "the first to agree" (using ʿUthmān's own words), thereby giving the appearance of a secret *a priori* wink-and-handshake agreement between him and ʿAbd al-Raḥmān, Ibn Kathīr's use of the dual form of the verb q-w-l, *qālā naʿm!* (They both said yes), implies ʿAlī's willingness, and the omission of his extraction of the anti-nepotism oath confirms that Ibn Kathīr has no desire to perform those aspects of his script. It is a small change, to be sure; however, the implications of the change are deeply significant to the meaning of the moment. Ibn Kathīr's ʿAlī agrees to the process without qualification; nowhere in Ibn Kathīr's narrative does ʿAlī extract any sort of anti-nepotism oath from ʿAbd al-Raḥmān. All three men deal with the issue of nepotism in one way or another. Al-Ṭabarī addresses it and flat out asserts that ʿAbd al-Raḥmān appointed ʿUthmān because of their relationship. Ibn al-Athīr allows the question of nepotism to remain in the nar-

9 Ibn Kathir, *Bidāya* vii, 141.

rative but removes any suggestion that it was the ʿAbd al-Raḥmān's primary concern (or a factor of which ʿAbd al-Raḥmān was even conscious). Ibn Kathīr skates by the whole issue with a performance that provides the critical factual information—"they both said yes," an agreement from both parties that each would accept ʿAbd al-Raḥmān's selection—but which transforms ʿAlī into a willing participant in the political process currently underway, and which eliminates the issue of nepotism, which is ʿAlī's primary (and justifiable) concern in earlier versions. In this way, Ibn Kathīr has pulled rank on Shīʿī objections about the legality or propriety of this electoral process. Who are the Shīʿa, after all, to disagree with ʿAlī himself?

One way or another, in each of the narratives, ʿAlī agrees to abide by ʿAbd al-Raḥmān's decision. It is at this point in al-Ṭabarī's narrative that the underhanded chicanery that comes to be associated with ʿAlī's political opponents reenters the story. We have already discussed the manipulation of the arbitration at Ṣiffīn. Here, like at Ṣiffīn, the guilty party is ʿAmr ibn al-ʿĀṣ, who apparently trails ʿAlī through the narrative, opposing him at every turn. As the *shūrā* prepares to meet, al-Ṭabarī reports that ʿAmr was lurking outside: "ʿAmr ibn al-ʿĀṣ and al-Mughīra ibn Shuʿba came and sat just outside the door. Saʿd [ibn Abī Waqqāṣ] threw pebbles at them and chased them away, saying, 'You two want to say, "We were there, we were members of the *shūrā*!"'"[10] Ibn Kathīr leaves this moment, and then, just to cast some doubt and set up his later rehabilitation of ʿAmr at Ṣiffīn, adds: "This is a narration of al-Madāʾinī, and God knows best whether it is true."[11] Ibn al-Athīr, for his part, omits this *khabar*; evidently, he wants the problematically divisive ʿAmr ibn al-ʿĀṣ as far away from his narrative as possible.

The fact that ʿAmr ibn al-ʿĀṣ was lurking around the initial discussion, however, is not his most important role in this section of the narrative. Despite not being a member of the *shūrā*, al-Ṭabarī reports that he planted some misinformation with ʿAlī, which caused him to flub a public question from ʿAbd al-Raḥmān when the community was gathered for the announcement of ʿAbd al-Raḥmān's decision.

> ʿAmr ibn al-ʿĀṣ had met ʿAlī during the nights the *shūrā* council was meeting, and said, "ʿAbd al-Raḥmān is struggling with his decision. The more you show (your) firm resolution, the less keen he is (that you be appointed). But [the more you say you will act according to] (your) effort and

10 Al-Ṭabarī, *Taʾrīkh* ii, 582.
11 Ibn Kathir, *Bidāya* vii, 141.

> ability, the keener he is (that you be appointed)." Then (ʿAmr ibn al-ʿĀṣ) met ʿUthmān and said, "ʿAbd al-Raḥmān is striving hard. He will not give you the *bayʿa* unless you show firm resolution. So accept (that stipulation).'"[12]

This report is a yet another perfect example of the way a small change of a seemingly insignificant moment can have a larger butterfly effect upon the story. Ibn al-Athīr and Ibn Kathīr specifically removed ʿAmr from this narrative. The former omitted the scene where he was lurking by the door of the council meeting, and the latter cast doubt on it by mentioning that al-Ṭabarī's source for that *khabar* was al-Madāʾinī, who was famously pro-ʿAlīd. Thus, Ibn Kathīr never bothered to reintroduce ʿAmr to the *shūrā* narrative, as al-Madāʾinī was obviously one of those "Rāfiḍī liars" whom Ibn Kathīr would decry just before his performance of the Karbalāʾ narrative. With ʿAmr's participation in these events omitted (in Ibn al-Athīr's case) or implicitly rejected (in Ibn Kathīr's case), ʿAmr could not sneakily undermine the political process. Thus, the implication is that the political process was never undermined.

The overriding objective for both Ibn al-Athīr and Ibn Kathīr in the narrative of the *shūrā* is to demonstrate first that ʿAlī was a willing participant in this election, and second that the election was carried out in a fair way. Both historians having carefully performed the *shūrā* narrative to downplay or eliminate any sense of improper nepotism, and in Ibn Kathīr's case, to downplay even the notion that ʿAlī was at all reticent about entering into what amounts to an arbitration in which ʿAbd al-Raḥmān would serve as the arbiter between him and ʿUthmān. All that remains is for them to demonstrate that ʿAlī willingly accepted the result.

The fact that al-Ṭabarī's ʿAlī is, in fact, quite unhappy with this process should come as no surprise; nor, indeed, should it surprise anyone that Ibn al-Athīr's and Ibn Kathīr's performances of what amounts to ʿAlī's moment of concession differ from that of their scripts. ʿAbd al-Raḥmān gathers the people together to tell them the results of a long narrative of consultation with the notables of the community (and this moment is essentially identical in all three versions of the narrative):

> [ʿAbd al-Raḥmān] spoke: "O people! I have asked you privately and publicly, and none of you has expressed any objection to either of these two men, ʿAlī or ʿUthmān. Get up, ʿAlī, and come to me!" So ʿAlī got up and

12 Al-Ṭabarī, *Taʾrīkh* ii, 586.

> approached him, and he stood beneath the *minbar*. ʿAbd al-Raḥmān took his hand and said, "Will you give me your oath by the Book of God, the Sunna of its Prophet, may God's prayers and peace be upon him, and the deeds of Abū Bakr and ʿUmar?" He replied, "By God, no! But I will swear to do my utmost to do so, in accordance with my own ability." He let go of his hand and said, "Come to me, ʿUthmān!" And he took his hand and said, "Will you give me your oath by the Book of God, the Sunna of its Prophet, may God's prayers and peace be upon him, and the deeds of Abū Bakr and ʿUmar?" [ʿUthmān] said, "By God, yes!" At that, he raised his head to the roof of the mosque, with his hand in ʿUthmān's hand, and said, "By God, listen and witness!"[13]

He then goes on to give his *bayʿa* to ʿUthmān. At the next moment, Ibn al-Athīr's and Ibn Kathīr's narrative performances diverge from al-Ṭabarī's script. Al-Ṭabarī reports:

> ʿAbd al-Raḥmān sat down where the Prophet had once sat upon the altar, and he sat ʿUthmān down on the second step. The people began to give him the oath of allegiance, but ʿAlī made as if to leave. ʿAbd al-Raḥmān quoted the Qurʾān: "He who breaks his word, does so to his own detriment; he who keeps the agreement he has made with God, He will bring him a great reward."[14] Then ʿAlī came back, pushing his way through the people, and gave the oath of allegiance, all the while saying, "Deceit! What deceit!"[15]

It is at this point that al-Ṭabarī relates the story about ʿAmr planting the disinformation about what ʿAbd al-Raḥmān needed to hear in order to choose him as caliph. Al-Ṭabarī's ʿAlī, in other words, is righteously bitter. Ibn al-Athīr, for his part, leaves out the cry of "deceit!" as well as ʿAlī grumble, "You have always been partial in his favor!" Instead, he presents the following, which, with those exceptions, is identical to the account of al-Ṭabarī: "ʿAlī said, 'This is not the first time you have all banded against me. I will be appropriately patient, and I will ask God's help against what you describe. By God, you have only appointed ʿUthmān so that you will get a favor in return. Every day, God exercises his sovereignty!' ʿAbd al-Raḥmān said, "ʿAlī, don't expose yourself to criticism.' And

13 Al-Ṭabarī, *Taʾrīkh* ii, 586; Ibn al-Athīr, *Kāmil* ii, 464; Ibn Kathīr, *Bidāya* vii, 142.

14 Qurʾān 48:10.

15 Al-Ṭabarī, *Taʾrīkh* ii, 586.

then ʿAlī left, saying, 'God's decree will have its day.'"[16] Ibn al-Athīr apparently feels unable to challenge the griping of ʿAlī at this point; ʿAlī's *bayʿa*, grudging as it is in al-Ṭabarī's script, is simply implied in Ibn al-Athīr's performance. But he does not miss the opportunity to have ʿAlī voice his intention to remain loyal to the unity of the community, with the words "I will be appropriately patient." Ibn Kathīr's performance of ʿAlī's reaction, however, is particularly noteworthy for its utter rejection of al-Ṭabarī's take of this moment:

> The people came to him and pledged allegiance to him, beginning with ʿAlī ibn Abī Ṭālib, who was the first to give the *bayʿa*. Others say this, as well. Most of the historians, like Ibn Jarīr [al-Ṭabarī] and others besides him do not know this, and mention that ʿAlī said to ʿAbd al-Raḥmān, "You cheated me! You appointed him because he is your relative by marriage, and he will ask your advice on every matter that comes to him every day [and so you will be able to rule through him or have great influence]," and that he tarried there [complaining] until ʿAbd al-Raḥmān said to him, "He who breaks his word, does so to his own detriment; he who keeps the agreement he has made with God, He will bring him a great reward."[17] [Those historians] recount other stories like this, containing contradictory *akhbār* regarding the order [in which people gave ʿUthmān the *bayʿa*], and how [ʿAlī] spoke and delivered it. God knows best.

At this moment, Ibn Kathīr revives his tack from the moment the *shūrā* was put into ʿAbd al-Raḥmān's hands: he changes the order of events. ʿAlī being the first to give ʿUthmān the *bayʿa* would clearly make it legitimate in the eyes of the Shīʿa (in the unlikely event they were willing to accept it in the first place). This is a playful little turnabout as well; Ibn Kathīr erased al-Ṭabarī's assertion that ʿUthmān had specifically been the first to accept ʿAbd al-Raḥmān as the deciding vote, and instead uses the "he was first" argument here, applied to ʿAlī in the matter of ʿUthmān's *bayʿa*. Furthermore, the moment is well-known enough that he calls al-Ṭabarī out by name and implies that al-Ṭabarī (and those like him, who claim that the moment was somehow tainted by controversy) either lied or were mistaken with his formulaic *Allāhu aʿlam*.

The strategy behind coopting ʿAlī's opinion, and having him express notions that are substantively opposed to the opinions of contemporaneous Shīʿa,

---

16 Ibn al-Athīr, *Kāmil* ii, 464.

17 Qurʾān 48:10.

seems like a cheap trick. It is nonetheless effective in undermining the meaning of the Shīʿī understanding of these events.

5 Looking Backward

Even if a reader accepts the truth of their entire *fitna* narratives—that al-Ḥusayn was rebelling against a legitimate ruler; that Yazīd was not so bad; that Muʿāwiya had legitimately assumed the caliphate and that his "rebellion" at Ṣiffīn did not disqualify him from ruler (or from Islam); that the rebels who murdered ʿUthmān were in error, because ʿUthmān's election had been untainted by chicanery or nepotism—there was a challenge from the Shīʿa that was more foundational in nature. Were the caliphs—not the Umayyads, but the *rāshidūn* themselves—legitimate as such? Was the caliphate the proper form of Prophetic succession to begin with? These became the fundamental questions that divided Sunnī and Shīʿa. If the establishment of the caliphate itself was a wrong turn for the community, then ʿUthmān cannot be considered legitimate, any more than Muʿāwiya or Yazīd could. In a way, establishing the invalidity of the caliphate would serve the Shīʿī narrative in the same way that establishing ʿAlī's assent with Sunnī norms would serve the Sunnī narrative. If this opinion is accepted as correct, the specifics of ʿUthmān's election and murder, the course of Ṣiffīn, and the entire Umayyad experiment become irrelevant, as they are all built on an invalid foundation.

The validity of the caliphate itself would be the next narrative battle to be fought. If the prize to be gained is the same size as the prize that may be lost, the careers of ʿUmar ibn al-Khaṭṭāb and Abū Bakr—and, once again, the actions and opinions of ʿAlī ibn Abī Ṭālib during those careers—are significant battlefields indeed.

PART 4

Further Ripples

CHAPTER 10

The Stories of Succession

1 Introduction

As this book has argued to this point, the most important narrative moment in the history of Islamic sectarianism is the Battle of Karbalāʾ. As a site of memory, Karbalāʾ not only stands on its own as a key moment in the emergence of Islamic sectarianism (Sunnī and Shīʿī in particular), but it also captures within its narrative a wide swath of thematic historiographical battlegrounds: the reputation of the Umayyad dynasty, the first *fitna*, and the divisive career of the third caliph, ʿUthmān ibn ʿAffān, are the most obvious examples of such battlegrounds. The Karbalāʾ event became not only the most important site of memory but also the supreme generator of meaning and context—context that, in a narrative endeavor, may be found both before and after the event. This approach means that we began with the entirety of the narrative in mind and, taking that narrative as an indivisible whole, understood that our authors shaped both the beginning and the end of the story to suit what they considered to be its chief purpose.

However, if one were to take a more standard view of Islamic history, the question of succession to the Prophet would easily replace Karbalāʾ—the battle is, after all, only a minor one-sided skirmish, albeit with a famous casualty or two—as the central question of the Islamic narrative. Such a "standard view" is one that approaches the events in question from a chronological perspective, understanding later events as manifestations of the results of earlier ones, rather than assuming—as we do here—that authors' concerns about the proper meaning of history shape the entire writing process, and that as such, later events may shape the narrative of earlier ones if their stakes are sufficiently high or if they are particularly central to the authors' moral assumptions. In the standard, chronological view, within the critically important early Islamic narrative, the earlier events almost by definition become more "important" than later ones because they become the supreme generators of context. Without the *saqīfa*, at which Abū Bakr was proclaimed the Prophet's successor over the protests of ʿAlī's supporters, or the *quid pro quo* appointment of ʿUmar ibn al-Khaṭṭāb to succeed Abū Bakr two years later, none of what follows—ʿUthmān's caliphate and assassination, the war between ʿAlī and Muʿāwiya (and the assassination of the former), the Umayyad dynasty, Karbalāʾ—would have happened. Indeed, the question of proper succession to the Prophet is at the

 | DOI:10.1163/9789004524255_012

heart of the Karbalāʾ story's importance, so it comes as no surprise that the moments of succession provide the authors with important opportunities to generate context.

2 The Death of the Prophet and the *Sāqifa*

When the Prophet Muḥammad died in the year 11/632, it was without a universally acknowledged succession plan in place. This lack of an agreed-upon successor would have profound consequences for the course of the Islamic community—we have already discussed the earliest and most important consequences in previous chapters. However, leaving aside for the moment the question of the identity of the proper successor, the nature of that succession was bound to be problematic. From the moment Muḥammad's first revelation was accepted by his close friend and eventual successor, Abū Bakr, and by the Prophet's own wife Khadīja, the Prophet Muḥammad was the *de facto* leader of a growing Islamic community; as he gained more followers, and especially after the *hijra*, his leadership of the community became *de jure* as well. As the acknowledged leader of the nascent community at Medina, he had the legitimacy of the support of his people; agreements with the Banū Umayya in Mecca, with whom he was at war for much of his Prophetic career, also implicitly demonstrate the Meccans' acknowledgment of the legitimacy of his leadership.[1] But the Prophet, and the early Muslims, would argue that the true leadership of the community came directly from God Himself, and that Muḥammad was just the human messenger chosen to relay God's messages to his people in the form of the Qurʾānic revelations. That the "Medinan *sūras*" are so focused on law, custom, and legislation (as opposed to the "Meccan *sūras*," which are proselytizing calls for repentance and submission to God's will) is proof of the early community's understanding of the notion that actual power and legitimacy lay not with Muḥammad but with God.

Such an arrangement was unproblematic so long as the Prophet was alive; indeed, it was quite convenient. Questions of legality, propriety, custom, and practice could easily and immediately be placed to the highest of high authorities, who could evidently respond directly, quickly, and with clarity (not to mention with extraordinary poetic flair). All aspects of life—not just the political—were eligible for divine guidance. As it pertains to the present discussion, at

1 The non-Muslim communities of Medina, like the three Jewish tribes of the Banū Qurayza, the Banū Qaynuqāʿ, and the Banū Nadir, would have disagreed, but their agreement was not necessary for the Prophet's legitimacy as leader of the Islamic enterprise.

least one relevant matter was unambiguous: Muḥammad was the "seal of the Prophets." In other words, although God had often communicated with humankind through the medium of prophets in the past, there would be no more prophets after Muḥammad: the time of God's direct intervention in human affairs would end with Muḥammad's death. This imminent shift was meant to have a dire warning for humanity attached to it: the message to the world that Muḥammad was reciting would be humanity's last, best chance to accept God's sovereignty. Whatever the spiritual consequences for the whole of humanity may have been, Muḥammad's standing as the last Prophet had profound consequences for the early Muslims themselves when he died, and the question of succession defined Islamic political life for centuries. With the direct contact between the community and the divine not only interrupted, but forever and irrevocably severed, by the Prophet Muḥammad's death, the community was faced with the challenge of not only finding a worthy successor to the Prophet but also with the fraught task of transitioning its leadership structure from direct divine instruction and intervention to a necessarily nonprophetic human's best attempt. Nothing recorded in the Qur'ān gives the community any unambiguous, universally accepted description of this office or clearly designates the identity of the successor. Very few communities or polities facing a power transition have had to contend with so many variables all at once. The loss of a charismatic individual leader, the doctrinal impossibility of anyone exactly filling his role as Prophet of God, the lack of communal agreement for even a mechanism by which a successor could be chosen, let alone that successor's identity: these were just the beginning of the challenges. Beyond that, tribal disunity and rivalry (not so overridden by the revelation of the Qur'ān as the Prophet may have hoped) and the presence of powerful, recently converted erstwhile enemies within the community complicated the question of succession even further. The fact that Abū Bakr's two years as caliph are most remembered for the *ridda* wars is testament to the fact that not all early Muslims were willing to make the transition from a divine executive to a human executive with the rest of the faithful community. Abū Bakr's skilled maintenance of the community's cohesion was impressive, but of limited narrative importance; the *ridda* wars could easily be cut or truncated, and the remainder of the narrative could generally continue unimpacted. They were a self-contained narrative episode, with little to no impact on what followed them or on what preceded them. This is not to say that the *ridda* wars were unimportant, but the wider historical narrative is not tinted by their impact; unlike Karbalā', there are almost no narrative callbacks to the *ridda* moment. In any event, there is every reason to treat the *ridda* wars, despite the religious branding, as politically motivated: as less of a rejection of the Prophet's message than an indicator that, less than a decade in, many members of the tribes originating in Eastern Arabia had not yet fully internalized a truly Islamic sense of devotion. With the charismatic leader gone and every reason to believe the benefits of the heretofore-successful enterprise were shortly to end, and absent the religious conviction of many of Muḥammad's followers from Medina and Mecca, the "apostasizing" tribes may have left the *umma* without even considering the potential spiritual consequences of doing so. In any event, even if their departure was a purposeful act of faith renunciation at its core, it led nowhere—the *ridda* event spawned no lasting theological movements that stood in opposition to Islam, nor did it give rise to any serious challenge to Islamic political survival. As a piece in the narrative, it is almost like a fable: a thematic episode with a clear beginning, middle, end, and moral of the story; every child can understand the explicitly narrated benefits of communal unity and the foolhardiness of abandoning the true faith of God. Most religions possess just such a cautionary tale, warning against the dangers of abandoning a religious tradition's central element.[2]

The seeds of a much more persistent problem—the questions of the source of legitimacy and identity of the ruler that would come to divide Sunnīs from Shīʿa over the course of the next few centuries—were also planted at the death of the Prophet, as ʿAlī was, for the first but not the last time, blocked from (what the Shīʿa would come to believe was his rightful) authority. Instead, the community (or, more accurately, a triumvirate of *muhājirūn*, Abū Bakr, ʿUmar ibn al-Khaṭṭāb, and Abū ʿUbayda ibn al-Jarrāḥ) conferred the job to Abū Bakr, apparently while ʿAlī was performing the pious task of preparing the Prophet's body for burial.

A slew of thematically loaded elements run through this story. The division between the *muhājirūn*—those Meccans who had been the first to convert to Islam and who had emigrated with the Prophet Muḥammad from Mecca to Medina—and the *anṣār*—those Medinans who had invited the Prophet to come assume leadership of their fractious town—is the most important thematic element in this narrative, as well as the subsequent succession of ʿUmar, discussed below. The histories are in accord that there was mistrust between the two communities, and the *muhājirūn/anṣār* division—which roughly doubled as a Meccan/Medinan division—took on a religious/political dimension as well, as ʿAlī would emerge as "an important focus for [*anṣār*] political loyalties."[3] For all their service to the nascent community, the *anṣār* would never produce from among their number a caliph (or a Shīʿī *imām*, of course,

2 The real antagonists of the Jewish Hanukkah story, for example, are not the Seleucid Greeks but rather the Hellenized Jews.

3 Kennedy, *Prophet* 51.

but that carried with it the requirement of ʿAlīd descent). Abū Bakr and ʿUmar both came from Mecca; so, too, did ʿUthmān, whose Umayyad clan was the dominant political force in Mecca dating back to before the Prophet's birth. ʿAlī, for his reputed egalitarianism on the subject of the status of believers, was the favorite of the *anṣār*; however, as previously discussed, his time as caliph was fractious and fraught. After ʿAlī's assassination at the hands of Ibn Muljam, a Khārijī—a sect spawned in part by ʿAlī's indecisiveness at Ṣiffīn, or as a result of the fractiousness of his camp there—came the establishment and the entrenchment of the Umayyad dynasty, beginning with Muʿāwiya, and with it the entrenchment of the power of the Meccan notables over the Medinan *anṣār* (or, more accurately, their descendants). That ʿAlī, as a general rule, was the favorite of the *anṣār* and their descendants, and a focus of their political hopes, was a seed that would grow into the partisan network of support that underlays the division of Islam into Sunnī and Shīʿī communities.

For later Sunnī legal scholars, including al-Mawardī, the *saqīfa* episode provided a number of important building blocks for theories of the caliphate. Philosophers and thinkers like al-Māwardī and al-Ghazālī, for example, would use the *saqīfa* to argue that the caliphate was a *fard kifaya* (communal necessity) for Muslims based on the jurisprudential principle of *ijmāʿ*, or consensus. The debated notion that the caliph should be a Qurashī or whether it was required to appoint *al-afdal*, the most excellent candidate, all have the *saqīfa* as their starting point.[4] But these were intra-Sunnī debates, and as Liew points out, the *saqīfa* has much more resonance and narrative potential for Sunnīs seeking to debate the legal boundaries of the caliphate—obviously, a Sunnī, and not a Shīʿī, institution—than it does for historians like Ibn al-Athīr and Ibn Kathīr, concerned as they were with the reputation of Syria rather than granular questions about specific strictures on Sunnī forms of communal leadership.

Abū Bakr's caliphate is remembered mostly for the *ridda* wars, the key challenge that plagued the early community upon the death of the Prophet. Traditionally presented as "apostasy wars"—in which multiple Arabian tribes that had converted to Islam attempted either to renege upon or renegotiate their relationship to the religion's governing forces—the *ridda* wars were more complex than a simple abandonment of the faith. In fact, they involved a number of factors, from attempts to renegotiate certain tribes' tax status to outright rebellion and even alternative anti-prophets.[5] Because the *ridda* wars ended in the

4 Han Hsien Liew, "History as Political Thought: The Saqīfa Meeting and the Sunnī Theory of the Caliphate" (paper presented at the Middle East Studies Association Conference, San Antonio, TX, November 2018).

5 See Kennedy, *Prophet* 54–57.

reunification of Arabia under the Islamic aegis, their narrative is essentially a dead end—one which is necessary for the story of Abū Bakr's caliphate, but one which does not much touch upon issues of concern to later historians.

3 The Caliphate of ʿUmar ibn al-Khaṭṭāb

When Abū Bakr died in 3/634, he left instructions for ʿUmar ibn al-Khaṭṭāb—the man most directly responsible for ensuring Abū Bakr's term as caliph—to be appointed as his successor. It was under ʿUmar that the dominance of the *muhājirūn* over the *anṣār* was bureaucratically consolidated. ʿUmar accomplished this by appointing important *muhājirūn*, including Abū ʿUbayda, Saʿd ibn Abī Waqqāṣ, and Muʿāwiya ibn Abī Sufyān to positions of power and importance, while offering the *anṣār* little in the way of advancement opportunities.[6] ʿUmar famously established the *dīwān*, the register of conversion precedence (*sābiqa*) of men and their families that formed the basis for government pensions. The *dīwān*, along with the rest of ʿUmar's domestic policy, meant that *sābiqa*, rather than ability or valor, became the key determinant of one's social and political potentialities. Precedence of conversion replaced tribal origin and familial notability as the most important qualification one could have; tribal origin was relegated to second place. The *anṣār*—coming, as they did, from Medina rather than Mecca, and not having had the opportunity for ground-floor conversion that the *muhājirūn* had enjoyed during the early days of Muḥammad's preaching—found themselves disadvantaged on both fronts. ʿAlī—despite his earliest of conversions and his tribal and familial closeness to the Prophet—became a natural outlet for their hopes, sharing their experience of being barred from power.

With Arabia apparently unified, ʿUmar set the sites of the community on Syria, in accord with the last wishes of the Prophet Muḥammad. It was almost an accident of history that Iraq was conquered, given that "its canals and agricultural landscape were much less attractive for nomads than Syria, or the Jazīra with their rich grazing grounds."[7] Because of the "official" sanction for the conquest of Syria, the men ʿUmar appointed to lead it were men with excellent *sābiqa* and important tribal ties: Abū ʿUbayda, Yazīd and later Muʿāwiya ibn Abī Sufyān, Shuraḥbil ibn Ḥasana, ʿAmr ibn al-ʿĀṣ, and ʿIyāḍ ibn Ghanm, for example. Most of the important conquerors of Syria were *muhājirūn*, and

6 Ibid. 57.

7 Ibid. 66.

all were at least Ḥijāzī. The conquest of Iraq, by contrast, were led by a large contingent of *anṣār,* as well as men from Ṭā'if and tribesmen from northeast Arabia. Looking up at the glass ceiling of Meccan *muhajirūn,* all the conquerors of Iraq saw in ʿAlī a convenient outlet for both their political frustrations and their aspirations.

4 The Stakes

Stories of political transition are rife with opportunity for authors to insert their own agenda into the narrative. There are, in fact, three elements to the narrative of any political transition: the character of the old regime, the means of transition, and the character of the new regime. A Shīʿī author looking back on the succession to the Prophet, for example, would have little-to-no disagreement with a Sunnī author on the nature and character of the Prophet's life; the disagreement enters the picture really only when it relates to the succession. By contrast, a Shīʿī view of the appointment of Abū Bakr by ʿUmar and Abū ʿUbayda would naturally emphasize the iniquity and illegitimacy of the process of selection. It would also criticize Abū Bakr as a usurper of power, even if it might acknowledge his virtues. In such a narrative, the later appointment of ʿUmar would be seen as an extension of the community's mistake in accepting Abū Bakr's caliphate in the first place.

By contrast, the accounts of Ibn al-Athīr and Ibn Kathīr, Sunnī as they are, see no problem in the accession of Abū Bakr and ʿUmar, and also no problem in the manner by which they came to hold their positions.

CHAPTER 11

The Prophet Muḥammad and His Role in the Narrative

The life and career of the Prophet Muḥammad, naturally, have their own important themes.[1] It would not be wrong to consider his life the most important element of the early Islamic story; there is little doubt that Muslims would rank the *sīra* of the Prophet as the foundational narrative of the entire Islamic story. Karbalāʾ is more important only in the sense that it colors the entire story. The Prophet's life begins the story, and in some ways *is* the story.

Consequently, by the time we get back as far as the life of the Prophet, we have entered the realm of another center of the narrative, with its own concerns, tropes, and rhythms. The reverse-chronological narrative considerations of Karbalāʾ are thus somewhat diffuse, as any Islamic historian treated the topic of Muḥammad; the Prophet's mission takes center stage and the sectarian intellectual conflict is largely relegated to waiting in the wings. This does not mean that concern with the meaning of Karbalāʾ disappears entirely from the narrative during the life of the Prophet. It is, however, decidedly secondary.

As an Islamic figure, the Prophet Muḥammad is unequaled in stature, regard, and narrative centrality. The "sources problem" with which this book opened is even more pronounced in the case of the Prophet. Not only do all the standard historiographical challenges already discussed apply, but as the center of not only the narrative but also the pious tradition of all stripes of the religion, the tendency to lionize this one figure above all others is pronounced. Even beyond Muḥammad's role in the revelation of the Qurʾān, which earned him the title "Messenger of God," the Prophet is remembered as the exemplar and often the originator of a great many practices of Islamic law, theology, ritual, and literature. The Prophetic *ḥadīth*, reports of stories of the Prophet's behavior, sayings, pronouncements, and arbitrations, provide for generations of Sunnī legal traditions with their preeminent non-Qurʾānic precedents, as well as the body of texts treating jurisprudential theory, *uṣūl al-fiqh* (the bases of the law). Shīʿī scholars, particularly Zaydīs, also (selectively) utilized the Sunnī *ḥadīth*

1 For an excellent overview, see Stephen J. Shoemaker, *The Death of a Prophet: The End of Muhammad's Life and the Beginnings of Islam* (Philadelphia: University of Pennsylvania Press, 2012).

 | DOI:10.1163/9789004524255_013

collection as early as the twelfth century CE, so the memory of the Prophet was not an exclusively Sunnī domain.[2]

The *sunna* of the Prophet was not confined to legalistic matters. Both Sunnī and Shīʿī *ḥadīths* treat the Prophet as an exemplar of the right way to live, which is one meaning of the term *sunna*.[3] Scholars spilled no small amount of ink delineating Prophetic practice, describing some practices of the Prophet as *farḍ* (obligatory) or merely *masnūn* (advisory). For example, *ḥadīths* treating the topic of *ṭahāra* (ritual purity) conveyed obligatory practice, while the washing of the knuckles—a practice in which the Prophet is said to have engaged—was not considered obligatory.[4] Sunnī and Shīʿī *ḥadīth* scholars might well have argued over the finer points of whether or not the Prophet was capable of committing a sin (Sunnīs argued that he was, but typically owned up to the mistake immediately; Shīʿīs tended to argue that he was not, and that on those rare occasions the Prophet did anything that was not recommended, it was by definition at least permitted),[5] but all sects of Islam regarded his personal practice as authoritative for pious behavior.

Law, ritual, philosophy, cosmology, spiritualism: the Prophet is the ideal character, the central figure, or the originator of practice in many areas around the Islamic religious and intellectual tradition. With a character of such eminence occupying the point in the narrative at which Islam begins, it is not surprising that the character of al-Ḥusayn—the Prophet's grandson, and quite young at the time of the Prophet's life—does not cast as deep a shadow over the Prophetic narrative as he does for events more immediately proximal to Karbalāʾ, whether antecedent or subsequent to his martyrdom at that battle. Such events include the key events in the life of his father and the Prophet's son-in-law, ʿAlī ibn Abī Ṭālib, which were previously discussed in this study, such as the Battle of Ṣiffīn and the *shūrā* of ʿUthmān ibn ʿAffān.

In fact, the Prophet as a figure is so unique in Islamic historiography that the scholarship about him is afforded a different name than for everyone else. A normal Muslim, even an early one, might have *akhbār* (reports) transmitted about them, and *taʾrīkh* (history) written that includes them. *Akhbār* of the Prophet (and his Companions, it must be said) are *ḥadīth*, and the story of the Prophet's life is not *taʾrīkh* but *sīra* (or *maghāzī*, if it treats a martial topic). Thus,

---

2 Joseph E. Lowry, "The Prophet as Lawgiver and Legal Authority," in Jonathan E. Brockopp (ed.), *The Cambridge Companion to Muḥammad* (New York: Cambridge University Press, 2010), 87.

3 Robert Gleave, "Personal Piety," in in Jonathan E. Brockopp (ed.), *The Cambridge Companion to Muḥammad* (New York: Cambridge University Press, 2010), 103.

4 Ibid. 106.

5 Ibid. 118–119.

the sources utilized by Ibn al-Athīr and Ibn Kathīr are of a different variety; they may present a version of the Prophet's life that is profoundly similar to that of al-Ṭabarī, but they clearly would have had access to the authoritative *ḥadīth* collections and biographies that were authoritative for information about the Prophet's life, mission, and practice.

The Prophet's love for his grandsons, al-Ḥusayn as well as his older brother al-Ḥasan, ʿAlī and Fāṭīma's eldest son, is well-attested in all *ḥadīth* collections, and typically the Prophet's weeping for al-Ḥusayn, as he foresees his grandson's death at Karbalāʾ, is inserted into the narrative—but not during the narrative of the Prophet's life, but rather later, when the authors are narrating Karbalāʾ.

In other words, for as long as the Prophet Muḥammad is alive and active in the story, he remains its central focus, and to the extent that the life of the Prophet has any bearing on the Karbalāʾ story, or the Karbalāʾ story on the life of the Prophet, the authors tend physically to remove it and place it within the Karbalāʾ narrative, rather than within the Prophet's own life. Perhaps this is testament to the (frankly expected) power of the Prophet's story to influence later events. Still, it is noteworthy that the disagreements about the Prophet, save obvious examples, like the Ghadīr Khumm *ḥadīth*, do not typically touch the sectarian divide. With the death of the Prophet, the *umma* exited the time of prophecy, and the historical narrative entered the realm of the political and the sectarian: Shīʿī grievances and Sunnī counter-grievances, whatever the validity of either, enter the story before the Prophet is even buried.

CONCLUSION

The Tapestry of History

Historians are never really engaged in the simple data-recording act of listing events for readers. On the contrary, the act of writing a history is an act of idealism, one that explains and contextualizes why and how the world has come to go wrong or right, and one that nudges its reader towards a hoped-for shared sense of a future ideal. Inasmuch as historians like al-Ṭabarī, Ibn al-Athīr, and Ibn Kathīr were indeed recording for posterity what they considered to be honest accountings, the fact is that true objectivity in history writing was and remains fundamentally unattainable. Personal bias, bias in the sources, lacunae in the sources, an overabundance of sources, and all the well-known problems of historical documentation essentially ensure that whatever picture a historian presents will be colored, slanted, incomplete, or factually inaccurate. Indeed, in the cases of Ibn al-Athīr and Ibn Kathīr, objectivity was never the objective. Ibn al-Athīr strove to create a picture of an early Islamic community at respectful odds with itself, and Ibn Kathīr tried to paint a picture of Shīʿī foolishness and Umayyad/Syrian righteousness wherever the narrative allowed. While each would claim that the history he presents is "true," neither could reasonably claim an impartial approach.

The act of digging out these perspectives is not particularly easy, given the similarities each man shares with his primary source of information for the first *fitna* and the events that are its echoes (like Karbalāʾ) and its heralds (like the *shūrā*). The act of copying a portion of al-Ṭabarī's text required no decisions, save for the determination that the section was: trustworthy; or too well-known to significantly alter; or dramatically essential to the narrative; and in accord with the subjective meaning each author wished to convey. The fact that Ibn al-Athīr and Ibn Kathīr very frequently copied al-Ṭabarī's words without alteration, on the surface gives us precious little insight into the later authors (and similarly little insight into al-Ṭabarī, who was copying the *akhbār* he received from other, earlier reporters). When they made a change to al-Ṭabarī's narrative, however, we can be certain that change was made with conscious purpose: forethought, desire, editing, and consideration of the impact of the change on the remainder of the narrative. Each of their works in this way became a performance of al-Ṭabarī's work: close, faithful renderings with carefully planned departures. These departures occurred at subsidiary moments to the famous ones. Changes during the *shūrā* of ʿUthmān altered the meaning of his assassination. Changes to the moment-by-moment conduct of Muʿāwiya and ʿAmr

 | DOI:10.1163/9789004524255_014

ibn al-ʿĀṣ at Ṣiffīn called into question the assumption of the Umayyad dynasty's illegitimacy. And finally, changes to the narrative surrounding Karbalāʾ, an event whose meaning was impacted by the narrative choices made at both the narratives of the *shūrā* and Ṣiffīn, altered the very course of the rest of Islamic communal history.

Even al-Ṭabarī's words give us more insight about the men who were his sources, such as ʿUmar ibn Saʿd, Abū Mikhnaf, and Naṣr ibn Muzāḥim, than they do about al-Ṭabarī himself. Unfortunately, since the complete works of these earliest accounts are lost to us, we are left in the dark about these tradent sources and their full take on the course and meaning of the early Islamic narrative, to which some of them may have been eyewitness. What this study did for Ibn al-Athīr and Ibn Kathīr, namely, drawing conclusions about their goals based upon their departures from al-Ṭabarī's text, could only be done for al-Ṭabarī on the basis of his own performance of his own sources if we had complete, original copies of them. With the complete works of those men lost, we have no "whole" or set of "wholes" with which to compare al-Ṭabarī's work. Ibn al Athīr and Ibn Kathīr each produced a copy of a copy of an original source, and composed comparatively little of their works themselves (the same must be said for al-Ṭabarī). It is a matter of no small irony that Ibn al-Athīr's and Ibn Kathīr's ideas and styles are easier to infer from their works than are the ideas and styles of the men who were the original composers of the accounts Ibn al-Athīr and Ibn Kathīr reproduced.

History is like a tapestry, with interweaving threads in the form of characters, events, and narratives. There is good reason, given his ubiquity as a source for later writers, to take al-Ṭabarī's history as defining the shape and form of the tapestry. His *Taʾrīkh al-rusul wa-l-mulūk* lets us know the major characters and events and movements. It is almost impossible for a later Muslim historian to challenge al-Ṭabarī on the historicity of the who, what, when, and where of his great narrative. However, by pulling on the tapestry's strings—altering characters, or changing or omitting the smaller moments—later historians like Ibn al-Athīr and Ibn Kathīr could fundamentally change the why and the how of al-Ṭabarī's historical narrative. Indeed, that was the point. Updated, carefully pruned and shaped performances of the most important historical narratives they knew allowed Ibn al-Athīr to perform an ideal of unity in the face of a terrifying external existential threat, and Ibn Kathīr to perform an ideal of Sunnī correctness in an age of intercommunal rivalry.

1 Karbalāʾ the Pebble

The preceding analysis has been chock-full of analogies: authors engaged in performance is the most prominent. An early draft of this study even contained reference to a white hole, the impenetrable counterpart to the inescapable, and much more widely known, black hole. That discussion was appropriately scrapped as inapt—who needs a physics section in the introduction to a historiographical study?—since the Karbalāʾ narrative, unlike white holes, could be changed and challenged, and was most certainly not totally impenetrable. But the wider point I was trying to make was that Karbalāʾ is the foremost narrative moment in the Islamic story, one that exerts its own gravity, which is perceptible by examining the differences among these three texts in the aggregate. But the "center of the galaxy" analogy or the "star at the center of the solar system" analogy do not quite fit either, since Karbalāʾ is an event that receives scanty treatment, no more than a few pages in most cases. Karbalāʾ, moreover, does not fundamentally shape the broad Islamic story in the same way that the life and career of the Prophet Muḥammad or the first *fitna* or, eventually, more globally tied events like the invasions of the Crusaders and the Mongols do.

The narrative exists not as an emerging set of chronological events but rather as a fully formed body of information that is, by the time our authors are born, already complete. Ibn al-Athīr and Ibn Kathīr would have been taught this story as children and had their opinions of it, its themes, and its characters formed through their lessons. When they first sat down to write *al-Kāmil fī al-taʾrīkh* and *Kitāb al-Bidāya wa-l-nihāya*, the narrative and their critiques of the narrative would have been fully conceived, if as yet unwritten. They clearly had enough critiques of the received narrative that they deemed a new performance of al-Ṭabarī's material worthwhile.

Al-Ṭabarī's opus was so ubiquitous by that point, though, that it may be considered as a well-known, mapped, lake of water. Its shape could not be altered. But Ibn al-Athīr and Ibn Kathīr could pick up a pebble off the shoreline, toss it into the water, watch it make a splash, and then watch the ripples skew the lake's surface. The pebble is not the water, nor is it the basin in which the water sits. It is not the river that fills the lake with water. But—with the skilled, well-aimed tosses of men like Ibn al-Athīr and Ibn Kathīr—for a few moments, that pebble is the center of a series of concentric ripples, traveling out in all directions, changing the shape of the lake and, for a few moments, drawing the attention of the observers. Karbalāʾ is the pebble: small, generally unassuming, and almost beneath notice in the grandeur of the lake, but nonetheless indelibly shaped, solidly composed, and possessed of the ability to change the nature of everything around it.

Bibliography

Primary Sources

al-Dīnawarī, Aḥmad ibn Dāwūd, *al-Akhbār al-ṭiwāl*. Leiden: E.J. Brill, 1888.

Ibn Abī al-Hadīd, ʿAbd al-Ḥamīd ibn Hibat Allāh, *Sharḥ nahj al-balāghah*, Cairo: Dār Iḥyāʾ al-Kutub al-ʿArabīyah, 1964.

Ibn al-Athīr al-Jazrī, ʿIzz al-Dīn Abū al-Ḥasan, *al-Kāmil fī al-taʾrīkh*, vol. 2, Beirut: Dār al-Kitāb al-ʿArabī, 1998.

Ibn ʿAsākir, ʿAlī, *Taʾrīkh madīnat Dimashq*, eds. ʿUmar al-Amrawī and ʿAlī Shīrī, Beirut: Dār al-Fikr, 1995–2001.

Ibn al-Athīr al-Jazrī, ʿIzz al-Dīn Abū al-Ḥasan, *al-Kāmil fī al-taʾrīkh*, eds. ʿAbdullah al-Qāḍī and Muḥammad al-Daqqāq, vols. 2 and 3, Beirut: Dar Al-Kotob al-Ilmiyah, ^{5}2010.

Ibn al-Jawzī, Abū al-Farāj ʿAbd al-Raḥmān, *al-Radd ʿalā l-mutaʿaṣṣib al-ʿanīd al-mānīʿ min dhamm Yazīd*, ed. H.ʿA. Muḥammad, Beirut: Dār al-Kotob al-Ilmiyya, 2005.

Ibn Kathīr, ʿImād al-Dīn Ismāʿīl, *Kitāb al-Bidāya wa-l-nihāya*, 15 vols. in 8 bindings, Beirut: Dar Al-Kotob al-Ilmiyah, 2009.

Ibn Muzāḥim al-Minqarī, Naṣr, *Kitāb Waqʿat Ṣiffīn*, ed. ʿAbd al-Salām M. Hārūn, Cairo: Al-Muʾassassa al-ʿArabiyya al-Ḥadītha, 1962.

Ibn al-Nadīm, *The Fihrist*, trans. Bayard Dodge, New York: Columbia University Press, 1970.

Ibn Saʿd, Muḥammad, *Kitāb al-Ṭabaqāt al-kabīr*, eds. Joseph Horovits and Edward Sachan, Leiden: E.J. Brill, 1904.

al-Iṣfahānī, Abū al-Farāj, *Kitāb Maqātil al-ṭālibiyyīn*, ed. Sayyid Ahmad Saqar, Beirut: Dār al-Maʿrifa, 1982.

al-Khaṭīb al-Baghdādī, Aḥmad ibn ʿAlī, *Taʾrīkh Baghdad*, ed. Muṣṭafā ʿAbd al-Qādir ʿAṭāʾ, 14 vols., Beirut: Dār al-Kutub al-ʿIlmiyya, 1997.

al-Ṭabarī, Muḥammad ibn Jarīr, *Taʾrīkh al-rusul wa-al-mulūk*, 13 vols., Beirut: Dar Al-Kotob al-Ilmiyah, 2012.

Yaʿqūbī, Aḥmad ibn Abī Yaʿqūb ibn Wadih, *Taʾrīkh*, Leiden Brill, 1883.

Yāqūt al-Rūmī, *Irshād al-arīb ilā maʿrifat al-adīb* (*muʿjam al-udabāʾ*) (W. Gibb Memorial Series 6), ed. D.S. Margoliouth, 7 vol., London: Luzac, 1907–1927.

Secondary Sources

Abbas, Hassan, *The Prophet's Heir: The Life of Ali ibn Abi Talib*, New Haven: Yale University Press, 2021.

Afsaruddin, Asma, *Excellence and Precedence: Medieval Islamic Discourse on Legitimate Leadership*, Leiden: E.J. Brill, 2002.

Afsaruddin, Asma, *The First Muslims: History and Memory*, Oxford: Oneworld, 2011.

Ahmad, M. Holmy M., "Some Notes on Arabic Historiography during the Zengid and Ayyubid Periods (521/1127–648/1250)," in Bernard Lewis and P.M. Holt (eds.), *Historians of the Middle East*, London: Oxford University Press, 1962, 79–97.

Al-Azmeh, Aziz, *The Times of History: Universal Topics in Islamic Historiography*, Budapest: Central European University Press, 2007.

Andrae, Tor, *Mohammed: The Man and His Faith*, trans. Theophil Menzel, New York: Books for Libraries Press, 1971.

Anthony, Sean W. (ed. and trans.), *Maʿmar ibn Rāshid: The Expeditions, an Early Biography of Muḥammad*, New York: New York University Press, 2014.

Anthony, Sean W. "Was Ibn Wāḍiḥ al-Yaʿqūbī a Shīʿite Historian? The State of the Question," in *Al-Uṣūr al-Wuṣṭa* 24 (2016), 15–41.

Arberry, Arthur J. (trans.), *The Koran Interpreted*, New York: Macmillan, 1955.

Barzegar, Abbas, "'Adhering to the Community' (Luzūm al-Jamāʿa): Continuities between Late Umayyad Political Discourse and 'Proto-Sunni' Identity," in *Review of Middle East Studies* 49 (2015), 140–158.

Berkey, Jonathan P., *The Formation of Islam: Religion and Society in the Near East, 600–1800*, New York: Cambridge University Press, 1994.

Borrut, Antoine, "Remembering Karbalāʾ: The Construction of an Early Islamic Site of Memory," in *JSAI* 42 (2015), 249–282.

Brockelmann, Carl, *Das Verhältnis von Ibn al-Aṯîrs Kâmil fit-taʾrîkh zu Ṭabarîs Aḫbâr er rusul wal mulûk* (PhD Diss.): Strassburg: Trübner, 1890.

Brockelmann, Carl, *Geschichte der arabischen Litteratur*, 2 vols. + 3 suppl. vols., Leiden: Brill, 1937–1943. = *GALS*

Bulliet, Richard W., *Conversion to Islam in the Medieval Period*, Cambridge, MA: Harvard University Press, 1979.

Bulliet, Richard W., *Islam: The View from the Edge*, New York: Cambridge University Press, 1994.

Chamberlain, Michael, *Knowledge and Social Practice in Medieval Damascus, 1190–1350*, Cambridge: Cambridge University Press, 1994.

Cobb, Paul M., *The Race for Paradise: An Islamic History of the Crusades*, Oxford: Oxford University Press, 2014.

Conrad, Lawrence I., "Ibn Aʿtham and His History," in *Al-Uṣūr al-Wuṣṭā* 23 (2015), 87–125.

Cook, Michael, *Muhammad*, Oxford: Oxford University Press, 1996.

Cook, Michael, and Patricia Crone, *Hagarism: The Making of the Islamic World*, New York: Columbia University Press, 1977.

Cooperson, Michael, and Shawkat M. Toorawa (eds.), *Arabic Literary Culture, 500–925*, Detroit: Thompson Gale, 2005.

Crone, Patricia, *Slaves on Horseback*, Cambridge: Cambridge University Press, 1980.

Crone, Patricia, *Medieval Islamic Political Thought*, Edinburgh: Edinburgh University Press, 2004.

Crone, Patricia, and Martin Hinds, *God's Caliph: Religious Authority in the First Centuries of Islam*, Cambridge: Cambridge University Press, 1986.

Daftary, Farhad, *The Ismāʿīlīs: Their History and Doctrines*, Cambridge: Cambridge University Press, 2007.

Dakake, Maria Massi, *The Charismatic Community: Shiʿite Identity in Early Islam*, Albany: SUNY Press, 2007.

Daniel, Elton L., "Al-Yaʿqūbī and Shiʿism Reconsidered," in James E. Montgomery (ed.), *Occasional Papers of the School of ʿAbbasid Studies*, Leuven: Peeters Publishers, 2002, 209–232.

De Somogyi, Joseph, "The 'Taʾrīkh al-islām' of adh-Dhahabī," in *Journal of the Royal Asiatic Society of Great Britain and Ireland* 4 (1932), 815–855.

Donnellan, Declan, *The Actor and the Target*, Great Britain: Theatre Communications Group, 2002.

Donner, Fred M., *Narratives of Islamic Origins*, Princeton: Darwin Press, 1998.

Dūrī, A.A., *The Rise of Historical Writing Among the Arabs*, trans. Lawrence I. Conrad, Princeton: Princeton University Press, 1993.

El-Hibri, Tayeb, *Reinterpreting Islamic Historiography: Hārūn al-Rashīd and the Narrative of the ʿAbbāsid Caliphate*, Cambridge: Cambridge University Press, 2009.

El-Hibri, Tayeb, *Parable and Politics in Early Islamic History: The Rashidun Caliphs*, New York: Columbia University Press, 2010.

Gleave, Robert, "Personal Piety," in Jonathan E. Brockopp (ed.), *The Cambridge Companion to Muḥammad*, New York: Cambridge University Press, 2010, 103–122.

Goldziher, Ignaz, *Muslim Studies*, ed. S.M. Stern, vol. 1 of 10, Albany: SUNY Press, 1967.

Gordon, Matthew, *The Breaking of a Thousand Swords: A History of the Turkish Military of Samarra* (*A.H.* 200–275/815–889 *C.E.*), Albany: SUNY Press, 2001.

Hagler, Aaron, "Repurposed Narratives: The Battle of Ṣiffīn and the Historical Memory of the Umayyad Dynasty," in *Journal of Islamic and Middle Eastern Multidisciplinary Studies* 3 (2013), 1–27.

Hagler, Aaron, "Sapping the Narrative: Ibn Kathir's Account of the *shūra* of ʿUthman in *Kitab al-Bidaya wa-l-Nihaya*," in *IJMES* 47 (2015), 303–321.

Hagler, Aaron, "The Shapers of Memory: The Theatrics of Islamic Historiography," in *Journal of Islamic and Middle Eastern Multidisciplinary Studies* 5 (2018), 1–28.

Hagler, Aaron, "Unity through Omission: Literary Strategies of Recension in Ibn al-Aṯīr's al-Kāmil fī l-Taʾrīḫ," in *Arabica* 65 (2018), 285–313.

Hagler, Aaron, "Sunnifying ʿAlī: Historiography and Notions of Rebellion in Ibn Kathīr's *Kitāb al-Bidāya wa-l-Nihāya*," in *Der Islam* 97 (2020), 203–232.

Haider, Najam, "The Myth of the Shīʿī Perspective," in Herbert Berg (ed.), *Routledge Handbook on Early Islam*, New York: Routledge, 2018, 209–222.

Hawting, G.R. (trans.), *The History of al-Ṭabarī*, vol. 17: *The First Civil War*, Albany: SUNY Press, 1996.

Helabi, Abdul-Aziz Saleh, *A Critical Edition of 'Akhbar Siffin,'* (PhD diss.) University of St. Andrews, 1974.

Hinds, Martin, "The Banners and Battle Cries at Ṣiffīn (657 AD)," in *al-Abḥāth* (American University of Beirut) 24 (1971), 3–42.

Hinds, Martin, "Kufan Political Alignments and the Background in the mid-7th Century," in *IJMES* 2 (1971), 346–367.

Hinds, Martin, "The Murder of the Caliph 'Uthman," in *IJMES* 3 (1972), 450–469.

Hinds, Martin, "The Siffin Arbitration Agreement," in *JSS* 17 (1972), 93–113.

Hirschler, Konrad, *Medieval Arabic Historiography: Authors as Actors*, London: Routledge, 2006.

Hirschler, Konrad, "Studying Muslim Historiography: From Source-Criticism to the Cultural Turn," in Stephan Conermann (ed.), *Ubi sumus? Quot vademus? Mamluk Studies—State of the Art*, Bonn: Bonn University Press, 2013, 159–186.

Hodgson, Marshall, "How did the Early Shiʿa become Sectarian?," in *JAOS* 75 (1955), 1–13.

Hodgson, Marshall, *The Venture of Islam: Conscience and History in a World Civilization*, vol. 1, Chicago: University of Chicago Press, 1974.

Howard, I.K.A., "Ḥusayn the Martyr: A Commentary on the Accounts of the Martyrdom in Arabic Sources," in *Al-Serāt* (*Papers from the Imam Ḥusayn Conference in London, July 1984*) 12 (1986), 124–142.

Humphreys, R. Stephen, *Islamic History: A Framework for Inquiry*, Princeton: Princeton University Press, 1991 (rev. ed.).

Humphreys, R. Stephen, *Mu'awiya ibn Abi Sufyan: From Arabia to Empire*, Oxford: Oneworld, 2006.

Jacobs, Andrew S., "Adversus Iudaeos," in Roger S. Bagnall, Kai Brodersen, Craig B. Champion, Andrew Erskine, and Sabine R. Huebner (eds.), *The Encyclopedia of Ancient History*, Oxford: Blackwell Publishing Ltd., 2013, 111–113.

Jafri, S.H.M., *The Origins and Development of Shīʿī Islam*, Oxford: Oxford University Press, 2000.

Juynboll, G.H.A., "The Qurrā' in Early Islamic History," in *JESHO* 16 (1972), 113–129.

Keaney, Heather, *Medieval Islamic Historiography: Remembering Rebellion*, New York: Routledge, 2013.

Keaney, Heather, *'Uthman ibn 'Affan: Legend or Liability?*, London: OneWorld, 2021.

Kennedy, Hugh, *The Armies of the Caliphs: Military and Society in the Early Islamic State*, London: Routledge, 2001.

Kennedy, Hugh, *The Prophet and the Age of the Caliphates*, Harlow, England: Pearson Longman, ²2004.

Kennedy, Hugh, *When Baghdad Ruled the Muslim World: The Rise and Fall of Islam's Greatest Dynasty*, Cambridge, MA: Da Capo Press, 2004.

Keshk, Khaled, "How to Frame History," in *Arabica* 56 (2009), 381–399.

Keshk, Khaled, "When did Muʿāwiya Become Caliph?," in *JNES* 69 (2010), 31–42.

Khalek, Nancy, *Damascus after the Muslim Conquest: Text and Image in Early Islam*, New York: Oxford University Press, 2011.

Khalidi, Tarif, "Al-Ṭabarī: An Introduction," in Hugh Kennedy (ed.), *Al-Ṭabarī: A Medieval Muslim Historian and His Work*, Princeton: Darwin Press, 2008, 1–9.

Kister, M.J., "On the Papyrus of Wahb ibn Munabbih," in *BSOAS* 38 (1974), 545–571.

Lalani, Arzina, "Ghadir Khumm," in Andrew Rippin (ed.), *Oxford Bibliographies in Islamic Studies*, https://www.oxfordbibliographies.com/view/document/obo-9780195390155/obo-9780195390155-0105.xml (accessed June 5, 2022).

Laoust, Henri, "Ibn Kaṯir Historien," in *Arabica* 2 (1955), 42–88.

Lapidus, Ira M., *A History of Islamic Societies*, Cambridge: Cambridge University Press, ^{2}2002.

Landau-Tasseron, Ella, "Sayf ibn Umar in Medieval and Modern Scholarship," in *Arabica* 67 (1990), 1–26.

Leder, Stefan, *Das Korpus al-Haytam ibn ʿAdī*, Frankfurt am Main: Klostermann, 1991.

Leder, Stefan, "The Paradigmatic Character of Madāʾinī's *shūrā*-Narration," in *SI* 88 (1998), 35–54.

Lewis, Bernard, and P.M. Holt (eds.), *Historians of the Middle East*, London: Oxford University Press, 1962.

Liew, Han Hsien, "History as Political Thought: The Saqīfa Meeting and the Sunnī Theory of the Caliphate," Paper presented at the Middle East Studies Association Conference, San Antonio, TX, November 2018.

Liew, Han Hsien, "Ibn al-Jawzī and the Cursing of Yazīd b. Muʿāwiya: A Debate on Rebellion and Legitimate Rulership," in *JAOS* 139 (2019), 631–646.

Lindsay, James E., "Caliphal and Moral Exemplar: ʿAlī ibn ʿAsākir's Portrayal of Yazīd ibn Muʿāwiya," in *Der Islam* 74 (1997), 250–278.

Lowry, Joseph E., "The Prophet as Lawgiver and Legal Authority," in Jonathan E. Brockopp (ed.), *The Cambridge Companion to Muḥammad*, New York: Cambridge University Press, 2010, 85–102.

Madelung, Wilferd, "ʿAbd al-Raḥmān b. ʿAwf," in *EI*^{3}, consulted online on October 13, 2017, http://dx.doi.org.du.idm.oclc.org/10.1163/1573-3912_ei3_COM_24664.

Madelung, Wilferd, *The Succession to Muḥammad: A Study of the Early Caliphate*, Cambridge: Cambridge University Press, 1997.

Marsham, Andrew, *Rituals of Islamic Monarchy*, Edinburgh: Edinburgh University Press, 2009.

Melchert, Christopher, *Ahmad ibn Hanbal*, Oxford: OneWorld, 2006.

Morony, Michael G., *Iraq after the Muslim Conquest*, Princeton: Princeton University Press, 1984.

Muir, William, *The Life of Mohammed*, London: Smith, Elder, and Co., 1851.
Noth, Albrecht, *The Early Arabic Historical Tradition: A Source-Critical Study*, trans. Michael Bonner, Princeton: Darwin Press, 1994.
Ohlander, Erik S., "Ibn Kathīr," in Joseph E. Lowry and Devin J. Stewart (eds.), *Essays in Arabic Literary Biography*, Wiesbaden, Germany: Harrassowitz Verlag, 2009, 147–158.
Petersen, E.L., *ʿAlī and Muʿāwiya in Early Arabic Tradition*, Copenhagen: Munksgard, 1964.
Richards, D.S., "Ibn al-Athīr and the Later Parts of the *Kāmil*: A Study in Aims and Methods," in D.O. Morgan (ed.), *Medieval Historical Writing in the Christian and Islamic Worlds*, London: SOAS, 1982, 76–108.
Robinson, Chase F., *Islamic Historiography*, Cambridge: Cambridge University Press, 2003.
Robinson, Chase F., "The Rise of Islam, 600–705," in Chase F. Robinson (ed.), *The New Cambridge History of Islam*, i, Cambridge: Cambridge University Press, 2010, 173–225.
Robinson, Chase F., "Al-Tabari," in Michael Cooperson and Shawkat M. Toorawa (eds.), *Arabic Literary Culture, 500–925*, Detroit: Thompson Gale, 2005, 358–369.
Rosenthal, Franz, *A History of Muslim Historiography*, Leiden: E.J. Brill, 1952, ^{2}1968.
Rosenthal, Franz, "The Life and Works of al-Ṭabarī," in *The History of al-Ṭabarī*, i, Albany: SUNY Press, 1989, 5–154.
Rosenthal, Franz, "Ibn al-Athīr," in *EI*^{2}, iii, 723.
Schacht, Joseph, "Introduction," in Joseph Schacht (ed.), *Ikhtilāf ʿulamāʾ al-amṣār fī aḥkām sharāʾiʿ al-Islām*, Leiden: E.J. Brill, 1933, i–xxiv.
Schönléber, Mónika, "Notes on the Textual Tradition of Ibn Aʿtham's *Kitāb al-Futūḥ*," in Jaako Hāmeen-Anttila, Petteri Koskikallio, and Ilkka Lindstedt (eds.), *Contacts and Interaction: Proceedings of the 27th Congress of the Union Européenes des Arabisants et Islamisants*, Leuven: Peeters, 2017, 427–438.
Sezgin, Fuat, *Geschichte des arabischen Schrifttums, Band I*, Leiden: E.J. Brill, 1967. = *GAS*
Sezgin, Ursula, *Abū Miḥnaf: ein Beitrag zur Historiographie der umayadischen Zeit*, Leiden: Brill, 1971.
Shahin, Aram, "In Defense of Muʿawiya ibn Abi Sufyan: Treatises and Monographs on Muʿwiya from the Eighth to the Nineteenth Centuries," in Paul Cobb (ed.), *The Lineaments of Islam: Studies in Honor of Fred Donner*, Leiden: Brill, 2012, 177–208.
Sharon, Moshe, *Black Banners from the East: The Establishment of the ʿAbbāsid State*, Jerusalem: Magnes Press, 1983.
Sharon, Moshe, "The Development of the Debate Around the Legitimacy of Authority in Early Islam," in *JSAI* 5 (1984), 1212–141.
Shoemaker, Stephen J., *The Death of a Prophet: The End of Muhammad's Life and the Beginnings of Islam*. Philadelphia: University of Pennsylvania Press, 2012.

Shoshan, Boaz, *The Poetics of Islamic Historiography: Deconstructing Tabari's History*, Leiden: E.J. Brill, 2004.

Sourdel, D., "Ibn K̲h̲āḳān," in *EI*², iii, 824.

Wansbrough, John, *The Sectarian Milieu*, New York: Prometheus, 2006.

Wensinck, A.J., *Concordance Et Indices De La Tradition Musulmane: Les Six Livres, Le Musnad D'Al-Darimi, Le Muwatta'De Malik, Le Musnad De Ahmad Ibn Hanbal*, vol. 1., Leiden: E.J. Brill, 1936.

West, E.J. (ed.), *Shaw on Theatre*, New York: Hill and Wang, 1958.

Index

al-ʿAbbās ibn ʿAlī 61–62
ʿAbbāsids
  Betrayal of ʿAlīd supporters 42–43
  Caliphate 5, 10, 10n32, 12, 25n80, 27, 30, 34n10, 43, 54n12, 59
  Civil war and anarchy at Samarrā’ 30
  Decline 43
  Destruction by the Mongols 40
  Patronage of history writing 76, 93, 121
  Revolution 34, 42, 44, 76
ʿAbd Allāh ibn ʿAbbās 90, 99, 99n10, 105
ʿAbd Allāh ibn ʿAmr ibn al-ʿĀṣ 110–111
ʿAbd Allāh ibn Ḥawza 64
ʿAbd Allāh ibn ʿUmar 79, 110
ʿAbd Allāh ibn al-Zubayr 51, 79
ʿAbd al-Raḥmān ibn Abī Bakr 70
ʿAbd al-Raḥmān ibn ʿAwf 35, 36, 126, 133–135, 139–147, 142n8
Abū Bakr al-Sīddiq
  At the Battle of Yamāma 96
  Death 4, 111
  Historical presentation of 37
  Reputation 56
  Ridda Wars 4, 115, 153–155
  Term as Caliph 23, 33, 56n16, 84n3
Abū ʿUbayda ibn al-Jarrāh 154, 157
Abū Mikhnaf, Lūṭ ibn Yaḥya 1, 2n2, 10, 14, 19, 25n78, 52, 53, 57, 58, 64, 87, 118
Abū Mūsā al-Ashʿarī
  Appointed as ʿAlī’s representative 89–91, 95, 105
  Appointed as Governor of Kūfa 132
  Description of character 90, 105, 113
  Negotiation with ʿAmr ibn al-ʿĀṣ 91, 100n13, 105, 116–117
  Revelation of arbitration decision 92, 106–110
  Tricked by ʿAmr 95, 104n, 120, 136
Abū Nuḥ al-Ḥimyarī 97
Abū Shāma, Shihāb al-Dīn al-Makdisī 19n72, 45
Abū Sufyān ibn Ḥarb 1, 85n4, 90, 94, 129
Adab 38
Adharbayjān 132
Aḥmad ibn Ḥanbal 11, 103, 104
ʿĀ’isha bint Abī Bakr
  At the Battle of the Camel 33, 109, 126
  Rivalry with ʿAlī ibn Abī Ṭālib 33
al-Amīn ibn Hārūn al-Rashīd 30
Aleppo 44, 45
ʿAlī ibn Abī Ṭālib
  Assassination of 21, 24, 26, 29, 34, 37, 77, 83, 84, 85, 91, 92, 96, 151, 155
  At the *shūrā* of ʿUthmān 125–133, 135, 136–148
  Erasure of title at the Battle of Ṣiffīn 63, 90, 105, 121
  Rivalry with ʿĀ’isha bint Abī Bakr 33
ʿAmmār ibn Yāsir
  As link to the generation of Companions 89, 96, 113
  Death at Ṣiffīn 66, 96–100
  Dispute over occasion of death 99–100, 104
  Hadith that he will be killed by “the rebel band” 96–99, 96n2, 98n4
Amīr al-Muʿminīn, title 63, 90, 91, 105, 115
ʿAmr ibn al-ʿĀṣ
  Appointed representative of Muʿāwiya at Ṣiffīn 90, 95, 105, 110
  Assassination attempt 84, 91
  Character of 80, 97, 98, 104, 110, 114, 115, 120
  Conquest of Syria 156
  Governor of Egypt 98, 112, 115
  Lurking around the *shūrā* of ʿUthmān 144–146
  Negotiation with and deception of Abū Mūsā al-Ashʿarī 90–95, 104–107, 113, 116–117
  Proclamation of Muʿāwiya as Caliph 85, 107, 121, 136
  Stratagems at Ṣiffīn 90–95, 100–104, 100n13, 107, 119, 137, 161
  Wooing of allegiance 110–115
ʿAmr ibn Saʿīd 58
al-Andālūs 76
Andrae, Tor 17, 17n62
Anṣār 4, 5, 29, 89, 110, 117, 125, 154–157
Apostasy 5, 66, 121, 155
  see also Ridda

Armenia 132
al-Ashʿath ibn Qays al-Kindī 95n1, 113, 127
al-Ashtar *see* al-Mālik al-Ashtar
ʿĀshūrāʾ 54–57, 61
Assassins (Ismāʿīlī *hashāshīn*) 40
Awāna ibn al-Ḥakam 14
ʿAyn Jālūt, Battle of 40
Ayyūbids 8

Badr, Battle of 3, 96, 140
Baghdad 2, 7, 11, 12, 42, 43, 43n24, 45, 57
  Destruction of 40, 45
  Founding of 30, 31
Bāghy (Rebellion)
  al-fiʾa al-bāghiya ("the rebel band") 96, 96n2
Bakhtiyār 31
Balādhūrī, Aḥmad ibn Yaḥya 25n78, 51n4, 52
Banū Hāshim 33, 125
Banū Nadir *see* Jewish Tribes of Medina
Banū Qaynūqāʿ *see* Jewish Tribes of Medina
Banū Qurayza *see* Jewish Tribes of Medina
Banū Umāyya 125, 152
Bayʿa
  Described 114
  Due to ʿAlī ibn Abī Ṭālib 89, 91, 94, 110, 114–116, 122, 126
  Due to al-Ḥusayn ibn ʿAlī 69
  Due to ʿUthmān ibn ʿAffān 145–147
  Due to Yazīd ibn Muʿāwiya 79
Burayr ibn Salīma 64
Burḥān al-Dīn Fazarī 9
Būyids 30, 31, 43, 44, 57
Byzantium 4, 41, 42, 44, 54, 128, 132

Cairo 40, 45
Camel, Battle of the 20, 22, 24, 27, 33, 85, 89, 91, 92, 94, 107, 109–111, 113, 126, 128, 139
Crusades 2, 40, 44, 46

Damascus 7, 8, 9, 27, 37, 58, 91, 125, 128
  As a center of scholarship 40–46
al-Dhahabī, Shams al-Dīn Muḥammad 6, 7, 9
Dhū al-Kalāʿ al-Ḥimyarī 97–98
al-Dīnawarī, Aḥmad ibn Dāʾūd 13, 51n4, 52, 112
Dūmat al-Jandal 86, 92, 105–106, 136, 137, 140

Edessa 44
Egypt 11, 30, 40, 45, 47, 59, 98, 110, 112, 127

Fāṭima bint Muḥammad 33, 56, 66, 69, 138
Fāṭimids 25, 30, 44, 45, 58, 59
Fiqh 7, 37, 39, 136, 137

Ghadīr Khumm *ḥadīth* 84n3, 137, 138n1, 160
al-Ghazālī, Abū Ḥamīd Muḥammad ibn Muḥammad 155

Ḥadīth 7, 9, 10, 12, 13, 23, 25n80, 37, 38, 54, 55, 57, 77, 84n3, 87, 96, 96n2, 97, 104, 104n19, 128, 137, 138, 158, 159, 160
Hamdānids 30
Ḥamza ibn ʿAbd al-Muṭṭalib 62
Hārūn al-Rashīd, Caliph 30
al-Ḥasan ibn ʿAlī 83, 160
Hāshim ibn ʿUtba al-Mirqal 98, 98n4
Ḥudaybiyya, Battle of 63, 65, 90, 104, 105, 121
Hujr ibn ʿAdī 64, 95n1
al-Ḥurr ibn Yazīd
  Death 64–65
  Fighting at Karbalāʾ 64–65, 68
  Interaction with al-Ḥusayn ibn ʿAlī 68, 69–74, 75, 79
al-Ḥusayn ibn ʿAlī
  At Karbalāʾ 61–66, 68–75
  Character 79–80, 137
  Charge of over-veneration of 53–60, 80, 136
  Corpse desecrated 51, 57–58, 66
  Death 21, 24, 29, 31, 34, 36, 43, 51, 53–60, 65–67, 75–77, 79n29, 83, 84, 108, 121, 137
  Denied water at Karbalāʿ 65, 75
  Grandson of the Prophet 76, 159, 160
  Inspiration for sectarian action 25, 36
  Interaction with al-Ḥurr 68, 69–74, 75, 79
  Leading armies in prayer 65
  Rebellion against Yazīd 26, 30, 51, 59, 75, 76, 78–79, 83, 86, 108, 136, 148

Ibn Aʿtham al-Kūfī 1n1, 3n5, 4n8, 25n78
Ibn Abī al-Dunyā 58
Ibn al-ʿAdīm 7, 9, 45, 120
Bughyat al-ṭalab fī taʾrīkh ḥalab 45, 97, 129
Ibn Mufliḥ, Muḥammad 78
Ibn Muljam 83–84, 85, 155
Ibn al-Nadīm, Muḥammad 12, 86
Ibn al-Qalānisī, Ḥamza ibn al-Asad 8n20, 45
Ibn Taymiyya, Aḥmad 9, 78, 79, 80, 107
Ikhshidīds 30
ʿIlm 138
Iraq, Conquest of 4, 4n8, 30, 156
Isnād/asānīd 3n5, 8, 39, 53
Isrāʾīliyyat 9

Jaʿfar ibn Abī Ṭālib 62
Jamāl al-Dīn al-Mizzī 9
Jarīr ibn ʿAbd Allāh al-Bajalī 89, 113, 114, 127
Jazīra 37, 156
Jerusalem 44, 45, 55
Jewish tribes of Medina 152n1

Kaʿba 97
Kaʿb ibn Jābir 64
Kamāl al-Dīn al-Isbahānī 9
Karbalāʾ, Battle of 51–80
As a historical event 31, 52, 75
As a site of memory 24–27, 36, 43, 52, 76
Consistency of presentations of 21–22, 53–60
Khabar/akhbār 39, 57, 100, 104, 128, 135, 144, 145, 147, 159, 161
Khalīfa ibn Khayyāt 52
Khārijī/Khawārij 13
Alleged hypocrisy of 101, 121, 136, 137
Assassinations and assassination attempts 83–84, 91, 92, 136, 155
Emergence of 26, 85, 103, 105
Historiographical reputation 88, 99–100, 104
Khūrāsānīs/*Abnāʾ al-dawla* 30, 43
Khurūj (disobedience to proper authority) 107
Kūfa 11, 51, 60, 64, 68, 69, 70, 89, 90, 91, 96, 110, 113, 127, 132
Abandonment of al-Ḥusayn's cause 51, 59
Bribery of notables against al-Ḥusayn 71–73

al-Madāʾinī, ʿAlī ibn Muḥammad 14, 87, 144–145
al-Mālik al-Ashtar 90, 101, 102, 105, 110, 114
Mālik ibn Nusayr al-Baddī 73, 74
Mamluk Dynasty 2, 8, 9, 40, 46
al-Maʾmūn ibn Hārūn al-Rashīd 30
al-Manṣūr, Caliph 30, 42
Marwān ibn al-Ḥakam 79
Marwānids 25n80, 47
al-Masʿūdī, ʿAlī ibn al-Ḥusayn 7, 12, 25n78, 52, 117
al-Māwardī, ʿAlī ibn Muḥamamd 155
Mongols 2, 40, 45, 66, 163
Sack of Baghdad 40, 45
Muʿāwiya ibn Abī Sufyān 9
Appoints Yazīd ibn Muʿāwiya as successor 51, 76, 78, 128
Assassination attempt against 84, 91
As *ṭāliq* 115–118
At the Battle of Ṣiffīn 14, 26, 31, 75, 84–122, 137, 151
Becomes Caliph 24, 34, 37, 42, 77, 83, 91–92, 95, 104–107, 121, 136, 155
Character 80, 92–93, 120, 161
Claim of vengeance for ʿUthmān's murder 26, 94, 105, 106, 110, 112, 115, 126–129, 131
Death 79
Governor of Syria 85, 88, 94, 125–6, 156
Legitimacy and legality of rule 80, 85–86, 92, 104, 115, 117, 121–122, 129, 136–137, 148
Refuses to give *bayʿa* to ʿAlī ibn Abī Ṭālib 26, 33, 85, 89, 94, 111, 114, 117
Rebellion against 64
al-Mukhtār 25, 30, 30n2, 52, 65
Muʿtāzila 13
Muḥājirūn 5, 29, 89, 109, 117, 125, 154, 156, 157
Muḥammad al-Nafs al-Zākiyya 25, 30
Muḥammad ibn ʿAmr ibn al-ʿĀṣ 110–111
Muḥammad ibn ʿUmar ibn Ṣāliḥ 58
Muhammad, the Prophet
As moral exemplar 46
As "Seal of the Prophets" 32, 153
Companions of 29, 33, 35, 46, 56, 89, 96, 107, 113, 133, 159
Death 4, 23, 28, 152–156

Narrative 151–156
Succession to 23, 28–30, 32, 34, 129, 137, 151–155
Muir, Sir William 17
Mujammiʿ ibn ʿAbd Allāh al-ʿĀʾidhī 71–72
al-Muʿtaṣim billah, Caliph 10, 30
al-Mutawakkil, Caliph 72

Nāʾila bint al-Furāfiṣa 125–128
Nahrawān, Battle of 103, 105
Naṣr ibn Muzāhim al-Minqarī 2n2, 16, 53, 87, 116–119, 162
Naṣṣ 138
Nubia 127
Nūr al-Dīn Zangī 43–45

Persia 4, 30, 40, 127

Qays (tribal confederation) 30
Qays ibn Mushir 71–72
Qurʾān 9, 13, 23, 25, 29n1, 37, 56, 74, 90, 95, 100–103, 100–101n13, 107, 114, 115, 116, 127, 132, 146, 152, 153, 158
Qurrāʾ 103, 103n18

Raqqa 88
Rāshidūn ("rightly-guided") caliphs 32–34, 32n8, 41, 84, 104, 121, 129, 131, 148
Ridda *see* Apostasy
Ridda Wars 4, 5, 115, 153–155

Saʿd ibn Abī Waqqāṣ 35, 110, 126, 132, 139, 141–144, 142n8, 156
Ṣaʿṣaʿa ibn Ṣūḥān 118–119
Sābiqa ("Precedence") 5, 111, 112, 156
Sabuktakīn 31
Sahl ibn Ḥanīf 104
Salāḥ al-Dīn al-Ayyūbī (Saladin) 40, 45
Saljūqs 44
Samarrāʾ, Anarchy at 30
Saqīfa 28, 151, 152–155
Ṣayf ibn ʿUmar 10, 14, 14n57, 16, 111, 115
Shams al-Dīn al-Dhahabī 9
Shams al-Dīn al-Isbahānī 9
Sibṭ ibn al-Jawzī 6, 8n20, 45, 78
Ṣiffīn, Battle of 83-
Arbitration at 21, 90–92, 94–108
As a piece of the *fitna* narrative 9, 20–21, 24, 83–86, 88–92, 120–122
As a political dispute 31, 109–111
As a site of sectarian grievance 37, 63, 84–86, 118–120
"Sunnī Revival" 40–46
Syria/al-Sham: Conquest of 44, 132, 156

Ṭāʾif 4, 134, 157
Ṭabaristān 10, 11, 132
Tahrīf 9
Talḥā ibn ʿUbayd Allāh 33, 35, 89, 92, 94, 107, 109–111, 117, 125–126, 139, 141, 143
Ṭalīq/ṭulaqāʾ 115–118
tawabbūn ("Penitents") 25, 51, 60
Tughril Beg 44
Tūlūnids 30
Turks 7, 30, 31, 43, 44

ʿUbayd Allāḥ ibn ʿUmar 98
ʿUbayd Allāḥ ibn Ziyād 64–74
Udhayb al-Hujanāt 70
ʿUmar ibn ʿAbd al-ʿAzīz, Caliph (ʿUmar II) 137
ʿUmar ibn al-Khaṭṭāb
Appointment of ʿAmmār as Governor of Kūfa 96
Appointment of Muʿāwiya as Governor of Syria 94
Appointment of *shūrā* 35, 126–127, 135, 142n8
As Caliph 4, 24, 28, 33, 84n3, 97, 133–134, 137, 146, 148, 156–157
Assassination and death 4, 33, 35, 35n13, 125–127, 133, 138, 139
At Hudaybiyya 104
Character 56, 111, 155
Election of 23, 140, 151, 154
ʿUmar ibn Saʿd 2n2, 16, 52, 53, 61, 130, 133
Umayyads
Dominance in pre-Islamic Mecca 4, 5, 12, 41, 125, 155
Dynasty 10, 29, 34, 37, 41, 42, 47, 86, 95, 97, 117, 129, 135, 136, 148, 155
Historiographical rehabilitation of 78–79, 92–93, 95, 107–108, 118–120, 161–162
Legitimacy 80, 85, 162
Negative historical reputation 2, 5, 26, 42, 57–59, 72–77, 84, 92–93, 95, 107, 112, 137, 140, 141, 151
Opposition to ʿAlī 90, 94–95, 105, 121, 125

Opposition to the Prophet Muḥammad 29, 105
Overthrow 29, 30, 42, 43, 76, 121
Rebellions against 30, 51, 64–75, 83, 121, 128
Virtues 34–35
ʿUsāma ibn Munqidh 56
Uṣūl al-fiqh 7, 37, 39, 158
ʿUthmān ibn ʿAbd al-Raḥmān 58
ʿUthmān ibn ʿAffān 33
As Caliph 127–128, 151
Assassination and death 21, 26, 33, 35, 36, 85, 94, 109, 112, 128–129, 151
Character 23, 33, 56, 115, 130–135
Demand for vengeance for murder 26, 85, 90–91, 98, 105, 106, 116, 117
see also walāya
Election of 23, 26, 28, 35–36, 66, 84, 95, 128, 138–148
Historical reputation of 33
Historical rehabilitation of 109
Killers of 26, 85, 88, 90, 94, 109, 116, 122, 128
Legitimacy 23, 26, 35–36, 122, 128–129, 136–148
Opposition to 96, 138
Rebellion against 14, 36, 75, 111, 119
Shūrā of 20, 24, 35–36, 95, 110, 126–127, 136–148, 159
Standardization of the Qur'ān 100n13

Wahb ibn Munabbih 20, 38
al-Walīd ibn ʿUtba 79, 79n29, 119
walāya 24, 25, 106, 116
al-Wāqidī, Muḥammad ibn ʿUmar 10, 87, 87n10, 133

Yamāma 4, 96
Yamānī (tribal confederation) 30
al-Yaʿqūbī, Aḥmad ibn Yaʿqūb 13, 52, 52n5, 112, 117
Yāqūt, Shihāb al-Dīn 7
Yazīd ibn Abī Sufyān 94, 156
Yazīd ibn Hāniʾ 101–102
Yazīd ibn Maʿqil 64
Yazīd ibn Muʿāwiya
Appointment as successor by Muʿāwiya 24, 51, 76–77, 83, 108, 109, 128
As Caliph 37
Legitimacy 78–80, 108, 129, 137, 148
Rehabilitation of character of 77–78, 136
Response to death of al-Ḥusayn 58, 66, 84
Responsibility for Karbalāʾ 42, 51, 64
Yazīd ibn Ziyād al-Kindī 73, 74

Zangī, Atabeg 44
Zangīds 8
Zayd ibn ʿAlī 25, 30
Zaydīs 158
Zaynāb bint Fāṭima 66
al-Zubayr ibn al-ʿAwwām 20, 33, 35, 89, 92, 94, 107–111, 117, 125–126, 139, 141, 143
Zuhayr ibn al-Qayn 61, 64, 70